The Ghost of Roark Ridge

And Other Stories

by Rufus Franklin Stephenson

authorHOUSE®

AuthorHouse™
1663 Liberty Drive
Bloomington, IN 47403
www.authorhouse.com
Phone: 1 (800) 839-8640

Published by AuthorHouse 10/19/2016

ISBN: 978-1-5246-4501-4 (sc)
ISBN: 978-1-5246-4500-7 (e)

Library of Congress Control Number: 2016917336

Print information available on the last page.

Table of Contents

Dedication 7

ACKNOWLEDGEMENTS 9

INTRODUCTION 11

LOUISE AND DAISY 13

FAMILY FRIENDS 23

SHINING HEAD 27

A POSSUM ON THE RAILS 39

BEEF TRIPE 47

THE KLAN 49

RUFUS AND ELMO 51

Danger on the Yazoo 58

Exploring Mint Springs and the Cemetery 67

Moving On 79

Another Night on the River 83

Summer Vacation 91

Problems with Elmo 97

Flood Water and Alligator Gar 111

Prayer Meeting and a Car Wreck 124

Crossing the River Bridge from Vicksburg to Louisiana 128

BOWIE 147

FIRST BALE OF COTTON.. 149

FEEDING THE CHICKENS 153

AN OLD WOOD STOVE.. 157

POOR FOLKS'FOOD.. 161

CORNBREAD AND BEANS.. 165

DRUNK BIRD STEW 167

A GIANT TURNIP.. 169

SQUIRREL STEW.. 173

TATER PATCH 175

A FISH STORY 179

COTTON PICKER.. 181

FROM RAGS TO RICHES 191

SLOPPING HOGS.. 197

BLACKSMITH SHOP 199

RUFUS AND HIS MULE 203

A TRIP TO THE GRISTMILL 209

BUCKY THE BEAVER 211

BILLY THE KID.. 215

ERNIE THE PIG 223

RUFUS AND JOE.. 229

A FOX HUNT 233

A NUT CASE 241

THE WATERMELON MAN 245

THE FUNNY FARM.. 257

MILKING A COW 261

KENNIE, ME, AND TUBBY LEE 263

CARTOAD 267

HOBO HOTEL.. 273

A CHRISTMAS ANGEL 301

A NEW LIFE 303

THE GHOST OF ROARK RIDGE.. 305

    Head 'Em Up, Move 'Em Out.. 305

    From Branson to Springdale, Arkansas.................................... 310

    Looking for a Home.. 312

    Tragedy in Colorado 318

    Moving into Our Dream Home 319

    New Friends and Sycamore Log Church 325

    Our Friend Willard Jones.. 336

    Our Early Visits to the Ozarks 338

Jammin' for Jesus and Barbara Fairchild 342

Adventures 343

The Ghost of Roark Ridge 356

Looking Back to Our Beginning 372

Temptation and Disappointments 379

Our Biggest Temptation Ever 384

A Change of Pace 387

Singing with The Gatlin Brothers 392

Clem School Reunion 394

Changing Seasons 397

PLAY THE SONGS 409

ALL ABOARD 411

FRIENDS 413

RUFUS AND THE LADYBUGS 433

LEON THE HERO RABBIT 447

Dedication

For Joyce, my sunshine girl, and for my family, past, present, and future.

ACKNOWLEDGEMENTS

Thank you to my family, not only for all their encouragement, but also the circumstances in life that gave me material to write about. There were good, bad and ugly times along the way that taught me many important lessons, but there were also times when I thought about giving up. At those times, it was my faith in God that kept me going.

In 1981, I began to write down my memories on scraps of paper. I threw them into a box, hoping that someday I would turn them into a book. I was 43 when that began, and I continued to do so until I retired in 2000. My wife and I then moved to Branson, Missouri the following August but after living there five years, we moved back to Colorado because of her health. After being back for three years, I signed up for a creative writing class at the local Red Rocks College in Golden. I was now 70, but I did learn a few helpful things that were needed to get me started.

This class took me out of the dark and opened a few doors, but I still knew very little about what was involved in putting a book together.

Then one day while searching through Craigslist, I came across a lady named Catherine Traffis. I contacted her and she agreed to edit my first book, *From Dixieland to Frisco Bay*. I felt God had answered my prayers and Catherine has been there for me from the start. Without her, none of what I wanted would have ever happened. I believe she was a God send from the very start.

I turned 78 in May of 2016. I've slowed down a little but still have many memories that keep my mind active. But who knows, I may give it another try if Catherine continues to be my editor!

INTRODUCTION

I was born on May 30, 1938 in Meridian, Mississippi. I had three brothers and a sister. Despite this, just one week after my youngest brother was born, our dad left our mother. So we spent our early childhood years growing up in Vicksburg, to be near my mother's parents, until I was 13. Mom married again on September 9, 1951 and with my stepdad and his four kids, we moved to a sharecrop farm in Jeff Davis County, Mississippi. I began attending the little country school of Clem on September 11, 1951.

With Mom, a new dad and nine kids, we worked a sharecrop cotton farm for five years. In January of 1957, when I was 18, I left home, riding a greyhound bus to San Francisco. On March 7th, 1957, I began a railroad career on the ATSF Railroad in Los Angeles. The other memories I've written about in this and my two previous books were meeting my wife, Joyce, getting married, and raising a family of four daughters while working 43 years and three months for five different railroads in California, Utah, and Colorado. Reliving these memories by writing three books was fun and I wanted to share them with my family and friends. After the first book, I had no thoughts of writing a second or third, but with much spare time on my hands, I decided to go for it.

11

I retired in 2000 and Joyce and I initially moved to Branson, Missouri, but came back to Colorado in January of 2005 when Joyce could no longer tolerate the hot, humid Missouri climate.

Being retired and needing something to fill the void, I began to write. I received much encouragement from my family. My reason for writing these books was to leave behind memories for my kids, grandkids, and great grandkids, along with future generations.

On completion of this project, Joyce and I have 13 grandkids, and 12 great grandkids. I hope they enjoy reading about the life and times of their Grandpa and Grandma Stephenson. God willing, Joyce and I will celebrate our 58th anniversary on November 24, 2016.

This book, along with the other two, are for my family, but I hope others who read them can relate in some way and find enjoyment in what I've written.

Rufus Franklin Stephenson
September 2016

LOUISE AND DAISY

They met back in the forties
On top of Givins Hill.
The town was north of Vicksburg
And was known as Waltersville.

They both were raising families
With babies on the way.
Louise was due in February
And was anxious for that day!

Louise had four children,
Daisy had just two,
But lost a son in forty-five;
In August she had been due.

Daisy and James felt sadness
Along with their two girls,
Losing that child in forty-five
Upset their entire world.

Faith, they had in Jesus
And they knew it was God's will.

13

Their tiny son would return to God
Because of Calvary's hill!

Time would pass by slowly
But soon the day would come:
On Valentine's Day of forty-six
Louise gave birth to a son.

Daisy had waited patiently
But when the day arrived,
Happy, she was, to see this child
Who was so much alive!

Losing a baby had broken her heart
But Daisy spent some time
With Louise and her newborn son
And soon she took a shine.

This tiny boy named Joseph
Was watched over day and night.
Louise and Daisy cared for him
And he was never out of sight.

Together, they worshipped God each week
A short way down the hill,
At a missionary bible Baptist church
In the town of Waltersville.

Close, they were, like sisters,
Their friendship grew each day.
On many Sundays after church

These families ate and played.

Their friendship never wavered
They helped in every way,
For each other's their doors were open
Twenty-four hours a day!

Daisy was called Ms. Henley,
Louise was Ms. Louise,
James was Mr. Henley
And all the kids were pleased.

Their lives were filled with hope and joy,
For Jesus there was love.
For him, they lived their life each day
And built their home above!

Life for them was a struggle,
Times were often tough.
Ups and downs, there were a few
But never did they give up.

One day the Henleys moved away
Not far from Givins Hill,
To the town of Kings on sixty-one.
They knew it was God's will.

No longer were they neighbors
But their friendship never swayed.
Sunday, Wednesday, and Thursday nights
They worshipped God and prayed.

These families would often visit,
The Sabbath was their favorite day.
Together they prepared a Sunday meal
And for the food, James would pray!

Their close friendship would continue
But hard times seemed to stay.
God was always there for them
And just a prayer away!

Together they went to church each week
As the months and years went by,
On September ninth of fifty-one
They said their first goodbye.

Louise got married and moved away
A hundred miles to the south,
With a husband now and four more kids,
She moved to a sharecrop house.

Times got worse and life would change
For Louise and her kids!
The cotton rows and long hard days
Seemed like they had no end.

They saw each other over the years;
Their visits were just a few.
They were short on time, money was scarce
And there was so much work to do!

The kids grew up and moved away

Then sharecrop life got worse.
Visits to Vicksburg rarely came
And they rarely went to church.

Help got scarce when the kids left home,
Farm life came to an end.
Louise and her husband of sixteen years
Went to work in the chicken pens.

One day they moved to Vicksburg
But their life was out of control.
Their marriage crumbled and fell apart.
The years had taken their toll.

Separation came but Louise survived
And moved close to her only daughter.
A phone call came that changed everything:
It was her five kids' father!

Cecilia, his wife, had passed away
So he called Louise the next day,
Wanting her to take him back!
She didn't know what to say.

A big decision was facing her
And she prayed to God every day,
Wanting an answer to all her prayers
And to pick the right words to say.

A decision was made that she felt was right
To her lost love, it was "yes"!
Plans were made for her special day

17

And she picked out a wedding dress.

For her, an airline ticket was bought,
In Jackson she boarded a plane.
Frightened, she was, on her very first flight;
She had always traveled by train.

In La Puente, California vows were said
And again they were husband and wife,
After twenty-five years of being apart
They were beginning a brand new life.

To a beautiful home, she moved that day,
Furnished with everything nice,
Life for her had turned around
But it came at an awful price.

Louise enjoyed the material things
But her family and friends were gone.
She missed them now and was lonely,
Yearning for her Vicksburg home!

Steve, her husband, was a railroad man
With two years left to go.
They settled down in a faraway town
So the weeks and months went slow!

Their plan was to sell when Steve retired
Then Louise got a new lease on life.
Vicksburg would soon be home again
For this newlywed husband and wife.

Two years went by and retirement came.
Their beautiful home was sold.
Everything they owned was loaded in a truck.
They headed east on the open road!

Two thousand miles they would travel,
Four days, it would take to get home.
To the state she loved they soon arrived,
No longer was she feeling alone!

From her sister, a tiny white house was bought
Not far from where they first met.
In 1935 they were young and in love
But their future hadn't started yet.

In Vicksburg the news was soon received
And Daisy was thrilled to no end,
Happy that Louise was coming home
And so were her family and friends!

Daisy and James lived in Vicksburg
And sometimes they felt all alone.
Their kids had married and moved away
But her long lost friend was coming home.

The year was nineteen seventy-one
And it was springtime in Dixieland.
These friends hadn't seen each other for years
But their future was looking better again.

In nineteen thirty-five, Louise met Steve

And for 34 years life was rough.
After struggling alone and raising five kids
Her future was now looking up.

Forgiveness took place and life become new,
Love brought them back together.
Steve was a Christian and a child of God
And life couldn't get any better.

Louise and Daisy were together again
And their husbands would soon become friends.
Brothers, they were, in a masonic lodge
And their friendship would have no end.

Visits with each other were many,
The months and years went fast.
This newlywed couple grew closer each day
But their good times wouldn't last.

On February 13th, nineteen seventy-four
After being back together five years,
Steve passed away two miles from where they met
And Louise was shocked and in tears!

Uncle Tom Marshall preached his funeral
While family and friends paid respect.
Mr. Henley did the masonic rites.
For some there were many regrets.

Steve was buried in Vicksburg,
Next to Kennie, his oldest son.

A plot next to him was left for Louise
But she had many miles left to run.

Sad, she was for a long, long time
But God gave her strength to go on.
Daisy and James would remain by her side
And love from her family was shown.

Out west, for many years, she visited her kids,
In Denver, Salt Lake, and L.A.
On a greyhound bus she made many trips;
For years she traveled this way.

In 1993 at the age of 72,
Daisy went to heaven one day,
Outliving the years God promised her
Following his teachings all the way!

Mr. Henley was blessed with 92 years
But in 2003 he joined his wife.
They had lived out their lives for Jesus
And their reward was eternal life!

Louise moved to Utah in 1993
To live out the rest of her years.
But on August 20th of 1996
Her family gathered around her in tears.

In Layton, Utah a memorial was held,
To Jackson her body was flown,
No longer would she travel on a greyhound bus

And this time she wouldn't be alone.

By way of Atlanta on to Jackson,
From there she took her last ride.
In a long, black hearse, she traveled to Vicksburg
But her family would be by her side.

Her celebration of life was attended by many
On a hot and humid August day.
At her graveside service kind words were said
As everyone stood by and prayed!

A meeting in heaven took place that day
With all of her family and friends,
First she saw Jesus, then Kennie and Steve.
Her reunion would never ever end.

Life goes on when we leave this earth,
Heaven or hell is our choice.
Salvation is free for those who ask
'Cause Jesus paid it all on the cross!

*In memory of my, mother, Louise Elizabeth Stephenson
And her best friend, Daisy Henley.*

FAMILY FRIENDS

When we were all just little kids
And had no dad around,
A family who we knew from church
Lived in our small hometown.

Their names were James and Daisy,
With two daughters our age.
We all grew up and went to church
And spent some happy days!

Mr. Henley was a sawmill man
Like many way back then.
He worked long hours every day
But took time out for friends.

In church, he played the old upright,
In a quartet, he would sing.
Along with Grandpa Conrad,
To God, their voice would ring.

The songs were from our old hymn book
That sat behind the pews.
The congregation sang along

23

And help spread God's good news.

Aunt Aggie and my Uncle George
Were part of their quartet.
They all praised God with songs they sang;
Satan never did like that.

Dinner was often on the ground
And that meant all-day singing.
When everyone would sing along
We rocked that old church building!

Good times were spent by young and old,
Great memories, we all made.
The lost were saved in that old church
On many happy days!

Sometimes on Sundays after church,
Our families got together
And loaded up Mr. Henley's car
No matter what the weather.

I still look back but can't believe
His old car held us all
As seven young kids and three adults
Made plans to have a ball!

Mama helped with the cooking
And brought along some food.
Between our moms, they cooked a meal
That always tasted good.

Us kids would play till it was time for church
Then we'd wash and comb our hair,
'Cause it was time to end our play
And meet in church for prayer.

Those memories I will not forget
But it seems so long ago
When two young families were best of friends
And unashamed to let it show.

Great memories were made back in those days
But the years went by too fast.
One day Jesus took our parents home
But the friendship still would last.

We all were blessed throughout those years
And Jesus never passed us by
Someday we'll see each other again
In heaven where no one dies!

Mr. And Mrs. Henley and their daughters, Barbara and Judy, were our good friends and were neighbors until we moved away from Vicksburg in 1951. Over the years, we were very close and even though our dad wasn't around during those early years, he became very close friends with Mr. Henley after he and mom remarried in 1969. They were both masons and belonged to the same lodge in Vicksburg, and when dad passed away, Mr. Henley conducted the masonic part of the services. To me, it was so strange when Dad wasn't around for Mom and us kids, but Mr. and Mrs. Henley were always there to lend a helping hand and were always close to our family. Mom and Dad

25

continued their friendship with Mr. and Mrs. Henley right up until they both passed away. I often wondered what kind of conversations went on between Dad and Mr. Henley after Mom and Dad were reunited in marriage. I guess it's not important but it made me feel good knowing that no hard feelings were ever shown between them. Dad always spoke very highly of the Henley family and always enjoyed visiting with them.

SHINING HEAD

Grandma Stephenson came to live with us in 1944. Her oldest son, James Lovell, was our dad; he had walked out on Mom and us five kids when we ranged in age between one week and nine years old.

Grandma arrived from Meridian, MS shortly after our youngest brother, Marshall, was born. She planned to take care of him and the rest of us while Mom worked.

We had few memories of our dad since he spent very little time with our family, always keeping busy instead with his friends or working on the railroad in Memphis.

Mom and her four oldest kids had lived in Memphis for a few years but the responsibility of raising a family without the help of a husband and father became too much for her, so we went to live with her parents in Vicksburg. This arrangement would last over two years before she could find a job and move out on her own.

During that time, Dad rarely came on visits and never stayed over two or three days when he did. There was never any financial support and on his last visit our youngest brother, Marshall, was just one week old. He never came back to visit us again.

On that visit, our family was living on Givens Hill in Waltersville and our house was one half of an old shotgun duplex three miles north of Vicksburg on Highway 61. Arrangements were made for Grandma Stephenson to move in and take care of us kids while Mom worked at Kress's department store in Vicksburg.

Grandma was a great storyteller and during those cold, rainy, winter months, we sat at her feet or on her lap and enjoyed her bedtime stories. There were many; some were about the Civil War but others were of her childhood while growing up in the late 1890s on a cotton farm in Lauderdale County, MS.

One of our favorite stories was the life of an Indian medicine man called Blue Feather. This story, along with many others, had been told to her by her Grandpa Gipson. From the beginning to the end the story took more than an hour to tell but never did we get tired of hearing it. My brother, Kennie, and I sat on the floor and the other three kids sat beside Grandma or on her lap trying hard not to miss a word. Here is the story.

It was 1854 in northeastern Mississippi. Many young Indian children often gathered on hot summer days and swam and played in a nearby river. Blue Feather had always been very happy but his life was about to undergo a drastic change.

Just before winter ended, fever broke out in the village and many older adults and small children died. This outbreak would last three months before everyone was well, but some of the effects lingered for weeks before going away.

At the age of eleven, Blue Feather had been very sick but he did recover after special care was given to him by the local medicine man. He lost both parents and this devastated him. The fever had left its mark on him and he became the butt of jokes when his long black hair began to fall out.

He was soon bald and many in his village laughed and made fun of him. This made him angry but also very sad.

His mother had named him Blue Feather after seeing a large blue jay feather lying on the ground shortly after he was born. It was tradition for mothers to name their children after the first thing they saw after giving birth. It was a great name and made him very proud.

Several weeks after his illness had passed, he was no longer known as Blue Feather. Instead, everyone began to call him Shining Head. He began to shy away from the village and only came around when he was sick or hungry. Never again did he swim in the river or play with his friends and he stayed in his tepee most of the time.

Losing his parents at such an early age was devastating for him and being an only child made it worse. He was now living alone in the family tepee and often had to beg for food.

He was an outcast and shunned by most of his friends and all the men. The women and young girls felt sorry and befriended him on his visits to the village and shared their food.

His hair never grew back and when the time came for all the young men to be taught the skills of hunting and fishing, the warriors and young braves continued to ignore him.

29

After he and many other young men turned twelve it was time to become young braves. They were taught to ride horses, shoot a bow, fish and hunt for their food, and survive alone in the wilderness. He had already learned a few skills from his father but was never taught all that was required of him.

He would not be allowed to participate because it was said that the bright sunlight reflecting off his bald head would frighten the animals away. This caused Blue Feather to become discouraged and choose to stay away.

One day, Wise Eagle, the village medicine man, saw him wandering alone and invited him for a visit to his tepee. He would try to build up Blue Feather's confidence by telling stories about his own childhood and the hard times he had experienced.

Wise Eagle had already prepared a meal and after eating, he began to speak of his own father and mother and how he loved and missed them very much. He talked about their good times together and how he was taught hunting and fishing skills before his parents died with the fever. He had then gone to live with his grandparents and his life was very hard but he survived all the hardships.

At an early age, Wise Eagle was taught by his mother the many cures of wild herbs. These plants grew in the swamp and across the hillsides and were gathered by him and his mother throughout the summer and fall.

From her teaching, Wise Eagle had learned to treat the sick and lame and was soon admired for making them well. He also treated the village animals and was appointed one day by the tribal council as head medicine man at the age of twenty.

Blue Feather became fascinated with his stories and spent many hours visiting Wise Eagle. Many lessons were learned and Blue Feather slowly became more confident in himself. He was soon spending time with many of his old friends.

Wise Eagle was the most admired person in the village and loved by the young and old. In the fall, his large tepee was always filled with dried wild herbs collected throughout the summer, ready to be prepared to treat any sickness or injury that needed attention.

With much knowledge being taught to him by Wise Eagle, Blue Feather began treating the sick and lame and learned all the uses of the healing herbs. He also helped Wise Eagle harvest them throughout the summer months.

While lying asleep early one morning just as the sun was coming up, Wise Eagle heard someone call his name. He opened the flap on his tepee and a young mother wanted help for her young son who had broken his leg. Treating a broken bone was something Blue Feather had never done but Wise Eagle invited him to come along. Blue Feather was anxious to watch and learn.

They followed the young mother down to the river and found her son lying on the ground in severe pain. A few yards away, his horse stood by and the young boy had fallen off after coming in contact with a low hanging tree branch.

The mother had heard his screams and came to his rescue but had to leave him behind while going for help.

Soon Wise Eagle and Blue Feather were by his side and saw that the break was clean and below the knee. Blue Feather was then sent to find two small pieces of dried ironwood and

31

brought them to Wise Eagle. With his sharp hunting knife, Wise Eagle cut them for length, then removed the bark and placed one on each side of the broken leg. The bones were now in place and wet strips of rawhide were wrapped to keep them from moving. When the leather strips dried they would shrink and hold the ironwood in place, allowing the bones to heal.

The young boy was in severe pain throughout the procedure but handled it like a true warrior. His mother was proud and thanked them both for helping her son.

It was a short distance back to his tepee but Wise Eagle had brought along a walking stick that was used by the young boy to get home.

Wise Eagle and Blue Feather helped while his mother led the horse back to the tepee. With everything happening so fast they were never told the boy's name and they wanted to know before leaving.

Little Acorn was his name: he had been born beneath a large oak tree. Wise Eagle praised him for his bravery and how well he handled the pain. He said someday Little Acorn would grow tall and strong like the big oak tree.

The shunning had nearly stopped for Blue Feather. He followed Wise Eagle's advice and tried to ignore cruel remarks and always made a special effort to be kind to everyone. Sometimes it was hard to follow his advice but soon it got easier. He continued to gain the knowledge of a medicine man's ways and his desire was to achieve the same goal as Wise Eagle.

Wise Eagle did suggest that Blue Feather wear a headband with a single blue jay feather in hopes it would take away the attention from his bald head. They both thought it was a good idea and after searching through the forest, they found a beautiful blue jay feather and returned to the village.

Wise Eagle then surprised him with a leather headband he had made and the feather was attached. Right away he put it on and walked outside. Four young girls were standing next to the tepee and thought he looked great and this made him feel much better!

Wise Eagle thought it was good for Blue Feather to be identified with a feather and suggested he add one on each full moon until the number reached his age. He also thought one should be added each year on his birthday. Again this made him happy and he continued to gather all the blue jay feathers he could find in the forest.

One day while walking on the riverbank, a strange noise was heard coming from the thick brush so he stopped to check it out. It got louder and suddenly a large black bear walking on its back legs appeared from behind the brush. He let out a loud, frightening growl and Blue Feather took off running toward the village. With an angry bear on his heels, Blue Feather began screaming for help. Out of nowhere, an Indian warrior with warpaint on his face and body appeared. The warrior told him to keep running and not look back. Blue Feather ran like a deer until he was in sight of the village. When he turned around he was surprised to find that the bear and the warrior were no longer in sight.

Where had they gone? He knew he had seen a huge bear chasing him and also a painted warrior coming to his rescue. He knew if he told anyone they would think he was making up the story for attention and decided not to tell anyone but Wise Eagle.

Soon he was sitting under a huge oak tree next to Wise Eagle's tepee and having a long discussion about his encounter. Wise Eagle listened to every word then tried to explain what had happened.

Blue Feather's parents had both died the same year he came down with the fever. It was shortly before his 12th birthday and he had been coming of age. What he had just witnessed was the spirit of his father and the spirit of an angry bear his father had killed two winters before his death.

In the spirit world, the bear had plans of taking Blue Feather's life in revenge for his own death. His father had watched over his son throughout his sickness and had returned to save him from the angry bear.

Wise Eagle explained to Blue Feather that his father would always be by his side but would never appear again unless he was in danger. It made him very happy to know that his father would always watch over him, and his fear of others soon went away.

Six years passed and Wise Eagle became sick and lame and could no longer travel without help. Blue Feather stayed by his side and began to gain trust from the older men and some of the young braves. While traveling with Wise Eagle he had learned the ways of a medicine man and soon took his place.

As fall arrived, everyone began to depend on Blue Feather to make them well. Weeks went by and after everyone saw him doing the job of Wise Eagle, the chief called him to his tepee and made him the village medicine man before he turned 19.

Everyone was happy and a celebration was planned in honor of Blue Feather's promotion.

Then came the day of celebration when all the villagers dressed in their very best and this made Blue Feather very happy. He wore clothes made by the women and dressed in his best from head to toe. A special head dress and moccasins were made and he wore them proudly.

He was also very pleased when the chief asked Wise Eagle to join in the celebration, although he had to be carried on a special bed by four young braves. He was now very old and could no longer walk on his own. His health was deteriorating fast.

The chief then came before the villagers and the ceremonies began! Food was prepared and the young braves painted their faces and bodies for the celebration dance.

A huge fire brightly lit the night skies and everyone was having a great time when a call for help was heard. They rushed over and discovered Wise Eagle was having trouble breathing. Blue Feather went to his side and moments later Wise Eagle was feeling better, but he asked to be placed on his favorite horse so he could speak to everyone. Two young braves helped him mount and with the help of Blue Feather and two other braves, Wise Eagle began to speak.

He wanted everyone to know he would be leaving soon for the happy hunting ground and wanted them to accept Blue Feather as their head medicine man. The villagers were sad but agreed to honor his wishes. Wise Eagle then asked to be taken to a special place in the forest and left alone to die in peace.

Blue Feather took the reins of Wise Eagle's horse and began walking, soon disappearing into the darkness. The drum beat changed and a death chant began.

The village became quiet for a short time, then Blue Feather walked back in the light of the fire. He had painted his face and placed another feather in his headband and told everyone that Wise Eagle was on his way to the happy hunting ground. The drums and the dance began and continued throughout the night.

When the sun rose, Blue Feather was sitting in front of Wise Eagle's tepee and promised to continue to be there for anyone needing his help.

The chief and tribal council were then taken to Wise Eagle's side and together they buried him in the mound as he had requested. Now Blue Feather was the head medicine man and ready to treat the entire village.

No one had slept that night so he spoke with the chief about returning to their tepees and resting for a while. Soon the village was quiet again and all that could be heard was the whinny of horses and barking from a few village dogs. Calm fell over the village as everyone slept.

The next day Blue Feather was busy treating the sick and lame and from that day forward, he got respect from everyone. He continued treating the sick and lame until he was 70 years old but in 1919, white man's medicine became available and he encouraged his people to get help from their doctors.

Blue Feather passed away in 1924 at the age of 80 and was buried on the reservation next to his parents. He was the last medicine man in his village and became a legend among his people. On his head was a beautiful bonnet of sixty-eight blue jay feathers; one for each year since he had turned twelve.

This was always one of our favorite stories but Grandma had many more that got our attention on cold, rainy nights. Her stories never got old and she was always our hero and a great storyteller.

She moved away in the fall of 1951 and I never saw her again until January of 1957, when I was 18 years old. She had moved to northern California with her son and daughter-in-law when I was 13 and my mother remarried. She lived to be 85. Grandma passed away in 1972 on January 6th and buried in San Leandro, California.

In her first 61 years there were many hardships but her last 24 were great and she had everything she ever wanted. Her son, Alton, and daughter-in-law, Evelyn, treated her like royalty and she was always pampered and loved.

Grandma had married Frank Stephenson in 1914 and their first baby had died before its first birthday. They had another daughter and three sons before her husband passed away in his early 40s from a massive heart attack. Grandma continued to raise her kids alone and never remarried.

She was a very devout Christian and she's now waiting in heaven for her family to join her. Grandma taught me and my three brothers and sister about Jesus and always set an example for us to live by. She read her bible and prayed every day and attended church when she could.

When Uncle Alton came and got her from the Ralph

Ramsey sharecrop farm we all had a hard time saying goodbye. Mom and we kids cried.

We had a lot to talk about when I saw her again but we never really got caught up before she passed away. She was a smart lady and loved Mom and us kids very much. We always missed not having her around.

Grandma loved to play checkers and dominoes and rarely did she ever lose. She knew everything about basic math and helped us kids many times with our homework. We learned a lot from her. I've always missed her, but someday I'll see her and all my family who have gone over to the other side. Thanks Grandma for always being there for our family and I love and miss you very much.

Your second grandson, Rufus Franklin Stephenson

A POSSUM ON THE RAILS

Many evenings after school, my brother Kennie and I walked the railroad track looking for scrap metal that had fallen off railcars. Whatever we found was taken home and thrown in our scrap pile and sold to the junk dealer when he came around on Saturday morning. We never made much money but it was enough to buy a few ten-cent movie tickets to the Saturday matinee, popcorn and a few treats.

One evening after school, we took a stroll north on the Illinois central railroad tracks and found a few pieces of scrap metal along with several old rusty railroad spikes. After walking more than a mile, we were turning around to head home when we saw movement about 100 yards down the tracks. We realized it was a big, fat possum.

We were always in need of fresh meat so we began to chase after him. When we got close enough, Kennie threw a piece of scrap metal and hit him in the head, planning to have him for supper the next night. He was big so we took turns carrying him home.

Soon we were walking in the front yard and Grandma wanted to know what we had. We laid our possum on the front porch and she thought he would make a good supper for the next day.

We took out our pocket knives and it didn't take long till we had him gutted and skinned. Grandma filled a pan with cold water and added a handful of salt, leaving the ole possum to soak overnight.

Grandma had supper ready so we cleaned up and took our places at the table. Mama blessed the food and we began to eat and talk about the adventure we had catching the ole possum. We were also looking forward to having him for supper the next day.

My friend John Harmon was coming home with me from school on Friday and would be spending the weekend. Kennie and I were proud of our kill and looked forward to sharing him with our friend.

We caught the school bus Friday morning in front of the Chinaman's Grocery Store and in less than an hour, we arrived and went looking for John. We found him in the hall. Since he had brought extra clothes for his visit, we headed for the locker room. The bell rang before we had enough time to tell him about the possum. It would have to wait till recess.

At 9 o'clock we went out to play and told John about catching the ole possum and how Grandma was cooking him for supper that evening. At first he wasn't looking forward to his evening meal but as the day went by, he got hungry and was preparing himself to eat his first ugly ole possum.

When school was out we boarded the bus and arrived in front of the Chinaman's Store in less than an hour. It was owned by Mr. and Mrs. Jue, whose five kids attended Redwood School with us.

Our little community of Waltersville was known to most folks as Negro Town. My family and I had lived there a long time and knew most all the families, both white and black.

In many ways this would be a strange weekend for John so we headed north on the railroad tracks and soon arrived at our little shotgun house. It was called a shotgun house because like many other homes, a shotgun could be fired from the front door all the way through the house and it would never hit anything if the interior doors were left open. Most of the old homes in Waltersville were built this way and ours sat 50 yards east of the tracks. Two hundred miles north of Vicksburg was Memphis, Tennessee and two hundred miles south was New Orleans, Louisiana.

All the houses in Waltersville were shacks and the neighborhood had a bad smell. We were used to it but John kept complaining and acted like he would rather be somewhere else.

Soon we were home and Grandma met us at the door. Since it would be a while before supper was ready, we changed clothes and went outside to play. Walking the rails was a favorite

41

game of ours; we would see who could walk the longest distance without falling off.

Anderson Tully Lumberyard was a few hundred yards south of our house and steam engines were always switching flat car loads of lumber. We were just a bunch of silly kids and never thought we were doing anything dangerous. Sometimes there were eight to ten of us trying to have a good time with this game.

At first John wasn't very good at walking the rails but he got better with practice. Another fun thing we did was climb stacks of lumber and jump from one to the other. They were 12 feet high and spaced about four feet apart. We could cross the entire lumber yard without climbing down. The watchman made his rounds often and we had to keep a lookout for him or we'd get chased away.

Like Kennie and I, John was having a good time and wanted to play longer but the 5 o'clock mill whistle blew and we had to head home for supper.

We left the lumber yard walking on the tracks but our fun soon ended when a northbound freight train showed up. We had to walk the rest of the way on a gravel road.

On the back porch was a bucket of water and a pan to wash up for supper. Soon we were sitting down at the table, with Mama at one end and Grandma at the other. All of us six kids took our places on two wood benches.

In the center of the table was a large baking pan and two plates of cornbread. At each end of the table was a large bowl of turnip greens and everyone had a mason jar filled with water. Mama said the blessing and Grandma removed the lid of the pan, and there in the middle of the table was our big possum with his legs sticking straight up, surrounded with lots of sweet potatoes.

Grandma offered each of us some possum. John was a little hesitant at first but did take a small piece. He also had some sweet potatoes and turnip greens and after eating a few bites, seemed to enjoy it. It had been a while since Grandma cooked a possum but it tasted the same as always to me - very greasy.

It was still early after eating supper so we played on the track for a while and then went back to the lumber yard and finished off the evening. Just before sundown we jumped a slow-moving freight and rode back to the house.

John had a great time and so did Kennie and I but he also enjoyed his first possum dinner. Walking on the railroad tracks, playing on stacks of lumber, and riding on a freight train were firsts for him, but they wouldn't be his last.

The next day was Saturday and we got up early and did it all over again, along with a few other fun things. We took our friend to the sawmill where Grandpa worked and to the Mississippi River to go swimming. It was Saturday and we would have an all-day adventure in Waltersville at the Anderson Tully Lumberyard, walking the railroad tracks till dark.

The day went by fast and soon it was time to go home and get cleaned up. We spent the rest of the evening listening to Grandma Stephenson tell our favorite stories. By 9:30 we were ready for bed since we would get up early Sunday morning for church.

Sunday school started at 9:00 am and was over at 10:00 am. Then there was an hour of singing before the preacher brought his message, which would last till noon. Our family then went over to Grandma Conrad's for dinner and spent the rest of the day.

Sunday afternoon at Grandpa's house was always a fun time, spent swinging on grape vines, climbing trees, picking wild berries and papaws, and shooting our slingshots.

John went to church regularly but never did the other things we did so this day would be another first for him. After dinner, Kennie and I found an extra slingshot for John and took him down to the creek to spend most of the evening shooting targets.

Before it was time to go back to church at 7:00 pm, Grandma and Mama heated up all the leftovers from dinner and supper was on the table around 5:30 pm. After eating, the dishes were washed and we all got in Grandpa's old car and headed for church.

The evening service was over before 8:30 pm and Grandpa took us home. We said our goodbyes and went inside to get ready for bed. We changed our clothes and said our prayers. We were soon fast asleep.

On Monday morning, Grandma cooked breakfast for the family while Mama got ready for work and we got dressed for school.

Then it was time to eat so we gathered around the table and Mama said the blessing. After finishing our meal, we headed down the old gravel road and caught the bus in front of the Chinaman's Store.

The nine-mile ride went by fast as we talked about the fun weekend we had. Soon we were getting off the bus and going to our classroom still thinking about the many happy memories we made with our friend John Harmon. He made several more visits to our home before we moved away with our new family to live on a sharecrop cotton farm in September of 1951.

BEEF TRIPE

In the '40s and '50s, beef tripe was the most inexpensive meat you could buy at a butcher shop. If Mama had extra money and went shopping at Jitney Jungle grocery store, she sometimes bought a few pounds for our family. It didn't happen often but we always looked forward to having it for supper. It was first seasoned with salt and pepper then boiled in a pot of water and later fried in a skillet with lard.

Tripe is beef stomach and is very tough and stringy! Our jaws and teeth got a workout. I don't remember seeing it being prepared any other way until I moved to California in 1957. I then learned it was used in a spicy Mexican soup called menudo, which was sometimes eaten for breakfast by those who had hangovers after a night of drinking. Tripe is white in color, is served in most Mexican restaurants and is enjoyed by many, even those without hangovers.

Tripe is as tough as or even tougher than beef jerky, but if it is cut in bite-size pieces and cooked in soup, it's much easier to eat. It took a long time to cook, but I remember enjoying it with my family as a young kid. I don't have it on my list of favorite

47

meat dishes anymore and will leave my share for someone else to savor. Today there are other cuts of beef that are much more appealing.

Organ meat from a hog was always a specialty for our family on butchering day. Grandma Conrad prepared a dish called hashlet and served it with cornbread and iced tea to all the kids and to those who helped with the butchering. Aunt Betty and some of the other family didn't like it but nothing from the hog was wasted. The only thing thrown away was the hair and the squeal!

THE KLAN

Bertha Mae Jones and Lela Mae Brown
Ate baked coon and hunted with hounds,
They both drank whiskey and cheap homebrew,
Loved grits and gravy and homemade stew.

Born in the middle of a saw briar patch,
They lived in a run-down shotgun shack,
Their mamas were sisters but also twins,
That's where Bertha and Lela Mae began.

They married twin brothers in a rock-and-roll band,
But they weren't just brothers, they belonged to the Klan.
They stirred up trouble every day and night
And nothing they did ever came out right.

Racist, they were, and so were their friends.
Their lives were messed up but were coming to an end.
All they ever did was stir up shit,
Next thing you know they were hiding in a ditch.

They had burned a church and killed two kids,
Took off running from the law and hid.

Bertha and Lela called nine-one-one;
In ten short minutes the sheriff would come.

A shoot-out ensued that would last for hours
But they were disarmed and lost all their power.
From the ditch they ran and crossed the road
But they got run over by a hundred-ton load.

Crushed on the highway were twin Klan members
But the fires of hell soon burned 'em to embers.
Here today, but gone tomorrow,
Very few eyes ever showed any sorrow.

Now there's two less members of the evil Klan.
They were not human beings and never a man,
So let this be a message to all the Klan members,
You better straighten up or you'll burn to cinders.

This sounds stupid but these kind of folks anger me and will
surely burn in hell unless they change their ways!

RUFUS AND ELMO

It was 1947 and the Tuesday after Labor Day. I was nine years old and attending my first day of fourth grade. It was a beautiful spring day as I rode the bus ten miles north on Highway 61 to Redwood School.

I always caught the bus each morning in front of Wilkerson's grocery store with my brother, Kennie, and, my sister, Mae. Summer vacation had ended but my first day back wasn't so bad; I met Elmo Blucher and we became good friends!

Elmo lived with his family on a run-down houseboat north of Vicksburg on the Mississippi River! Many folks lived this lifestyle and were known as "river rats". Like so many others, Elmo and I were poor and life had always been hard for our families.

For eight dollars a month, Mama rented us a three-room shotgun duplex on Givens Hill and I lived there with her, my three brothers, my sister and our Grandma Stephenson. Times were hard but we took life one day at a time and did whatever it took to get by. We survived on faith in God and a firm belief that someday life would get better. My dad had abandoned our family when my youngest brother, Marshall, was just a week old. Right away Mama got a job and arrangements were made for Grandma Stephenson to take care of us kids while she worked.

My dad had been the oldest of four kids, and at twelve years old he had found his dad lying on the ground early one morning in the summer of 1927 on his way to the cotton field. He had died from a massive heart attack. This was devastating to the family but Grandma continued to raise her three sons and a daughter on their little cotton farm in Lauderdale County, Mississippi. Times were never easy and got even worse as the years went by. Grandma never married again and kept her family together as best she could. They survived on what they made on the farm and with some help from family. At the time, Dad was twelve years old and his sister, Ruth, was the youngest at just four years old. Joel, the second son, was eight and Alton, the third son, was seven. Over the next eight years the two oldest boys grew up and left home and farm life withered away. Grandma continued to raise her youngest son, Alton and daughter, Ruth until they were eighteen, when they moved away and left her all alone.

Grandma had been having a hard time and moving in with us had been good for her. It also gave Mama a chance to work. With five kids and two adults, our small duplex was crowded but we made the best of a bad situation and got by.

Grandma received ten dollars a month from her youngest son, Alton, and with Mama's income from Kress's department store and help from our family and church, we managed to survive.

Mama couldn't afford to give us kids an allowance so Kennie and I sold worms and scrap metal for spending money. We didn't earn a lot but it was enough for movies and a few treats. Movie tickets and popcorn were a dime each but candy bars and pop were only a nickel.

Fifty cents went a long way and rarely did we miss going to the kiddie matinee in Vicksburg on Saturday. If there was extra money, we took Alton Ray and our sister, Mae, but Marshall had to wait till he was older.

Earning money was easier during the summer months but if luck was on our side, we could earn three dollars or more each week. Red worms brought fifty cents a hundred but the price of scrap metal was always up and down.

The junk man came once a week and sold worms to the local fish bait shops on Saturday morning. There was always a limit on how many worms we could sell; sometimes we had a thousand but sold only four or five hundred. When this happened, the leftovers were put in a bucket of dirt and cornmeal and sold later in the week.

When funds got low, we rode our bikes to the lake and sold what we could to local fishermen. They never paid more than bait shop prices but this gave us a little extra spending money.

This was our way of life at the time I met Elmo. My first visit to his houseboat was just before school ended in 1948, just two weeks before I turned ten. It was Friday and Mama had given me permission to visit over the weekend and return to school on Monday.

My new friend and I had a lot in common; we both lived a life of poverty and came from large families. Like me, he had three brothers, but also two-year-old twin sisters. Elmo had always lived on a houseboat and times for him and his family had

53

been tough. The only thing he had that I didn't was a daddy.

On Friday after school, the bus driver dropped us off on Highway 61 less than a hundred yards from the Mississippi River. It was a hot, muggy, spring afternoon but I was looking forward to a fun weekend.

Elmo and I, along with his three brothers, made our way down a dirt path to the riverbank. To reach the houseboat, we used a rickety old wood ramp that squeaked and swayed back and forth each time we took a step.

The river was calm and the old houseboat sat very still on the water. Elmo's dad was repairing trotlines to get ready for a night of fishing and his Mama was in the kitchen cooking supper. The twins were playing on the floor, and Luther, his old hound dog, met us at the door with a bark that was much worse than his bite.

Elmo's mama told him to change clothes and take care of his evening chores. After school he always helped his dad get ready for a night of fishing and could finish much sooner with my help.

For many years Mr. Blucher had fished the local rivers and lakes to support his family. He fished mostly at night but sometimes went out during the day when his catch was low.

His four sons knew all about fishing and learned to swim before walking. I thought I was a pretty good swimmer but they put me to shame!

Elmo and I were both wearing cut-off jeans without shirts and Elmo was wearing a big, wide brimmed straw hat. Later in the evening he found one for me. Neither of us wore shoes. Our feet were tough as leather since we wore shoes only when attending school or church!

Earlier in the day, Mr. Blucher had caught a bucket of sucker fish. He gave each of us a knife, along with instructions on how to cut them up for bait. The knives were very sharp and we finished the job in a short time. I had grown up close to the river and knew all about night fishing with trotlines. My friends, family, and I had fished the rivers and lakes most of our lives and I was looking forward to a fun night with Elmo and his dad.

After the chores were finished, it was time for supper so we washed up in an old porcelain pan and then sat down on wood benches around the kitchen table. The twins sat in highchairs next to their Mama and Mr. Blucher sat at the head of the table and blessed the food.

On a long wood table anchored to the floor were two large platters of fried catfish along with two bowls of fresh Polk salad covered with chopped boiled eggs.

That day, Mrs. Blucher had taken the twins along the riverbanks and gathered wild Polk salad for the evening meal. Also on the table were two pans of fresh baked cornbread and a bowl of oleo margarine. To drink, we had pint jars filled with our choice of tea or Kool-Aid.

With seven hungry kids and two adults, it didn't take long till the table was bare. The food was good and Polk salad just happened to be one of my favorites. Mrs. Blucher had prepared plenty and no one would leave the table hungry. Mama had always taught me good manners and I made sure to let her know how much I enjoyed her cooking. I knew it was important wherever I visited and she deserved the thanks.

After being excused, Elmo and I walked outside and took a seat on a wood bench attached to the side deck of the houseboat. We had always been told it was unsafe to swim right after eating so we rested and let our food settle.

Everything inside the houseboat and on the deck was anchored to the floor or walls! Rough waters would rock the houseboat in all directions; anything not properly secured would slide across the floor and everything on the walls would come crashing down. Oil lamps were securely attached to the wall (there was no electricity) and the stove and icebox got extra support on the floor.

A wood-burning stove was used for cooking and also supplied heat during the winter months. Cast-iron cook stoves were great and used by many families. Since they were used to prepare three meals each day, they rarely cooled down before it was time to build another fire.

The family drinking water was collected in fifty-five-gallon barrels placed at all four corners of the houseboat. The fresh rainwater ran off the roof through filters into wooden barrels, and if there was ever a need for extra water, it was hauled in from Vicksburg. This method of collecting water supplied most of their needs and they seldom ran out.

The Bluchers' transportation was an old, beat-up, half-ton Studebaker pick-up truck. When the family traveled together, Elmo and his three brothers rode in the back and the twins sat up front with their mama.

Mrs. Blucher used a rub board to scrub their clothes clean and hung them out to dry on a single clothes line attached to the outside eaves of the houseboat.

Everyone took baths in the river and the only toilet facility was a porcelain bucket with a lid and bail, better known as a "slop jar". It was carried to a ditch above the river each morning, emptied, and put back under the bed. Since the houseboat was docked on the river, there was no outhouse.

Mrs. Blucher ironed their clothes with heavy metal irons heated on top of the cook stove. Six were often heated at the same time; one was used until it cooled, then it was put back on the stove and another one was used until the ironing was finished.

Life on the river for Elmo and his family was much worse than my home life but the Stephenson family also used slop jars at night. We did have a two-seat outhouse out back but used it only during the daytime.

Mama also cooked on a cast-iron wood stove which was used to heat our house during the winter months. Our source of light was kerosene lamps and Mama also scrubbed our clothes clean on a rub board in a galvanized washtub on the back porch and hung them out to dry on clothes lines in the backyard. It was our way of life and we never gave it much thought. Most everyone lived this way.

After thirty minutes of sitting outside, our food had settled so we were given carbide lights that we attached to special brackets on our caps. After lighting them, we climbed aboard a fourteen-foot flat bottomed boat and were soon ready to begin our night of fun and adventure. We untied the boat and Mr.

Blucher headed upstream.

The safest way to travel was to stay to the right side of the main river channel, keeping close to the trees. Our headlights lit the way as we began an exciting night of fishing.

The sounds of locusts and bullfrogs could be heard, as well as the spooky sounds of the hoot owl and other birds and creatures of the night. A few feet from the boat, water moccasins and turtles could be seen swimming in the muddy water. There was danger all around but these sights didn't frighten us. They simply added more excitement to the evening.

The humidity was high and sweat ran off our bodies like we were standing in the rain. The movement of the boat was our only relief and created a breeze that helped keep us cool. When we stopped, the sweat began flowing again and to quench our thirst, we were constantly drinking fresh rainwater from a jug we brought along.

Our headlights attracted many bugs and mosquitoes that constantly swarmed around our heads. We had to keep our mouths closed to keep them out. We did get a few bites but that was expected during the spring and summer months. Everything about the evening was getting off to a great start for a fun night of fishing.

Danger on the Yazoo

It didn't take long till we reached the mouth of the Yazoo River. Hundreds of years before, it was known by the Indians as the "River of Death". The headwaters began north of Greenwood, Mississippi and ran one hundred and eighty-eight miles south, emptying into the Mississippi River a few miles north of

Vicksburg. It got its name from the Yazoo Indians, fierce fighting warriors who lived in the Mississippi Delta region. Part of their homeland later became known as Yazoo City, where many ancient burial mounds can still be seen.

According to legend, a tribe of giants once lived and farmed in the fertile, north Mississippi Delta region who were exterminated by the Yazoos. The Yahoos continued dominating the area for many years but the Choctaw and Chickasaw tribes, living west of the Mississippi River, eventually waged war and annihilated the entire Yazoo race. Around the campfire, we enjoyed this story and others like it, as so many other kids and grown-ups did in the past.

We continued upstream, our headlights lighting the way as we bucked the slow-moving current of the Yazoo River. After searching along the way, Mr. Blucher soon found a good place to set out our first trotline.

Even with our small boat, it was hard to get close to the riverbank with all the thick trees and brush growing in the shallow water. Mr. Blucher got as close as he could before turning off the engine. We then used the oars to get closer to shore.

When we made it to shallow water, Elmo and I got out of the boat and began baiting the hooks. First we tied both ends of the trotline to large willow branches and after an hour in the water, we had fifteen hooks baited. Before leaving, we marked the area with strips of white cloth and made our way back to the main river channel.

While Elmo and I were busy baiting the hooks, Mr. Blucher stayed in the boat and kept an eye out for any danger around us!

The river had many water moccasins and turtles; alligators were rarely ever seen, but to be on the safe side, he kept his pistol handy.

He smoked an old, crooked stem, briarwood pipe that was always filled with rum and maple tobacco. Elmo and I enjoyed the sweet smell of the smoke and it had the added benefit of helping keep the bugs and mosquitoes away. The aroma of pipe tobacco filled the air as we made our way upstream, searching for more places to set out more trotlines.

After traveling more than a mile, we heard the sounds of a high-speed boat and saw two bright headlights coming our way. Since our boat wasn't equipped with headlights, Mr. Blucher tried getting the operator's attention by waving his carbide light but it kept speeding toward us and never slowed down. By the sound of the motor, we could tell it was a big boat and would soon run over us if we didn't get out of the way. Mr. Blucher turned just in time and the big boat went by like a rocket. The two men were screaming and cussing, obviously drunk.

Their reckless action frightened us so Mr. Blucher pulled in close to the riverbank and hid behind thick brush and trees. After turning off the engine and putting out our lights, we kept quiet and sit very still. The speeding boat continued a short distance downstream, then turned and headed back our way. Elmo's dad reached under the seat and took out his pistol in case there was trouble.

Our boat was powered by a small outboard motor but these two drunks had a high-speed inboard equipped with two bright headlights. Both men held spotlights in their hands and shined them along the riverbank while looking for us.

60

There was nothing we could do but sit still and hope they didn't see or hear us. We did have one advantage over them: we were able to get closer to shore and maneuver through the thick trees and brush with our small boat.

They came within fifty yards of us; we could see them clearly and hear every word they were saying! This had us scared out of our minds but Mr. Blucher kept the gun in his hand and we prayed they didn't find us. He knew they were up to no good and urged us to keep quiet and not make a move. We did what he said as they searched the trees and brush for ten minutes before giving up and heading downstream.

It had been a close call but hopefully the danger was over. When they were out of sight and hearing, Mr. Blucher started our engine and we continued upstream in search of more places to set out our lines. Elmo and I felt much safer knowing that Mr. Blucher was keeping his pistol handy. We weren't exactly relaxed and still kept a sharp lookout for any strange boats coming up behind us.

We soon found a good fishing spot and got close to shore before turning off the engine. Out came the oars and we made our way through the thick willows and brush. In less than an hour, we had fifteen more hooks baited and the lines were tied between two large cypress trees.

We got back in the boat but Elmo's dad wanted to go ashore and have something to eat. Mrs. Blucher had put hot dogs in the cooler along with all the fixings and this made us happy. Elmo and I walked in front of the boat, pulling it as close as we could to the bank to unload what was needed. Then we gathered dry wood and built a roaring campfire.

61

With our pocket knives, we cut three small willow branches and used them for roasting our hot dogs. Mr. Blucher surprised us again when he gave us a bottle of Coke! This was new to us; not once had we ever thought we would be cooking hot dogs and drinking Coke on the banks of the Yazoo River!

After we had finished eating, Mr. Blucher wanted to walk the riverbanks and set out hooks instead of fishing out of the boat. This sounded like fun so we each got out a machete and began cutting fishing poles from cane that grew along the riverbank. Before long we had fifteen poles cut and were ready for fishing. Mr. Blucher suggested we try to find salamanders for bait. We liked the idea and ventured out in the swamp to begin turning over rotten logs. It was very dark so we stayed together and looked under everything we could, only to find a few salamanders.

We were about ready to give up but discovered a huge, rotten log half buried in the mud. The first thing we saw after turning it over was a five-foot water moccasin! Lucky for us we didn't get bitten. In seconds he made his escape into the safety of the swamp.

We searched the area for more snakes and when none were found, we broke up the rotten log, revealing twenty salamanders and dozens of huge white grub worms. This was encouraging so we continued our search until we had several dozen in our bucket.

Perhaps salamanders isn't the proper name for these slimy little creatures; they are better known as "puppy dogs" to most fishermen. They were five to six inches long and many different colors. Some were solid black but most had yellow, white, or red spots. To most folks they were the best fish bait no matter what the size or color.

We put out the fire and headed upstream to look for more fishing spots. Each time we found one, a hook was baited with a puppy dog and set out while Mr. Blucher followed behind with his light. It was fun, but after setting out the last pole we decided to take a rest before checking the hooks. We gathered more dry wood and built a camp fire. The area around the fire was cleaned off to make it safe from snakes and wild animals.

Overhead, the trees were very thick and we could hardly see the stars. The flashing lights of the fireflies helped light the darkness and the sound of hoot owls and bullfrogs were all around us. In the water, the beaver were splashing their tails and wild hogs could be heard grunting and squealing off in the swamp.

The campfire provided safety from wild animals and snakes on the ground around us, but one important thing we had to remember was to never let the fire go out!

While relaxing, Mr. Blucher told us a story about the S.S. Cairo, a powerful Civil War gunboat. It got its name from the city of Cairo, Illinois and was operated by the Union Navy. On December 12, 1862, Confederate forces launched a torpedo from shore and sank the Cairo to the bottom of the river in just twelve minutes. It went down in thirty-six feet of water but the crew survived with only a few injuries. This was the first electrically detonated torpedo ever fired. The spooky thing about this story was that we were not far from where it all happened. Upstream from our camp, the Cairo gunboat was still lying at the bottom of the Yazoo River and it would stay there for more than a hundred years before being raised from its grave.

It had been an exciting story but Elmo's dad thought we should get more rest. We got comfortable and soon fell asleep.

After an hour of rest, Mr. Blucher woke us and it was time to check the lines. We recharged our headlights with water and carbide, then put out the campfire and headed out.

It was still very hot and muggy as we made our way downstream. One by one, the lines were checked and after removing the fish, the hooks were baited again with puppy dogs and the poles reset.

Our string of catfish was getting so heavy we could hardly carry them by the time we got back to the boat. According to Mr. Blucher we had over seventy-five pounds. He helped carry the biggest share.

We put our fish in the boat tank and filled it with water. Another fire was built but Mr. Blucher thought we should take another short nap. It was still hot even in the early morning hours! We were also tired but after the campfire was burning well, we went off to sleep.

Two hours later, it was time to check the hooks so Mr. Blucher got us up and after putting out the fire, we headed out. At first we were sleepy but it wasn't long before we were wide awake. Instead of checking the lines on our way up the river, we waited until we got to the last pole and checked them all on our way back.

The first pole was pulled under the bank and we knew right away something big was on the line! Mr. Blucher removed the pole from the ground and felt the heavy weight of something tugging. It was tangled in dead tree limbs so Elmo and I got in the water and made an attempt to retrieve our mystery catch.

We used a long stick to feel our way to the end of the line then discovered our mystery catch was a huge turtle. We reached down in the water and grabbed him along with what he was tangled up in, and tried lifting everything out at once. It was way too heavy for Elmo and me, so Mr. Blucher jumped in and with his help, our leatherback turtle was soon lying on the riverbank. He was more than three feet in diameter and weighed close to fifty pounds. He was still very much alive and active when we got him out of the water.

We wanted to keep him but Mr. Blucher said he was way too big to take back to the boat. We removed the hook from his mouth and put him back in the water. At first he lay very still, then swam away like nothing was wrong. We had fourteen lines left to check but now we were much more excited about it!

There was nothing on the next two poles. The fourth, however, was pulled under the bank but not tangled up in limbs. Mr. Blucher removed the pole from the ground and began pulling in a huge fish. When he was close to the bank, we could tell it was a buffalo weighing close to thirty pounds. He had been hooked for a long time and didn't have much fight left. We removed the hook from his mouth, put a rope through his gills, and took turns carrying him.

Our stringer of fish was getting heavy but we continued checking the lines. Each of them had a three- to five-pound catfish and our load was more than sixty pounds when we finished.

All the fish were put in the tank and in fifteen minutes our carbide headlights were recharged and ready to go. It was after five o'clock and nearly daylight, but it was still dark enough for us to use our lights. Mr. Blucher pulled away from the bank and headed downstream.

In less than twenty minutes we arrived at our second fifteen-hook trotline. We spotted the white cloth markers and got as close as we could before tying up. When we got back in the water and thirty minutes later, we had removed fifteen more fish. This batch weighed close to fifty pounds and nearly filled the tank.

The sun was up and we no longer needed our headlights so we stored them under the seat and headed down the river.

It had turned into another beautiful Saturday morning when we arrived at our first trotline. Again we pulled up close to the riverbank so Elmo and I could get out and begin checking the lines.

Right away we saw strange activity in the water and noticed one end of the line was broken. Something big was splashing in the water so we stood back and let Mr. Blucher check it out. He got in the water and discovered a huge alligator gar on one of the lines. It weighed close to forty pounds and had pulled the other lines into thick willows. Everything was tangled up.

Mr. Blucher retrieved his pistol from under the seat and made his way over to the big alligator gar. He was still very active but was soon shot in the head. It was all Elmo and I could do to get him in the boat. It didn't take long until the other fish had been removed from the tangled lines and put in the tank.

Our night of fishing was coming to an end. We had caught more than two hundred and fifty pounds and now it was time to go home. It had been a fun and exciting night of fishing for us. In less than twenty minutes we were leaving the Yazoo River and entering the Mississippi. Immediately, we saw heavy barge traffic moving up and down the river. At a far-off distance, we heard sounds of a calliope, then saw the Delta Queen steamboat rounding the curve. It was heading south to New Orleans but would be stopping in Vicksburg. The old paddle wheeler was popular with the gamblers but also a beautiful sight for everyone to see.

We were tired and hungry and looking forward to having breakfast. Mr. Blucher headed for home and was soon tied up next to the houseboat.

First we unloaded the fish and cleaned out the boat. Before going inside, we grabbed a bar of soap and jumped in the river to get washed up and ready to eat. We took our seats at the table with all the family, then joined hands and bowed our heads as Mr. Blucher said the blessing.

Everyone enjoyed toodlum gravy, biscuits, and salt pork, along with a special treat of hot chocolate with marshmallow cream. Breakfast hadn't tasted that good in a long time!

Exploring Mint Springs and the Cemetery

After breakfast, we laid on the deck and took a nap, but after an hour of rest, it was time to make plans for another day of adventure.

Most of my Saturdays consisted of a movie in Vicksburg at the Strand or Singer Theater. There was always candy, popcorn, and my favorite soda, but today my brother, Kennie, and our friends would be enjoying that without me. Thinking about it made me sad so I tried not to dwell on it too long. Elmo and I were planning another adventure and I was looking forward to a fun day.

Elmo had no chores that day, but his dad had to clean and cut up all the fish and pick up crushed ice to keep them cool. Riding in Mr. Blucher's old truck sounded like fun so we decided to tag along.

The ice house was in an area of Waltersville called Negro Town. Sometimes on Saturdays, I went there with my Grandpa Conrad to get ice for the family. Grandpa worked five and a half days a week and got off work at noon on Saturday, so I would often walk over to the sawmill and ride with him to pick up his paycheck. He was paid in cash and stopped off at Harlen's Grocery Store and got whatever Grandma needed. Plus a piece of candy for me! From there, we went to the ice house and got fifty pounds for Grandma's old wood icebox.

I had friends living in Negro Town and often went fishing with them or swimming. Sometimes we even got together for a baseball game.

They were colored and one was a year older than me. His name was Tank. He looked much older than all of us and came to our rescue if we ever needed help. He was only eleven but was twice as big as me and all the others, weighing nearly one hundred and fifty pounds and towering above us all.

Two more of my colored friends were the Droan brothers, Little Boy and Boogs. Little Boy was the youngest at only eight, and was very small for his age. Boogs was much bigger than his brother and they lived in an old, rundown, two-story hotel on the north end of Negro Town. It was just about falling down, with most of the windows missing and some of the screens torn. A fire had burned out one room on the ground level. On the south side of their house was a honky-tonk where loud music and partying went on many nights. We never felt in danger while visiting there and very seldom heard about bad things happening to anyone.

There was one street in town and it ran north and south. Most of the buildings were in need of repair; some were built before the turn of the century and had rarely been painted or fixed up. The street was always in need of repair, with huge holes that filled up with water after a rain. The town had an awful smell since there were few public utilities other than electricity. Most of the houses had no indoor plumbing or toilets.

All the commercial buildings had electricity and running water along with indoor plumbing and toilets, but they too were in poor condition. Laced throughout town were one hotel, less than a dozen houses, several juke joints, a few grocery stores, and an ice house. There was one colored barber shop. Bill Windom owned the only white barber shop and I was his shoeshine boy.

When the heavy rains came, most of the town was under water but that didn't chase folks away. Houses were built several feet above ground and rarely did the water reach the inside. Folks just waited till the water went down and life continued as it had for many years.

The Wilkerson family was white and owned a grocery store on the south end of Negro Town. On the north end were two more grocery stores: One was owned by the Harlen family, who were white, and other by the Jue family, who were Chinese. There was another store in the middle of town owned by a white family but rarely did we go there.

The Jue family had five kids who attended Redwood School. They were Johnson, Anna Rose, Pansy, Maylee, and the youngest, who I never knew. They were the smartest kids in school and also attended the Missionary Bible Baptist Church in Waltersville with our family. Mr. and Mrs. Jue rarely attended but furnished ice cream and other treats for Vacation Bible School. They were a great family, known by everyone around Vicksburg.

While driving through Negro Town, I looked for Tank and the Droan brothers but never saw them. Tank lived with his mom, stepdad, four brothers and a sister in a two-room, rundown shack. His house was like ours and had no indoor plumbing or electricity. We were all poor but he and his family were much worse off than we were. My friends lived in poverty like all the other families in Negro Town and Waltersville. Tank didn't own a good pair of shoes and his clothes were ragged and torn. He was a good kid and a great friend!

Tank, Little Boy, and Boogs often went with me and Kennie to dig worms. Our favorite places were behind houses that backed up to the railroad tracks. We sold red worms for fish bait and when we earned three dollars, we divided it and went to Harlen's or the Chinaman's Grocery Store for treats. With sixty cents each, we could buy all the candy and pop we wanted and have money left over.

On Highway 61 next to Anderson Tully Paymasters' Office, a World War II veteran who had lost his right leg in

70

combat owned a bait shop. He liked all the whites but was very mean to the colored kids. While making our sale, our friends had to stay out of sight or there would be trouble. After we were paid, our colored friends joined us and the money was divided.

Many times when we were with our colored friends, the white folks gave us dirty looks but we never let it bother us. It was always fun being with them and that was all that mattered. At the end of the day we went to our house and they went to theirs.

Many Saturday mornings, we walked up to Highway 61 together and caught the city bus to Vicksburg. Our colored friends had to pay the driver at the front of the bus then get off and walk to the rear and enter again. The whites, however, entered at the front door and could sit wherever they wanted all the way back to the dividing line. After paying our fare and if there was extra room in both sections, we all sat at the dividing line and talked on our way to town. When we arrived at Washington and Clay Street, we got off and walked up the hill to the Strand Theater.

The white kids bought tickets at the Whites Only ticket booth and went in on the bottom level of the theater. The colored kids bought their tickets at their own booth and went upstairs and sat in the balcony.

Our afternoon and evening was spent watching double features of our favorite cowboy heroes and cartoons while enjoying our many treats.

After watching the movies two or three times, we met back at the bus stop. Mama worked at Kress's and at six o'clock we all

71

rode home together. Many great memories were made with my friends during those years on Givens Hill, Waltersville, and Negro Town.

Once in the early '60s while standing in line at a supermarket checkout stand in Maywood, California, I saw a picture of a huge colored man on the front page of the National Inquirer. Right away it caught my eye and I noticed his name was Tank! I bought a copy and discovered it was my old childhood friend from Negro Town.

The story described him as being one of the largest men in the U.S.A. I could hardly believe what I read because the picture didn't look anything like the Tank I once knew. It was plenty sad that he had lived in poverty in his early childhood, but he was much worse off now. Apparently, he had a health problem of obesity; Tank was twenty-four and weighed over one thousand pounds. I never heard or read any more about him but often wondered what happened to him.

Elmo's dad was soon ready to go so we got in the pick-up and rode along. When we got to the ice house, Mr. Blucher backed under the loading shoot and three hundred pounds of crushed ice was loaded in his truck. We each got a small piece to eat on our way home.

When we got home, Elmo and I helped pack the fish on ice and Mr. Blucher left on his route. He sold fish in the residential area of Vicksburg and Saturday was his busiest day. Generally, he fished five nights a week and sold his catch on Saturdays. The only day he didn't fish was Sunday, since it was the Lord's Day and he always spent it with his family. They attended church on Sunday morning and sometimes the evening service, but that was his day to rest.

Mrs. Blucher prepared a special meal on Sunday just like Mama but since I wouldn't be home, I was looking forward to having dinner with Elmo.

The rest of Saturday was free so we decided to visit Mint Springs, since Elmo had never been there. It was a beautiful place and located at the bottom of Fort Nogales in the Vicksburg Military Park. For me and my friends, it had always been a fun place to spend a day. Elmo's mother had given us permission to go provided that we were home before dark.

In less than thirty minutes we were at the west gate of the military cemetery. Using this route was faster and a fun way to go. Mr. Bell was the caretaker and if he caught us on our way through, we were escorted to the nearest exit. We had to be on the lookout and get as close to the east exit as possible or be taken back where we started.

There were two entrances and there was no other way to get in or out unless you were a kid. If or when we were ever chased by Mr. Bell or the park ranger, we got out the fastest way we could. Sometimes that meant climbing over the wall.

The roads through the cemetery were gravel and very crooked, with lots of hills and many places to hide. Mr. Bell made his rounds often and if we heard or saw a car coming, we hid until it passed. Visitation was seven days a week and the gates were open from 8:00 am to 4:00 pm, but kids were not allowed without adults.

Our house on Givens Hill was less than a hundred feet from the west cemetery wall. Kennie and I and our friends spent many days there and knew every crook and turn in the road. Our house was close enough to throw a rock from the back porch and hit the wall. During the wet season, for days at a time, a pink liquid that looked like Jell-O could often be seen on the hillside and around the back porch. It would appear after the rains stopped and the ground dried up. It had a strange smell and some folks thought it came from the cemetery. We never knew what it was or where it came from, but we stayed far away from it.

Grandma Stephenson's ghost stories during the time we lived near the cemetery were always the best. She told one each night and never got tired of telling them. We kids started out on the floor around her feet and by the time the evening was over we were sitting in her lap or close as we could. It would scare us half to death if someone said, "Boo"!

Mr. Bell and his family lived in a beautiful red brick home at the east entrance of the cemetery just inside the gate. There was a visitor's center next door and if we got thirsty, a drinking fountain was available under the gazebo. Getting a drink of water or going to the restroom was okay but that was the end of the line and we had to leave when we were finished. "Whites Only" was spelled out in big bold letters above our drinking fountain and restrooms, but there was also one for the colored.

The cemetery was beautiful and was a very quiet and peaceful place to visit so we treated it with respect. After World War II, I attended the funeral of my Uncle Leon McMullen. He was my Aunt Lela Mae's husband and though he was killed in Europe, he was later brought back and buried as a hero. I remember the loud twenty-one-gun salute and how sad it was for

Aunt Mae and all our family. I never forgot where Uncle Leon was buried and visited his grave often with Kennie and our friends.

There were many monuments throughout the cemetery and park and we always visited them. My friends and I often climbed huge magnolia trees and sat on the big limbs for hours, just talking.

The cemetery and park grounds were maintained year round and nothing was ever out of place. For me, my family, and friends, there was no place on earth more beautiful than the military park and the hills and city of Vicksburg. It was the only home I had ever known and was simply my Heaven on earth.

When my dad was a young man, before he and Mama met in 1935, he served in the CCC camps and his duty was maintaining the grounds of both the cemetery and the battlefield park. He met Mama while serving his time and they were married in December of 1935.

Vicksburg had always been a big part of my life and Grandma and Grandpa Conrad had lived in the area most all their lives. Some of our family on the Stephenson and Conrad side had fought in the Civil War and some had fought at the Battle of Vicksburg. For me there is no place like home even though I've lived far away from Dixieland my entire adult life.

One morning, while eating breakfast during summer break from school, sounds of fire trucks could be heard down the hill from where we lived. It was coming from Highway 61 just below Givens Hill. Kennie and I took off like a bullet and our friends, Wayne, Ralph, and Allen soon joined us. We made our way down the hill and saw fire trucks in front of an old grocery store in Negro Town.

It was exciting seeing all the firemen so we hung around until everything was under control and the trucks were gone. The burnt-out store was roped off and no one was allowed inside, but we kids were very curious and went back later in the day. Hardly anything was worth taking, but we found several cartons of wet cigarettes and many boxes of cigars after digging through the ruins. We loaded up all we could carry and hid them behind the burned-out building, with plans to go back and get them after dark.

At home we made plans to hide our stash. Wayne's house would be the best since it had a tall crawl space, so later in the evening we went back to the store with burlap sacks and hauled everything back to his house.

It took a while, but our cigarettes and cigars were soon separated, knowing it would take days to dry.

After more than a week had passed, we filled our pockets with cigars and cigarettes and headed for the cemetery. Magnolia trees were our favorite gathering places so we found one and climbed up on the limbs and took a seat. We all had matches and took out what we wanted to smoke and lit up. As we puffed away it didn't take long till the big magnolia tree looked like it was on fire. We were laughing and coughing and thought it was funny until Allen fell out of the tree and hit his head on a tombstone. He was crying his eyes out so we climbed down and went to his rescue. He had a big knot on his head but was able to walk after a few minutes, so we helped him over the wall and took him home.

When we arrived on the front porch, his Mama met us at the door and let him in. He was still crying and when we told her what had happened, she got all excited and called the doctor. He came right over but after examining Allen and his bump, the old doctor said he would be okay, though he advised us to stay out of the cemetery and quit climbing trees. His last and most important piece of advice was to stay away from cigarettes and cigars.

In a few days Allen was okay and ready to join us for more exciting times in the cemetery. He continued living on Givens Hill and many years later become a Baptist minister. He was the only friend we had who lived in a fancy house with a phone on Givens Hill.

Indian Mound Monument, located on the south side of the cemetery, was another place we often met. Built on top of the mound was a stone and brick gazebo that had a table and seating area overlooking the Mississippi River. From there it was a beautiful sight and we often had picnics there. You could see Louisiana across the river and also Highway 61, which went south to Vicksburg and north to Greenville and Memphis.

Many years before there was ever a cemetery, Indian Mound was used by the local Indians to escape the rising spring floodwaters. With their families, they left behind the dangers of rising waters, took everything they owned, including livestock, and retreated to higher ground, staying until it was safe to return to their village. The mound and the surrounding area was once much larger before it was part of the military park.

Elmo and I were lucky and made it through the cemetery without getting caught. After getting a drink of water at the east gate, we continued down the hill and soon arrived at Mint

Springs.

The spring water that flowed over the road was six inches deep and the natural limestone bridge was part of the road. A waterfall on the west side fell fifteen feet and created a crystal-clear pool below. We used grapevines to get down the waterfall, and after reaching the bottom we took a swim to cool off.

There were many trees and vines along the banks of Mint Springs and it was a beautiful sight very few adults ever got a chance to see. The stream continued west and emptied into the Mississippi River not far from where Elmo's houseboat was docked.

After a quick swim, we continued downstream and spent the rest of the afternoon exploring my favorite playground. Before leaving for home, our adventure took us to many waterfalls, each with a crystal-clear pool below. In these pools you could see many sun perch and blue gills, along with hundreds of crawfish. The water was so clear you could see all the way to the bottom.

We never bothered the fish but caught many crawfish and put them in small pools we made at the edge of the creek bank. They could live out of water and when we got tired of playing with them, they were put back in the pools.

We often threw rocks at targets while making our way downstream. Elmo saw an abandoned squirrel's nest in a big cottonwood tree and began throwing rocks at it. After a few tries he hit it but nothing happened. He continued until he hit it again but this time something in the nest began to move and small twigs began falling to the ground. Then a big raccoon walked out on a limb so we got scared and took off running, leaving him alone. He wasn't hurt but he sure didn't like his sleep being disturbed.

Moving On

Along the creek bank and on the hillsides, we picked and ate wild fruit and berries. Green plums were a special treat to eat with salt, but too many would give you a belly ache. There were many plum trees along the way and the ripe fruit was sweet as sugar.

Later in the summer months, pawpaws were ripe and so were wild grapes. Pawpaws grew on many small bushes but some grew on trees twenty feet tall. Most grapevines grew close to the ground but others grew on vines high in the trees. Pawpaws had the shape of a giant six-inch peanut but had a taste of bananas. Grapes were plentiful and so were huckleberries, blackberries, dewberries, mayhaws, blackhaws, redhaws, and mulberries!

In late summer and early fall, pecans, black walnuts, chinkapins and hickory nuts were ready to gather. These trees also grew on hillsides and creek banks – there was never a reason to go hungry while exploring Mint Springs.

There were a few times when Kennie and I, along with our friends, caught fish and killed birds with our slingshots and cooked them on an open fire. All we needed was salt so we never left home without it. Another important thing was to never leave home without matches.

We continued our adventure downstream toward the last waterfall. A hundred yards away we could hear the sound of roaring water as it fell twenty feet to the pool below. Getting to the bottom wasn't very easy since we made our way down on grapevines.

There was a four-foot rock ledge wide enough for both of us halfway down the falls. A few feet away, but behind the falling water, was the entrance to a large cavern. Making it through was tricky but most of us kids had done it before.

We would take a ten-foot plunge into the pool below if we lost our balance while stepping through the falling water. But if we made it through, we were rewarded with the beautiful rainbow colors of the sun shining through the water. I led the way with Elmo right behind me. I reached the ledge first and waited for him. Soon we were standing side by side.

He was in awe of this rare adventure and had never seen anything like it before. We stood there several minutes before I made an attempt to enter the cavern. There was nothing to hold on to, so I lost my balance and fell in the pool below.

I was a little embarrassed at first but it had happened before and there was no danger in the fall. In less than three minutes I made it out and was soon standing on the bank. I looked up and Elmo was still on the ledge, laughing out loud. He yelled out and said he was going to give it a try and then disappeared behind the waterfall.

I began climbing up and was soon back on the ledge. The roaring water was very noisy and I could hardly hear Elmo, but I could see him through the water. I rested a few minutes then made it through on my next attempt.

The sun was shining through and the dirt floor was

smooth and dry. Against the wall was a ledge wide enough to sit on. Elmo was thrilled to see everything for the first time; it was such a beautiful sight with rainbow colors brightly lighting the cavern.

Now it was time to take the plunge! To exit the cavern, we had to jump through the falling water and I led the way. With only a few feet to get up speed, I ran fast as I could and did a cannonball through the falling water, landing in the pool below. I got out and looked up just as Elmo made his leap. He landed with a big, thrilling splash!

He wanted to do it again and this time we both made it through without a problem. Now Elmo jumped first and I followed. After a perfect landing, we were soon stepping out of the pool. It had been exhilarating for both of us, but it was time to make our way back to Elmo's houseboat.

We could see the highway and the Mississippi River and were only a mile away from Elmo's house. We continued downstream and finally made it to Highway 61. Going beneath the road would be another adventure as we made our way through a long dark concrete culvert. It was part of a drainage system that carried water from Mint Springs to the Mississippi River. It was always best to go through in the evening when the sun was shining in the west end.

There were many drainage pipes that emptied into the main system but it was best not to venture into them. It was an easy place to get lost and no one would ever find you!

We finally entered the east entrance and traveled over two hundred feet before reaching the west end. We burned pine knots to light our way. They created lots of black smoke and had a strong smell of pine tar, but using them eliminated the risk of stepping on water moccasins. We were very lucky to have made it through without encountering any danger.

After reaching the halfway mark, the bright evening sun began providing light and our torches were no longer needed. We dropped them in the water and made our way to the west end without any problems. Once outside, we were less than two hundred and fifty yards from the river.

The railroad tracks were a few yards away and we heard a train whistle to the north. It was heading toward Vicksburg and it took about fifteen minutes to get to us. Since there was an hour of daylight left, we jumped in an empty boxcar when it went by.

Elmo had never hopped a freight train before and this was another adventure for him. Our ride went by fast but slowed down when we got to Vicksburg. We didn't want to go any farther south so we jumped off at Ryan's Coal Yard.

The Illinois Central Depot was less than a block away so we walked over there to get a drink of water and use the restroom. After a few minutes in the depot, we went over to the river and watched the tugboats push barges up and down the river. Seeing the busy river traffic was exciting but we soon headed north toward Elmo's houseboat.

While walking north on the railroad tracks, we could see the Mississippi River on the west side and Highway 61 on the east. Along the way we picked up pieces of scrap metal and had all we could carry. We would have plenty for the junk man when he came that week!

It didn't take long till we were crossing the wood ramp to Elmo's houseboat. The sun was disappearing behind the trees and Mr. Blucher was sitting on the bench smoking his pipe. Elmo's three brothers were swimming in the river and the twins were inside with their mother. Mrs. Blucher told us to get ready for dinner so we jumped in the water and washed off with soap. Attached to the west end of the houseboat was a rickety old diving board; after a few dives we dried off and got ready to eat.

The food was blessed and Mr. Blucher told us about how he had traded gar fish for a burlap bag of fresh mustard greens. He had made the trade with a colored lady living north of Waltersville. There were a few white folks who ate gar fish and buffalo, but nearly all the colored folks liked them. Our own family fish fries at Grandpa's always consisted of catfish and buffalo, although Mama and Grandma would rarely let the kids eat buffalo because it had too many small bones.

On the table, Mrs. Blucher had two big bowls of mustard greens and lots of fried catfish that we had caught the night before. There was also a big pan of hot cornbread, along with plenty of oleo margarine and fresh wild onions she had picked on the hillside. We had a choice of tea or Kool-Aid. Everything was great.

Another Night on the River

After supper, everyone except Mrs. Blucher and the twins went out on the deck. Elmo and I attached two kerosene lamps to wall brackets above the deck and Mr. Blucher was puffing away on his briarwood pipe. Elmo's three brothers were playing jacks on a fold-down table attached to the wall. Everyone was suffering from the heat so we jumped in the river again and cooled off.

After a short swim we got out and Mr. Blucher told us a story about Booger Dan and how he was abandoned by his mother and raised by an old wild sow and thirteen little pigs. It took over an hour and even though we had heard it many times before, we enjoyed it.

The bugs and mosquitoes were thick so we took the lamps and went inside at ten o'clock. The twins had been put to bed earlier and Mrs. Blucher had covered them with a mosquito net. There were screens on the windows and doors but many flies and mosquitoes had gotten inside when the doors were left open. Mr. Blucher turned up the lamps and the bright light began attracting the pesky little critters. We each took a fly swatter and the battle was on, seeing who could kill the most. Mr. Blucher nearly broke a lamp shade while swinging his fly swatter. After battling an hour or more, most of them had been killed so we put the fly swatters away.

Since we had worked up a sweat, we were given permission to take yet another swim before going to bed. Our kerosene lamps helped light the area but it was much brighter once we had lit the carbide lights.

We were having fun but Mrs. Blucher yelled out the window and said the twins couldn't sleep. It was time for us to go to bed. The carbide lights were put out but Elmo and I took the lamps and made our way to bed, hanging them on the wall. It was a tiny room with six built-in bunk beds. There were three on each side so we each had our own bed with one to spare. With only one window, there was very little air circulation and we could hardly see our hands in front of our faces when the lights were put out. It took a few minutes but the reflection from the moon on the river gave off enough light for us to get settled.

Outside we could hear strange sounds but we were well used to it. Our day in the park had been great and our boxcar ride to Vicksburg was something Elmo would never forget. A day like this was always fun but when bedtime came we were ready to go to sleep.

The river was a little choppy and rocked the houseboat, but the motion, combined with the outside sounds of the swamp and water slapping against the houseboat, put us to sleep.

The night went by fast and Sunday morning came before we knew it. We got up and took turns using the slop jar, and after our business was finished, we went out on the deck and jumped in the river. It was already hot but the cool water woke us up. Mrs. Blucher called us for breakfast so we got out and dried off.

It was another beautiful day and we took our seats at the table. A big bowl of macaroni and cheese was on the table, along with a pan of hot biscuits. Mrs. Blucher then brought out a pitcher of hot chocolate syrup, which was always a big treat at our house on Sunday mornings. Everyone agreed that it tasted great over hot biscuits. At my house we were not allowed to drink coffee, but Elmo had a cup and one was offered to me. I said yes and it tasted great with sugar and cream. The other kids had milk and we all enjoyed our breakfast.

Sunday school was at nine o'clock, so Elmo, his brothers, and I grabbed a bar of soap and took another swim. We then got dressed and slicked down our hair with rose hair tonic. We were soon ready for church and waiting on deck for the others.

After everyone was ready, we made our way up hill to the

85

old Studebaker pick-up. Mr. and Mrs. Blucher and the twins got up front and we five boys got in the back.

In fifteen minutes we were parked in front of the Hilltop Pentecostal Church and went to our classrooms. Elmo and I were together but the other kids went to different rooms. There was no air conditioning and the sweat was pouring off of us. It didn't take long till our clothes were soaking wet. All I could think of was taking another swim in the Mississippi River.

I was a little scared at first when we walked inside because of the stories I had heard about the shouting and running up and down the aisles at the Pentecostal church. I was Baptist and our church frowned on the Pentecostal's ways. We called them holy rollers. They were good people but worshipped with a little more excitement than most!

After Sunday school, everyone went to the sanctuary. Elmo and I took a seat on the back pew and it didn't take long till all the seats were full. It wasn't a big church but there was standing room only when the service started.

The choir and the musicians took their places on stage and the preacher walked over to the pulpit. All the adults were cooling off with their hand-held paper fans furnished by the local mortuaries. The babies were fussing from the heat but the pianist began to play and the band joined in. This type of gospel singing and dancing was some of the first rock and roll before Elvis came along.

My eyes bugged out when everyone began to sing and shout. The preacher waved his bible in the air and pounded on the pulpit. The babies continued to cry and all the adults were raising their hands toward Heaven. Some were running up and down the aisles but Elmo and the other kids didn't think anything about it. I was shocked at what I was seeing - now I knew everything I had heard was true!

After an hour of singing and shouting, everyone got quiet and took their seats. By now all the congregation was soaking wet with sweat but the preacher soon finished his sermon.

A special healing service began and anyone wanting to be healed could come to the altar so the preacher and deacons could lay hands on them while praying in tongues. I couldn't understand anything they were saying but those who came forward began dancing in the aisles and falling on the floor. Some got up and made a few rounds in the church then came back and knelt at the altar. They were screaming and crying but Elmo and all the others just sat there like nothing was happening! I was all eyes and ears and didn't know whether to laugh out loud or get up and run.

This went on for a long time but then the service returned to normal. The preacher soon dismissed the congregation with prayer and before long, the church was empty. Everyone went outside and milled around in the parking lot trying to cool off. It didn't take long till the Blucher family and Rufus were on their way home. I was tired just watching everybody run up and down the aisles; I was ready to get out of there and go cool off in the river.

I was glad when we were parked and making our way down the ramp to the houseboat. Mrs. Blucher told us we could change out of our church clothes and go swimming. It felt great!

Like most ladies, Mrs. Blucher had prepared most of her food before leaving for church and told us kids to stay close because dinner would soon be ready.

While we were swimming in the river and having fun, we heard gunshots. Mr. Blucher told us to get out of the water. We didn't ask any questions but were curious to know what was wrong. While standing on the deck, Elmo's dad pointed toward some willow trees a few feet from where we had been swimming. To our surprise there was a big water moccasin floating belly up in the water. We watched him float out of sight then got back in the water and continued having fun till Mrs. Blucher called us for dinner.

We were all starved and quickly gathered around the table. Mr. Blucher obliged us with the blessing.

Sunday dinner was my favorite at home. Mama always made the best of everything. I thought about what she was fixing and how good it must be, but today I would have to settle for whatever Mrs. Blucher was making. I had never missed Mama's Sunday dinner before.

The usual platters of fish were on the table but also a big bowl of collard greens with fatback. A bowl of rice and brown gravy was steaming hot, along with leftover biscuits from breakfast. A big platter of cornbread was on each end of the table and to drink there was tea, Kool-Aid and coffee.

The food looked great and over the next half hour we enjoyed our dinner. Mrs. Blucher later surprised us with a big banana pudding that smelled like what Mama made. She gave each of us a bowl and Elmo and I had a cup of coffee while the other kids had a glass of Kool-Aid. Dinner had been good but the dessert was great and I had a chance to enjoy another cup of coffee with cream and sugar.

When we left the table, Mr. Blucher got out his fishing rod and cast out into the river about fifty feet. He had a big red bobber on the line and let it sit in the moving current while resting. His old pipe was lit and he leaned back against the wall and told us kids some more stories. After an hour of rest, it was time to take another swim. This was our only way to cool off so we played in the water and dove off the deck most of the afternoon.

Radio was everyone's home entertainment and on Sunday evening several of our favorite programs were broadcasted. The old radio was powered by a big Rayovac battery placed next to the cook stove and charged up overnight when it got weak.

Elmo's battery was fully charged so we went in the front room and turned on the radio. All of our programs were on the same station so we set the knob and settled down for an evening of radio fun.

Each program was thirty minutes long. Our favorites were the Lone Ranger, Straight Arrow, Sky King, Mr. and Mrs. North, B-Bar-B-Ranch, The Squeaking Door, and Amos and Andy. It took over three hours but eventually it was time to end the evening. We took another swim and got ready for bed.

Off to bed we went and it didn't take long until we were fast asleep. My weekend with Elmo had been great and we were already making plans for summer break.

We were up early Monday morning and after a swim, we

dried off and got dressed for school. Again our hair was slicked down with rose hair tonic and we got ready for breakfast. There were grits, biscuits, gravy, and my last chance for another cup of coffee.

Now it was time to say goodbye to Elmo's mama and dad. I thanked them for a great weekend. Elmo and I had made great memories and we looked forward to the many more we would make.

Up the hill we went to the highway where the bus was waiting. We climbed aboard and all the kids began calling Elmo and his brothers river rats. It made us mad but we took our seats and in forty minutes, we were getting off in front of Redwood School.

My attention span wasn't very good that day because I couldn't get my mind off the good time I had on the Mississippi River. I was angry about my friend and his brothers being called river rats but there was nothing I could do about it.

When school was out at three o'clock I said goodbye to Elmo since we would be riding different buses. I was looking forward to seeing my family again.

It seemed like a long ride before we got off in front of Wilkerson's Grocery Store. Together Kennie, Mae, and I walked up Givens Hill and climbed the stairs to our little shotgun duplex. I was gone only a weekend but it seemed much longer. When we opened the door, Snowball greeted us, followed by Mama and the boys. Grandma had problems with her feet but soon came out and hugged me. It had been a fun weekend but I was glad to be home. Kennie and I changed clothes and went outside to meet with Ralph and Wayne before supper. They asked all about my weekend and I shared some of my adventures.

Behind the house we crossed the cemetery wall, climbed a big magnolia tree and talked. Our house was a short distance from the wall and we soon heard Mama calling. We climbed down and crossed the wall and in less than five minutes, we were washed up for supper.

We took our seats and Mama blessed the food. Everything looked like it always did – my favorite macaroni and cheese, along with a big pot of mustard greens and Mama's favorite cornbread were on the table. There was no dessert but to drink we had Kool-Aid. It was great being home and I was making plans to spend more time on the river with my friend Elmo during summer break.

Summer Vacation

Over the next two weeks, Elmo and I saw each other every day and were looking forward to summer break. My tenth birthday came and went, with nothing very exciting happening except that school was out. My birthday always fell on Memorial Day but very few people other than the colored folks celebrated. I was often kidded about it falling on what most folks called "Nigger Day". It seemed to generate a few laughs but for me, it was never funny at all. I tried to grin and bear it till the day was over.

The first Monday morning after school was out, Kennie and I had plans to visit our cousins for two weeks. They lived in the country and I would be staying with Aunt Estus and Uncle James Cowart and their three kids, Charles Wayne, Arlene, and Jimmy. It was always fun and there was never a dull moment.

Fishing, hunting, horseback riding, and swimming created many memories. The time always went by way too fast.

Kennie would be visiting Aunt Marie and Uncle Aubrey Williams and their five kids, Gene, Mickey, David, Ronnie, and Peggy. They lived a mile west of Aunt Estus so we all got together often during those two weeks.

Being with my cousins kept my mind off the adventures Elmo and I were planning but those two weeks were over before I knew it. It was sad to leave but it was soon time to say goodbye and return home to continue my summer vacation. Before long, we were back in the swing of having fun with our local friends. We sold worms and scrap metal, earning money for summer treats and our favorite comic books. There was always enough left over for tickets to see our favorite cowboy heroes on the big screen at the Strand and Singer theaters.

We attended church both Sunday morning and night but also went to prayer meeting on Wednesday night. We never missed the revivals and church was always a big part of our life. Most of our family and friends attended Waltersville Missionary Bible Baptist Church, which was less than a mile from our house.

Bible school would last two weeks each summer and we learned all about Jesus. We memorized bible scriptures and each class performed plays on the first Sunday after it was over. There were special treats prepared each day by the mothers and at the end, a big picnic was held for which the Jue family furnished ice cream and other treats. This was a fun day we all looked forward to and each kid recited bible verses that we memorized. We learned a lot about Jesus, doing what was right, and staying away from the evils of Satan. It was a great way to start summer vacation and ensured we were reminded of the sins of the world.

When I accepted Christ as my savior at nine years old, my outlook on life drastically changed. Before becoming a Christian, I was always worried about dying and each night after attending church on Sunday, I would go home and find it hard to fall asleep. I was always scared and thought I would go to Hell and never see my family and friends if I died. Those frightening feelings went away once I made things right with God. I never worried about it again.

There was no way I could ever be perfect but when I did some things I shouldn't have done, I always asked God to forgive me. This happened now and then but forgiveness gave me hope that the gates of Hell were closed to me. I knew I would go to Heaven if I died. It gave me a good feeling knowing Jesus forgave me. He fought my battles and never lost one.

The Boogie Man was no longer a fear and I could now grow up and have fun without having any worries. But if I did slip along the way, forgiveness was just a prayer away and my sins would be forgotten. For a little kid, this was a great insurance policy and it didn't cost me a penny. Christ paid it all when he died on the cross and I was also taught that once I accepted God's plan of salvation, I was saved and his protection would be with me forever. My sleepless nights went away and never again did I have any more nightmares. As a little kid, I had been carrying a burden since reaching the age of accountability, but that had been lifted forever.

The hot summer days would come and go but one day in late June, I walked over to Elmo's houseboat. It was early in the morning so I told Grandma where I was going and when I would be back. Kennie wouldn't be going since he had plans to visit Fort Nogales with friends.

When I arrived at Elmo's house, he and his dad were loading fishing gear on the boat so I helped. Together it didn't take long until we were finished so Elmo was given permission to play. Dinner wasn't ready so we went swimming and played a few games before eating.

I was invited to eat and Mrs. Blucher had catfish, a big bowl of fried squash, two platters of cornbread, and to drink we had cherry Kool-Aid. Mr. Blucher had left early so Elmo said the blessing. After eating, we rested awhile and then cooled off in the river.

Our plan that afternoon was to explore an old abandoned sawmill not far from where Elmo lived. It was less than a mile away and it took about fifteen minutes to get there. The old, dilapidated mill building sat on the west side of the railroad tracks and most of it was built over the backwaters of the river. The trees and vines were thick and the buildings were pretty much falling down. I had been there before but this would be Elmo's first time.

We kept a lookout for snakes and spiders and made sure we didn't step on rotten boards or rusty nails. Like always, we were wearing shorts and straw hats but no shoes!

Sometimes we were as high as fifty feet above the river. If we found large pieces of wood, we lined them up with an opening below and yelled out, "bombs away" as we dropped them in the water below. Sometimes they hung up and didn't fall all the way but we kept trying till we hit the water. If we got lucky there was always a big splash. It always gave us a thrill to hit our target.

Our favorite place to explore was an enclosed area once used to transfer logs from the river. Years before, when the mill was in operation, logs were taken out of the water and moved on transfer belts to a location where they were dried and cut up for lumber.

It was an enclosed area with very little light coming through the gaps in the boards so we had to be careful of nails and rotten wood. Walking through it was like being inside a cave.

While making our way through the old building, we caught many lizards and put them in a glass jug we found along the tracks. These lizards were hard to catch but by the time we were ready to leave, our jug was nearly full. It was always fun catching them but it was also fun setting them free.

Our adventure had lasted nearly two hours when we decided to go somewhere else and not keep pushing our luck. The old sawmill was dangerous; we were always lucky and never got hurt too badly!

We headed north to Negro Town and stopped at Tank's house. He had extra fishing poles so we decided to try our luck on the river. Tank had a bucket of worms so off we went with hopes of catching a few catfish before it got late.

It didn't take long till we were sitting on the banks of the Mississippi River. We baited our hooks and sat by our poles for a while, but our luck wasn't good. We got bored from not catching anything, so we secured our poles in the ground and began exploring the sand bars.

The sand and dirt were dry and crusty, but very smooth along the edge of the water. We each carried a long stick to test for quicksand ahead of us as we made our way slowly downstream. We must have walked a half mile before finding a safe place to wade in the river. Soon Elmo and I were standing in water up to our knees. Tank was lagging behind about a hundred feet.

All of sudden the dry crusty sand and mud gave way and Tank went down to his chest and began screaming. All we could do was throw him our sticks hoping they would give him enough support to keep from sinking deeper. We were much lighter and able to walk without breaking through the crust. Tank weighed more than both of us together and the sand couldn't support his weight. Holding all three sticks kept him from sinking while we took off toward the trees, desperately hoping to find something to set him free. Tank screamed as we ran away, but there was nothing we could do but try to find a way to rescue him.

No sooner had we reached the thick trees and brush when we found a ten-foot board left behind when the river was flooded out of its banks. We each grabbed an end and took off to the sandbar. When we reached Tank he hadn't sunk any deeper so we got on our hands and knees and crawled as close as we could while sliding the board to him. He still clung to all three sticks to keep from sinking.

He reached out and grabbed the board while we held tight to the other end. Slowly he made his way to safety and we all began crying tears of joy. Tank had always been there for us, but this time we were there for him.

He was covered with mud up to his neck but he soon

found a safe place in the river for him to clean up. We had forgotten all about our fishing poles so we hurried back to check them. It had been an unlucky day for Tank and a frightening day for all of us. But our luck was about to change!

When we reached the poles, each of them had a catfish that weighed over five pounds. We thought it was best not to press our luck any further, so we took our fish and headed for home.

We were soon saying goodbye to Tank and heading out of Negro Town. When we reached the bottom of Givens Hill, Elmo said goodbye and headed south on Highway 61, and I took off for the house. The sun was nearly down so I made my way up the hill and was soon washing up for supper.

It had been another fun day but also frightening. We nearly lost our good friend but God had saved his life and protected Elmo and me. A good lesson was taught that day as we learned more about the dangers that lurked on the banks of the great Mississippi River. We had been told stories about fishermen being sucked down in quicksand before, but now we knew firsthand just how dangerous it really was.

We didn't want to upset our folks with this narrow escape so it would be our secret. Thank God for looking after three ignorant little kids and giving Elmo and me the strength and knowledge to save our friend from the dangers of quicksand. This was just one of my friends' secrets that were never forgotten.

Problems with Elmo

One evening while I was sitting alone on the front porch, I heard my name called. I didn't see anyone so I walked down the hill toward the highway and heard it again. *Rufus! Hey, Rufus, what are you doing?* I couldn't tell where it was coming from but I saw someone standing in the shadows of a big chinaberry tree. I was surprised as I got closer to see it was Elmo, who had been crying. I asked what was wrong and said he just wanted to stop by and see me before it got dark.

I asked if there was something he wanted to tell me but refused to say anything so I invited him to eat supper with us.

Snowball, our family dog, was in the back room and came running when the door was opened. He was a big white fur ball and wouldn't harm a fly; he was a puppy when we got him and had always stayed inside.

Mama told us to get ready for supper so we washed up and took a seat at the table. She said the blessing. Elmo's silence continued until Grandma spoke up and asked where he lived. I think she already knew but this was her way of getting him to talk. He answered her question, which did break the ice and everyone began to talk.

Marshall hadn't been walking very long so he was sitting in his highchair next to Mama at the end of the table. Grandma sat at the other end and the rest of us kids filled up the wood benches on each side.

For supper there was cornbread along with three fresh vegetables from Grandpa's garden. He had dropped them off on his way to work that morning. He had a beautiful garden that supplied most of the family's needs, and he also raised the hogs and chickens that supplied their meat and eggs. He had one cow that supplied their milk and butter. We thought Grandpa was rich because he had lots of food and always helped our family.

There were two bowls on the table: one filled with fried squash and the other had mustard greens. There was also a dish of fresh sliced cucumbers in vinegar along with a plate of green onions. Grandma had sent along a pound of fresh churned butter she made the day before. The cornbread was hot out of the oven and smelled great. Mama made it with left over cracklins given to us by Grandpa. We enjoyed our supper but after finishing, Kennie, Elmo, and I went out on the porch.

Elmo still hadn't said why he stopped by and it certainly wasn't like him to be out that late by himself. We could tell he didn't want to talk and didn't ask any more questions.

It was still hot and muggy and the lightning bugs were everywhere. We caught dozens and put them in mason jars but we released them before going inside. We went in and washed our hands, then gathered around Grandma Stephenson and enjoyed one of her favorite bedtime stories.

Elmo hadn't said anything about going home so Mama asked if his folks knew where he was. He began to cry and said he ran away and wasn't ever going home. Mama tried to find out what happened but he didn't have much to say other than he'd had an argument with his dad and left shortly before dark.

We didn't have a car and nobody had phones, so Mama didn't know what to do. It was getting late and she didn't want his folks to worry. After talking with him a few minutes, he had a different view of what happened and decided to go home. He never did say what the problem was. He was scared so Mama told Kennie and me to walk him home.

He lived more than a mile away so we headed down to the

highway then south toward Vicksburg. Mama told us to be careful and come home as soon as we could.

In twenty minutes we were crossing the wood ramp to Elmo's houseboat. His dad's pickup was gone but his family met us at the door and were glad to see Elmo. His mother didn't scold him. Instead, she gave him a hug and was very happy that he came home. Mr. Blucher was still out searching the neighborhood but there was no way to let him know that his runaway son had come home.

We stayed a few minutes and Elmo walked us up to the railroad tracks. Just before leaving, Mr. Blucher pulled up in his truck and jumped out and gave Elmo a hug, simultaneously scolding him for what he had done. It was plain to see he had been worried but was very happy now that his son was home.

Kennie and I said goodbye and headed north on the highway. In twenty minutes we were climbing Givens Hill and walking in the front door. Snowball greeted us then went back to his bed. It was late so we washed our faces, hands and feet in a pan of water and got ready for bed.

Our house was tiny so Kennie, Grandma, and I slept in the back room. Grandma slept on an old army cot and was already in bed but still awake. She was worried but happy we were home. Mama, Eula Mae and Marshall slept in a double bed in the front room and Alton Ray slept on a pallet made up on the floor. Kennie and I shared a single bed but he slept on one end and I slept on the other. We said our prayers and jumped in bed. Mama said goodnight and blew out the lamps.

As the house grew dark and quiet and I couldn't get my

mind off Elmo and wondered what happen between him and his dad. I thought he was lucky to have a dad in the first place and even though Elmo ran away, his dad was happy that he came home.

Eventually I went off to sleep and the night went by fast. I was up early the next morning. Like always, Mama had breakfast ready and we kids washed up and took our seats around the table. She blessed the food and we enjoyed a breakfast of biscuits, gravy, and chocolate milk.

Mama had to pinch pennies so our weekday breakfast was always the same. If there was extra money, she tried to make something special on Saturday and Sunday, but we never did complain no matter what she made.

I asked Kennie after breakfast to go with me to see Elmo but he had other plans so I sat around till mid-morning reading comic books and playing marbles with my friend Ralph.

Each morning, Ralph's mother left at ten o'clock for work but his dad was on a disability pension and in a wheelchair. He was in a mining accident in South Dakota that had left him paralyzed from the waist down and he couldn't be left alone. Ralph always stayed with him till his Mama got home from work at six o'clock.

Mama was at work so I asked Grandma if I could go visit Elmo. She said it was okay but to be home by six o'clock. I took off running down the hill and was crossing the wood ramp to Elmo's houseboat in twenty minutes. At first I thought he couldn't play since he was busy helping his dad repair fishing lines.

He motioned for me so I walked over, not knowing what to expect. Mr. Blucher spoke and Elmo got out of the boat and began talking. It was close to dinner time but he still had a few chores left before it was time to eat. I started to leave but Mr. Blucher asked me to stay and eat with them.

I helped Elmo and in less than an hour the job was finished so we got permission to take a swim. We jumped in the river and cooled off until it was time to eat.

Mr. Blucher blessed the food and thanked me and Kennie for walking Elmo home the night before. He also thanked Mama for letting him eat with us and for persuading him to go home.

Now everything was back to normal! After dinner, we went out on the porch and I asked if it would be okay for him to visit the park that afternoon.

At first he was a little hesitant but then got up enough courage to ask his dad. We were surprised when he said we could if Elmo was home by five thirty. To us that was great and since I had to be home at six o'clock. This would give me time to stop by Elmo's and continue on home.

I was carrying a slingshot in my back pocket so Elmo found his and we left for the park. We walked to the railroad tracks and began filling our pockets with rocks from between the rails.

We reached the cemetery and there was no one in sight, so we stayed on the road up to the east gate and got a drink of water. Then we heard a loud noise and when we looked up, Mr. Bell was closing the gate. We were trapped and there was no chance of escaping! We waited for our punishment.

We were scared, especially since Elmo had gotten in trouble the night before; he knew his dad would ground him all summer if he found out.

Mr. Bell was very angry and told us to empty our pockets and then took away our slingshots. We hadn't shot anything, but he didn't believe us so we just gave up and took a seat on the bench.

He was friends with Grandpa Conrad and knew he would soon be passing the cemetery gate on his way back to work. He made us sit on the bench and wait till Grandpa showed up. A few minutes later we heard Grandpa coming in his Oldsmobile. The dust was flying in the air and he was breaking the speed limit like always but running on time!

Mr. Bell flagged him down and they began to talk. We couldn't tell what they were saying but in less than a minute Mr. Bell came over and took Elmo by the hand and Grandpa took me and walked us to the car. Grandpa got in and Mr. Bell thanked him for his help. He took off in a cloud of dust and broke more records the rest of the way to work.

He never spoke a word but kept his eyes on the road and was soon parked in front of his saw filing shop. The eleven thirty whistle blew and he told us to get out of the car and come with him. Grandpa had made it back on time even though he had been delayed about two minutes.

He made us take a seat inside the mill room and wait until he had time to deal with us.

We were worried but sat still and spoke very little to each other. After waiting an hour, Grandpa got a break and began quizzing us. We knew kids weren't allowed in the park without adults but told him it was our shortcut to Mint Springs, which was true. He wasn't satisfied with our reason and read us the riot act. He made us solemnly promise not to do it again.

This was the first time Grandpa had met Elmo and this encounter with Mr. Bell had Elmo scared that his dad may find out. I didn't think he would tell Mr. Blucher but I was pretty sure he'd tell Mama and I would be the one in trouble.

After the lecture we felt a little better. What upset us more than anything else was that our slingshots had been taken away, and Grandpa knew it.

Before we left, Grandpa walked over to the tool room and brought back two slingshots he had made. They had nice custom-made wood stocks, red rubber shooters and a nice leather pouch. They were the best-looking slingshots a kid would ever want. He handed them to us and said stay out of trouble and don't let Mr. Bell catch you in the cemetery again. That was a good piece of advice and we knew we'd better lay low for a while.

It was time to leave so we thanked Grandpa and went on our way. Once on the gravel road, we stopped and filled our pockets with rocks and practiced with our new slingshots all the way back to the highway.

This delay had put a damper on our earlier plans and we had to think of something else to finish out the day.

When we reached the highway, I suggested taking the path from Highway 61 over the hill to Grandma's house. It was just over a mile through the woods with many places to shoot our slingshots.

We walked a short distance north on the highway then took the path east that would take us through the woods to Sherman Avenue. Mama had traveled with us kids across the hill many times and always had fun.

There were several houses on the north side of the path just off the highway, but after passing them, we came to a heavily wooded thicket at the bottom of the hill. Mama had told us kids many times to stay close to her and not venture too far away from her side when we passed the place.

A tale had often been told about a band of gypsies that traveled the area during the summer months and camped in the nearby woods. According to the story, they stole from the locals and kidnapped little kids who were never heard from again. This spooked us so we always stayed close to Mama.

I had heard the story many times over the years but it didn't frighten me now that I was ten. It worked when I was younger, but now that I was older it didn't stop me from venturing off the path.

After walking past the houses, we began looking for more rocks. There was a small creek a few yards south so we walked over and cooled our feet in the shallow water. It wasn't deep enough to do anything else so we began filling our pockets with rocks.

We headed back to the path after restocking our ammunition and started up the hill. After walking a few yards we heard loud music coming from the north and headed that way. The trees and vines were thick but soon we reached the top of the hill. Down below and along the side of a much bigger creek were

105

four trailers parked in a circle and a half dozen old trucks. A campfire was burning and several horses were tied to hitching post. Two horse trailers were parked next to the creek and several men and women dressed in strange clothes were dancing around the fire. Some were playing instruments. Oddly, there were no kids amongst them.

To get closer without being seen, we had to crawl on our bellies through the thick brush. Since we were on top of a tree-covered ridge we weren't worried about water moccasins but kept our eyes out for rattlesnakes.

It was slow moving but we continued until we could get a better view and understand what they were saying. They were speaking English but their singing was in another language.

A jug was passed around and it was plain to see most of them were getting drunk. We were concerned about dogs but we never saw any animals other than the horses, a few dozen chickens, and a big parrot in a cage.

It was midafternoon and the longer we watched, the more exciting it got so we crawled closer to their camp.

Our last drink of water was at the cemetery and we were getting mighty thirsty again. The creek was only a few yards away but the safest place to drink would be upstream from their camp.

Several times the men had walked off in the woods and relieved themselves. We were high above their camp and could see every move they made, so we continued making our way upstream.

As we crawled through the brush, I suddenly looked up and saw Elmo swinging his arms. At first I couldn't tell what was going on but then I realized he was on top of a yellow jacket nest. They were everywhere and he was trying to keep quiet and not get stung. It was a miracle we weren't discovered.

Elmo got lucky and was soon clear of the nest without getting stung. I wasn't far behind but had to make a detour while he waited a few yards away.

After catching up with him, we continued east and soon made it to the creek. We got a cool drink of water, then headed downstream and got close enough to see what was going on.

Two ladies were building a fire under a big black pot hanging from a pole. They first filled it with water and then added other ingredients. It looked like they were preparing supper and it didn't take long till we could smell whatever it was, making us both hungry.

The sun was getting lower in the sky and we didn't have much time before we had to head for home.

The music was still loud and the dancing and singing had never stopped. One of the men took time out to feed the horses and put more wood on the fire. It was strange seeing all the chickens running loose and the big parrot sitting soundlessly in his cage.

Just as we were getting ready to leave, I heard a strange sound and when I turned around, a big rattlesnake was coiled up less than three feet away. We were in great danger since the snake was big and in striking range so we sat still, hoping he would crawl off in the bushes. He just lay there coiled up on the ground, shaking his rattlers, without any indication of leaving anytime soon.

We didn't know what to do but had to take a chance on moving out of striking range without getting the attention of our visitors. Waiting for him to crawl away might take a long time so we had to do something fast.

We whispered to each other and finally agreed to make an escape attempt from the fangs of this deadly rattlesnake.

Just as we were ready to make our move, a loud shot rang out and the head of that big rattlesnake disappeared right before our eyes. We were shocked but much more frightened after turning around and seeing a huge man with a beard standing less than ten feet behind us. He held a shotgun in his hand and was dressed in strange-looking clothes. He had a big smile on his face as more men showed up with guns.

The rattlesnake was still moving on the ground but one of the men reached down and picked him up. He pulled out a knife and in less than a minute the hide disappeared from the big snake.

They all knew we were scared but the old man who had saved our lives let us know we were no longer in danger and invited us to join them for supper.

All our fears went away as we walked down to their campsite. The pot hanging over the fire was full of mutton stew and smelled great. The man who skinned the snake was now frying him in a skillet.

We had nearly an hour left and enjoyed visiting with our

new friends. Some were still drunk but they were very good to us. The mutton stew was a first for us but it tasted great with fresh bread that was baked in their strange-looking ovens.

I wondered if the stories told to me as a kid had been made up about these strange people we had just met. They were different, but not dangerous like the people in the stories we had heard.

We did ask if they were gypsies and they smiled and said they were. They had been coming to Vicksburg many years and always spent part of the spring and early summer months here before traveling north to Canada, where they spent the rest of the summer.

They had always hunted and fished for food and sold crafts they made to support themselves. There was one old lady with a crystal ball who would tell your fortune for a few pennies. We didn't have any money so we didn't get our fortunes read.

They had strange names that we had never heard before. Our big question to them was, where are the kids? Their answer made sense; they told us the kids were left behind on this trip to be taught family crafts by their grandparents.

Our new friends were old enough to be our parents and grandparents but very kind and at no time did we feel in danger. They wanted us to come back and visit again and the man who had shot the snake said we were always welcome, but to be sure to come before the first day of July. After that, they would be leaving for Canada and spending the last days of summer and early fall there before returning to Florida for the winter.

We did ask if the parrot talked and one of the ladies

109

brought him out. His cage was covered with a big red cloth which was removed by an older man who looked like a river pirate. He opened the cage door and the parrot flew on his shoulder. He then reached in his pocket, took out something and called the parrot by name. He asked what he wanted and in a clear loud voice the parrot said, "Polly wants a cracker!" At that, one was given to him. We thought he was a smart bird and he spoke a few more words before being put back in his cage.

The chickens that supplied their meat and eggs never left the area other than when roosting in the trees. They were many different colors and sizes but several were big, red roosters with long, sharp spurs. We suspected them to be fighting cocks but we never asked any questions about that.

The horses were used for riding but one had been trained to perform tricks. They wanted to show us a few but it was getting late and we had to leave soon. Everybody had sobered up by now and had gathered around to say goodbye. It was time to leave so we took the old path and headed for Highway 61.

We never made it to Grandma's house that day but planned on trying again before summer was over.

I said goodbye at the bottom of Givens Hill and headed for the house while Elmo continued south. I was getting home much earlier than expected and he had plenty of time to make it without being late.

When I walked in the front door, Snowball met me. Kennie was sitting in front of the radio listening to the Lone Ranger and Eula Mae was playing jacks on the front room floor. Marshall and Alton Ray were sleeping on a pallet and Grandma was sitting on the back porch in her old rocking chair. Mama was finishing supper but since I had eaten a big bowl of mutton stew and bread I wasn't very hungry. It wasn't long before we gathered around the table and Mama blessed the food. Everything looked and smelled good but I spent more time talking than eating.

They all wanted to know where I had been and what I had been doing all day. I didn't go into all the details but I told them about spending time with Grandpa and going through the cemetery with Elmo. I also told them about traveling the path to Grandma's house but never making it before having to come home. I told them about Grandpa giving Elmo and me new slingshots and about the fun we had shooting at targets. I didn't mention the problem we had in the cemetery in the hope that Grandpa never said anything to Mama. The excitement with the snake and the gypsies was a particular secret we never shared for many years afterward. What a day it had been! Clearly, God had been there to watch over us. He had protected us from harm and made sure we were around to have many more fun days of childhood in Mississippi.

Flood Water and Alligator Gar

I saw Elmo several days later at Wilkerson's Store in Waltersville. It was Monday and Grandma had sent me to buy kerosene for the lamps. He and his dad were looking at fishing equipment so I paid my nickel for a gallon of kerosene and Elmo walked out with me. Elmo's dad stayed in the store.

I filled my can, set it on the ground, and climbed up with Elmo in the back of his dad's old Studebaker pickup. He said everything was going great with him, but he wanted to know if I got in trouble for being in the cemetery. I assured him that Mama

111

hadn't said anything and I thought Grandpa hadn't told her. This made Elmo feel much better.

Our family always went to church on Wednesday night so I asked if he could go. He had to ask his dad first.

Mr. Blucher soon came out with an armload of fishing equipment and got in the truck. Elmo hollered out the window as they drove away, "See you Wednesday morning at ten o'clock!" I picked up my can of kerosene and headed up Givens Hill.

This made me happy and I began thinking of things we could do before going to church Wednesday evening.

Grandma had instructed me and Kennie to clean the lamp shades, trim the wicks and fill the lamps with oil when I got home. There were six lamps and this chore would take a while.

On my way up Givens Hill, I had to pass a mean dog that roamed a yard on my route. He always looked vicious and often tried jumping the fence. Just as I got to the gate, here he came like always, so I took off running for the house. He had never made it over the fence but I worried that someday, he would.

Our house was a short distance up the hill so I took off running fast as I could with my gallon can of kerosene. After reaching the house, I looked back and to my surprise, this mean dog, a chow, had jumped the fence and was right on my heels. When I opened the front door, Snowball ran out on the porch and they began to fight. Grandma heard all the commotion and came running outside with her broom. The chow was on top of Snowball but after she hit the chow a few times he took off running.

Snowball was bleeding but his wounds weren't as bad as they looked. I got out the Watkins salve and Grandma doctored the bites while I went to see where the chow had gone.

He was back in his yard so I told Grandma this. She was a tough lady and after cleaning the blood off her hands, she went next door with her broom and a baseball bat. She walked through the front gate then up on the porch and pounded on the door. A big, fat man stepped outside and wanted to know if there was a problem. In a loud, angry voice Grandma told him what his dog had done and that he had better keep him in the yard or she would kill him. He said very little but I think he believed every word he heard. That was the last time his ole dog ever jumped the fence.

I wasn't brave like Grandma but I heard everything she said while standing out by the gate. She left the porch and walked over to where I was standing and together we went to the house.

From that day on, when I walked in front of the neighbor's house, his dog was always called back if he started barking. He was never a problem again and I felt much safer walking up and down Givens Hill. Snowball lay around the rest of the day of the encounter but wasn't very frisky. He ate very little but his appetite slowly returned and he was back to normal in a few days.

When the supper dishes were finished, Grandma wanted to play checkers. We kids took turns but rarely ever beat her. She wouldn't give us a chance and said the only way to learn the game was to practice till we got good. If I judged my ability to play against Grandma, I must have never learned the game very well because she beat me and everyone else ninety-five percent of the time. We also played dominos, and she was very good but we kids beat her more often than we did at checkers.

Later in the evening we gathered around Grandma while she told our favorite bedtime stories. She was good at everything, but storytelling was her best talent. We never got tired of listening, even though she told the same stories over and over.

Grandma had been born in Meridian, Mississippi in 1887 and her maiden name was Eula Lee Gipson. Most of her family was still living there but we rarely saw them. By the time I was thirteen, I had seen her family four or five times but they never invited her or any of us to visit. They kept in touch by letter. The distance was just over a hundred miles and we couldn't afford to ride the bus there. We didn't own a car.

Her two brothers had law degrees from Cumberland University in Lebanon, Tennessee and were Mississippi state politicians. The youngest, Ray Gipson, was a city judge, and the oldest, Vannoy Gipson, was a well-known criminal lawyer. At one time he was District Attorney of Meridian and also represented the Chicago & Northwestern Railroad for many years. They were both later elected to state and municipal political offices.

Many stories Grandma told were about our great- and great-great- grandparents, and aunts and uncles on the Gipson and Stephenson side. Some took place during the Civil War. She also told stories about her life with Grandpa Stephenson before his heart attack.

Two years before the Great Depression, when dad was only twelve years old, he had found his dad lying face down on his way to the cotton field. He had died from a heart attack and left behind his forty-year-old wife, three sons and a daughter! Life for the Stephenson family was never the same. Grandma and her four kids grew up in poverty on a small cotton farm and she never remarried. Her two oldest sons, James and Sydney, left home at an early age but her youngest son, Alton, graduated from high school and joined the army air corps after Mama and Dad got married in 1935. Ruth, the only daughter, suffered from mental illness but graduated from high school. She got married and had a family but was committed to the state hospital while her kids were still young. She spent most of her adult life confined to a mental hospital before passing away in her late 70s. I was told she received straight A's in school and graduated at the top of her class. Most of her problems started after graduation but she never received proper medical treatment. I have vague memories of her but the last time I remember was in 1945 when I was seven years old.

That time, Uncle Alton came down from San Francisco and took Grandma along with Mama and all us kids to see Aunt Ruth at the Whitfield Mental Hospital in Jackson, Mississippi. We kids weren't allowed to visit but Mama and Grandma brought her out on the second floor balcony. She waved at us and I thought it was awful for her to be locked up, unable to come and go when she wanted. It always made me sad just thinking about her.

My connection to dad's family had been through Grandma Stephenson and the only stories she ever told were the good ones.

I was also born in Meridian and moved away at three years old. I had very few memories of dad's family. All I ever knew was told to me by Mama and Grandma, but much of our history on the Stephenson side had been left out. I grew up in

115

Vicksburg around Grandpa and Grandma Conrad and Mama's five sisters, three brothers and their families. Living around them had always been my life and I had no other family. Times were hard but Mama did the best she could at raising five kids.

Wednesday morning came and I was up at my regular time. I played marbles with my friend, Wayne, after breakfast. He lived at the top of Givens Hill with his mama, dad, two brothers and a sister. We attended school together and had known each other most of our lives. His mother's twin brother, Tom Marshall, married my Aunt Mae after her first husband, Leon McMullin, was killed in World War II.

Wayne and his family were Pentecostal and we were Baptist, but we were very good friends. They went to their church and we went to ours but there was never a problem. The adults spoke to each other but never became close friends. There was a difference in church doctrine and this kept the two denominations apart. They were always polite but that was the best they could do. I never understood why it had to be that way. It was their problem and we kids never had any control over how the adults got along.

Each denomination thought they were right and the other was wrong so the best way to get along was to spend as little time as possible together. This didn't go for the kids because we never let our beliefs or our families get in the way of friendship. Elmo and his family were also Pentecostal but again this didn't affect our friendship.

I was glad Elmo would be attending Wednesday night prayer meeting with me. Now he could see how our church services were conducted and I'm sure he would see the difference.

After finishing my game of marbles with Wayne, I sat down on the front porch and waited for Elmo. About ten o'clock I saw him coming and met him half way down the hill. On our way back to the house, we had to pass the mean chow again but this time he never bothered us.

We still had most of the day to play but hadn't yet decided what to do. Whatever it was we had to be home early for supper because church started at seven o'clock. The cemetery and park were out of the question but there were other fun things we could do.

Elmo said the river was out of its banks and his houseboat had risen about three feet over the past week! We put his clothes away and decided to check out the floodwaters. I told Grandma we were leaving and she said to be home by five thirty. Elmo had brought his sling shot and pocket knife so I got mine and we took off for Waltersville.

We stopped on our way at the Chinaman's Market and we both bought a bottle of Coke and a bag of Tom's Roasted Peanuts. This was one of our favorite treats and it only cost us a dime each. After taking a few sips of Coke, we poured in the peanuts and shook them up. This concoction created a great taste that we loved like so many other kids.

We left the store with our Coke and peanuts and headed west across the railroad track. After passing Anderson Tully Sawmill offices and the turnoff to Grandpa's saw filing shop, we went another mile and found that the road was closed and was flooded with high water.

117

Many boats were tied to trees along the road and had been left there by folks who couldn't drive their cars. Boats were their only transportation when the river was high.

Sometimes the spring and early summer floodwater would last for weeks before going down. Everyone affected would follow the road in their boats and make their way as far east as they could, then continue on foot to where they were going.

Discarded trash was a big problem along the roadside, attracting hundreds of gar fish when the river was up. These huge fish were scavengers and we kids would wade out in the water and chase them with sticks and poles. Some were bigger than we were but at no time did we fear them. It was hard to get close but the best way to see these huge alligator gar was to stand still and let them find us. Rarely did we get in water over our waists and it was always clear enough to see a gar fish swimming three feet under the water.

This was the first time Elmo had done this and he was excited. After walking off the road about two hundred feet, we found a small boat floating next to some bushes. There were no oars or tie-down ropes and it appeared to have floated there on its own. It was a small boat but very solid without any leaks. The water was shallow so we climbed aboard and took a seat. There were dead trees and brush all around so we found two long poles that we used to push our boat through the water.

This was getting to be more fun than we expected and we continued making our way through the floodwaters. So far we hadn't seen any garfish but using the boat was already a thrill. Our pockets were full of rocks so we got in some practice with our sling shots.

118

It was a beautiful day so we lay back in the boat and floated around without a single care. We did see snakes and turtles now and then, but we chased them away with our slingshots.

While floating through the trees and brush, we had to pay close attention or get lost.

After an hour, Elmo spotted a school of huge gar fish just three feet from the boat. Some were over six feet long and swimming less than a foot under the water. There must have been a dozen or more so we sat still and watched them swim around the boat. They were big and ugly with lots of teeth and heavy thick body armor. They are definitely a prehistoric fish from the past. They didn't spend much time around us before swimming away.

Each year a gar rodeo was held at the lakes and river west of Waltersville. A cash prize was always given to the winner and many fish measured eight to thirteen feet long.

Some folks ate these ugly-looking things but most fishermen would cut the line and let them go. Some of my colored friends thought they were good and used special cutters to scoop out the meat and deep fry it. It was called "garballs" and I ate my first at the rodeo. It wasn't too bad but the more I chewed, the bigger it got. It had a strong taste though and since there were many other good fish to be had, we never took time to prepare them at home. Cutting through the heavy armor and preparing the meat was a big job and not worth the work.

Uncle James Cowart fed fish scraps to over two hundred head of hogs. Each week he went to Furr's Fish Dock with several

119

fifty-five-gallon barrels in his trailer and hauled scraps left over after the market processed their fish. Sometimes there were small alligators in the barrels that had been skinned and also three- and four-foot alligator gar. He never knew what was in the barrels until they were emptied.

When Uncle James would arrive home and open the gate to his farm, all the hogs would begin squealing and running toward the trailer. After the barrels were emptied, it was nothing to see a big boar hog grab a four-foot skinned alligator or gar fish and run off in the woods like a dog with a bone. It was always a sight to see and a smell you never forgot. He fed fish scraps to his hogs for many years.

His two sons, Charles Wayne, Jimmy and I, would go along for the ride on my visits each summer. On our way home from the fish dock, Uncle James would stop off at the local Dairy Queen and buy our favorite treats. Summer vacation with Uncle James and his family was always great.

Thinking that we had checked out all the compartments in the boat, Elmo reached inside the center seat box and discovered a roll of set hooks we had missed. There must have been twenty-five rolled up on a piece of wood and stuck back in the corner. Each line was eight feet long, had a big hook, and small lead sinkers.

The poles used to push the boat were just right for fishing and we tried to catch a lizard for bait. After a few failed attempts, we finally caught one that was bright green and six inches long. I held the pole while Elmo put the hook through the lizard's tail, and I threw the line in the water. He was very much alive and since the lead weight was small, he was able to float and swim without sinking.

As our lizard swam and floated just a few feet from the boat, we kept our eyes on him but he never attracted anything. Soon we got discouraged and removed the line from the pole and tied it to a metal ring attached to the front of the boat. The lizard was still alive so we left him in the water and sat back to relax again. Now and then we used our poles to push the boat but never got in a hurry to go anywhere.

It wasn't long before we were floating in clear water with only a few dead trees and brush around us. All of a sudden we felt something banging against the boat and discovered we were surrounded by dozens of huge alligator gar. They were all around us so we began poking them with our poles. They were jumping and splashing in the water and we were having the time of our lives.

During the excitement, we had forgotten about our baited hook, but suddenly we noticed we were being pulled west toward open water. We scrambled to the front and saw an eight-foot gar on our line. He had swallowed our green lizard and was pulling our boat through the water. At first we thought it was fun but there was nothing we could do but let him pull the boat slowly till he got tired and stopped. This kept up a long time, but eventually, we stopped moving. After checking to see if he was still on the line, we saw him swimming but not going anywhere. It was plain to see he was tired and didn't have the strength to continue.

It had been a fun ride but we were eager to turn our fish loose and head for home. There were no trees around so we had no way of telling how deep the water was. I jumped in the water but couldn't touch the bottom. Here we were far from shore without any oars and our poles weren't long enough to push our boat through the water.

The huge gar kept swimming but he couldn't move the boat anymore. He was too tired to do anything but stay afloat. We thought if we waited long enough, he may get his strength back and pull us to shallow water. We waited awhile but then decided our fish was all washed up.

The three thirty mill whistle blew and we had to be home by five thirty, but as it stood, we wouldn't be going anywhere for a while. The wind was calm and we slowly and helplessly drifted south.

We didn't know what to do other than wait it out and see what happened with our big alligator gar. The fun was over; fear had set in.

It had been a hot day and we were badly sunburned. All we had eaten since breakfast was a bag of peanuts and a bottle of Coke; we had been thirsty all afternoon. We finally gave in and drank river water even though it didn't taste very good.

We lay down in the boat and waited but nothing changed. We were still very thirsty and since we hadn't gotten sick from the river water, we decided to have another drink.

Another hour had passed when we heard the sound of a motor boat coming our way. We began waving our poles when it got closer and the operator saw us.

It didn't take long till he was pulling up close to us. An old man was at the controls. He began scolding us and wanted to know where we got our boat, and why we were out in the floodwater without an adult! We tried to explain but he wasn't satisfied with our explanation until he saw the big gar fish swimming beside the boat. He was shocked at what he saw and began laughing. At least he now believed our story.

I took out my pocket knife and was getting ready to cut our big fish loose but he stopped me. The old man then took out a gaff pole and pulled him in his boat.

We already knew our fish was huge but he looked much bigger once out of the water. The old man got out his tape measure and our trophy alligator gar was nine feet seven inches long. He wanted to keep him and that was okay with us. Our fish didn't break any records but it was a mighty big catch for two little boys.

The old man, whose name was Jessie, pulled in front of our boat, tied on with a rope, and towed us to Eagle Lake Road.

Before long, we were heading east following the flooded road toward Waltersville. Soon we arrived at the same place where our adventure had started, unhooked the boat and pushed it back where we had found it. The piece of fishing line was still connected so we tied it around a small tree limb and left it there. That ole boat and our alligator gar had made fun memories for us that day, but it was time to head home. The mill whistles blew again so we knew it was five o'clock and that we would make it home on time.

After thanking Jessie for rescuing us, he thanked us in return for the big gar fish and started his engine. He headed west into the floodwaters and soon was out of sight. Elmo and I believe God had sent Jessie to help us. We never saw him again.

It was time to go home and in twenty minutes we were climbing Givens Hill. We made it home safe and on time. It had been another exciting day and it was time to wash up for supper. Kennie wasn't home yet; he walked in later with Mama from the bus stop. We took a seat at the table and she said the blessing. Our family and Elmo enjoyed a great meal cooked by Grandma and we all spent a long time visiting at the table. Everybody talked about their day and Elmo and I shared some of our adventures. A few were carefully left out. We didn't want to worry Mama or Grandma so we kept those few secrets to ourselves. This day had been fun and left us with more exciting memories that we would share in the years to come. God had allowed two little skinny Mississippi kids to enjoy a day on the flooded Mississippi River, protecting us with his angels.

Prayer Meeting and a Car Wreck

After supper we hurried around and got ready for the prayer meeting. It was a fifteen-minute walk to the church but with bunions on both of Grandma's feet, she set a slow pace for us.

Grandma and Grandpa Conrad and their three kids were the first to arrive and unlock the doors. The Henley family, with their two daughters, along with Mr. and Mrs. Bounds and their daughter, were never far behind. Preacher Guy, our pastor, was blind but he and his wife always got to church on time. The congregation was always small with less than twenty-five attending, but that was normal for Wednesday night prayer meeting.

124

After everyone was seated, in walked Aunt Betty, Uncle
Fount and their son, Terry. With them was their friend and
neighbor, Buddy Jones. He was a friend to everyone but the
young boys in particular thought he was the greatest.

Many times on a Sunday afternoon, Buddy would take us
for rides through the military park in his old Buick. We always
had a great time and looked forward to his visits. We loved his
stories and he always treated us well. He had worked for the
Coca Cola bottling company in Vicksburg since leaving high
school. I whispered to Elmo that we may get a chance to ride in
Buddy's old car.

He was in his early twenties but acted much younger. The
Coca Cola bottling company in Vicksburg was the first in the
United States and was located on Washington Street. Local school
kids would visit at least once a year and I had been there several
times with my class. It was always fun and each kid was given a
bottle of Coke at the end of the tour. On my visits I had seen
Buddy a few times working on the bottle line and he always
waved when we went by.

He and Uncle Fount were neighbors and had known each
other for years. There were times when Uncle Fount took Kennie
and I to the movies on Sunday afternoon and Buddy would join
us. Between the two, they bought all the treats we could eat and
drink.

Church was over about eight thirty but since Mama had
the next day off, we would be spending the night with Grandma
and Grandpa Conrad. But first, Grandma Stephenson had to be
taken home because of her bunions. She rarely spent time away
from home and had to soak her feet in Epsom salts after walking

to and from church.

Grandpa's old car wasn't big enough for everyone, so I asked Mama if Elmo and I could ride home with Buddy. He would be passing Grandpa's house on his way home but she still didn't want us to go with him. We didn't give up and after we begged her for a few minutes, she gave in and said okay.

Grandpa took Grandma Stephenson home and came back and got the rest of the family. His old 1938 four-door Oldsmobile was soon loaded down with seven kids and three adults.

Buddy had left with Elmo and me the same time Grandpa took Grandma home and would be taking Sherman Avenue through the battlefield park to get home. Buddy's old Buick had bad passenger door locks and had to be tied shut with bailing wire, so Elmo and I got in on the driver's side and took a seat! We were both excited and soon turned off Highway 61, passing the Vicksburg Military Cemetery. It didn't take long before we were at the east gate and heading up the hill toward Grandpa's house. The hill was very long and steep but the old car was making the grade without a problem. But just before reaching the top, it began to spit and sputter and the engine died! It was pitch black and Buddy figured he was out of gas.

His plan was to roll backwards down the hill and try starting the engine just in case he wasn't out of gas. He turned the lights off and after his eyes adjusted to the darkness, he decided to give it a try.

The transmission was in reverse and with the clutch pushed in, the old Buick began rolling down the hill. When the speed increased enough, he popped the clutch, but the engine didn't start and the transmission popped out of gear. He couldn't get it back in reverse and the speed began to increase. A short distance down the hill was a sharp curve and when Buddy applied the brakes, the old car didn't slow down. Instead, it turned over twice in the middle of the road.

I was next to the door with my window rolled down and went flying out on the second turn. I tried holding on but nothing kept me inside. I landed on my right elbow and shoulder in a concrete drainage ditch. Buddy and Elmo had managed to stay inside and weren't hurt.

I was walking around like a zombie when I saw Buddy and Elmo climbing out the window. My arm was bleeding and my shoulder was hurting when Buddy got to me. I didn't have any broken bones but I was scared to death. It was too dark to see but we knew Grandpa would be coming along soon. We just waited in the middle of the dark road.

It seemed like forever before we saw headlights coming up the hill. It was Grandpa and he pulled up close, leaving his headlights on. Mama and Grandpa jumped out and saw my arm was skinned and cut. She checked me over and saw I wasn't hurt too badly. Elmo and Buddy were banged up a little but were okay.

The old Buick was sitting on its side with oil running out of the engine, but there was no danger of fire since the gas tank was empty.

Buddy stayed behind while Elmo and I squeezed into Grandpa's car and headed for home. It took about ten minutes and I was in pain all the way. Once we were home, everybody

127

went inside except Uncle George and Grandpa, who went back to get Buddy.

When they got back to the car, Uncle Fount was already there and all four men were able to roll Buddy's car over on its wheels. Uncle Fount had a can of gas in his trunk and after pouring it in the tank and priming the carburetor, the engine started. Buddy poured two quarts of oil in the engine and drove away. After the accident our rides with Buddy came to an end, but we still enjoyed our time with him. He was a good man and a friend to everyone.

Over the next two weeks my arm healed and my adventures with Elmo continued. With most of our summer vacation left, there was never a problem finding something to keep us entertained and when danger showed up, God and his angels kept watch over us. He was there all the time and never did we forget to give him thanks.

Crossing the River Bridge from Vicksburg to Louisiana

Summers were always hot in Mississippi and since we had no air conditioning, all the windows and doors were left open to keep the house cool. My friends and I went to the river and lakes four or five times a week from April first through October each year. For us, this was a fun way to cool off when the temperature reached the upper 90s, and sometimes a hundred and above.

Fishing and swimming was our favorite pastime. We never left home without our fishing poles and a can of worms. If we got lucky there would be fried catfish on the table for dinner.

Early one hot July morning in 1948, I was bored with nothing to do and walked over to Elmo's houseboat, thinking he and I could think of something fun. After a short visit, we decided to go down to the river bridge and watch the big trucks and cars cross over to Louisiana. The bridge was over a mile long and a short distance on the other side was the little farm town of Mounds. I had family members on my Grandpa Conrad's side who were sharecrop cotton farmers there and who we visited once or twice each year.

I had crossed over several times with my Grandpa and Grandma Conrad and their daughter, Aggie. On those trips, Mama, my three brothers, my sister and I went along and everyone had a day of fun. We always made those trips during summer school break when watermelons and cantaloupe were in season. In July, the melons were huge and tasted great. Some weighed over fifty pounds. Cantaloupes and quill melons were also in season. We always ate what we wanted and took a few home. Many fresh vegetables were gathered from their garden and prepared for dinner and supper. Some were even taken home for Grandma and Mama to can. Grandpa's old Oldsmobile was always loaded down when leaving Vicksburg, but the trip took less than an hour. Time went fast with six kids in the back seat and three adults up front singing songs we had learned in vacation bible school. Going over to Louisiana was a big treat for everyone and we always looked forward to going each year.

At nine o'clock, Elmo and I left his house and were soon walking down Washington Street, making our way south through the main part of Vicksburg. In less than an hour we reached the bridge, which was on Highway 80 and on the south end of town.

129

There was a toll charge for crossing but dozens of trucks were lined up waiting to be weighed and inspected when we got there. This delay didn't take long. It was an old steel bridge built back in 1928 and opened for traffic in 1930. It was used by many cars and trucks as well as by the railroad. The lanes were narrow, only nine feet wide with a speed limit of fifteen miles per hour. Still, it was an exciting ride for everyone making the trip.

After waiting in the bright hot sunshine for nearly thirty minutes, we got thirsty and walked over to a service station and bought ourselves a Coke and a bag of peanuts. On our way back, Elmo surprised me when he suggested we climb aboard one of the big trucks and ride over to Louisiana. At first I didn't know what to say but it did sound exciting! It didn't take long till we had a plan and began looking for a place to hide. There were many trucks and trailers loaded with all kinds of cargo in line. We had to find the right one to make the trip without being seen.

After checking dozens without any luck, we were ready to give up. But then we spotted a trailer loaded with bales of cotton. They were spaced eight to ten inches apart and we thought we could safely fit between them without being seen. We climbed aboard, found a comfortable place to lie down, and settled down for the ride.

The big rig pulled up and stopped several times but we could tell when we reached the scale. It took a few minutes to get inspected and weighed, then the toll was paid and the truck headed across the bridge.

We hoped that the driver would stop in Mounds for gas once he reached the other side, but if not, somehow we would have to get his attention and pray he stopped and let us off. This was all new to us so we played it by ear and prayed everything went well.

It was a rough ride all the way and at no time could we tell where we were. At last, the big rig slowed down and came to a stop. After not moving for a few minutes, we peeked out between the cotton bales and saw the driver filling the gas tank at a Rose Oil truck stop. There were many cars and trucks doing the same and we thought it was a good time to make our escape.

We climbed off the trailer and ran as fast as we could. Surprisingly, no one paid any attention to us. It was a busy truck stop with many adults and kids in and out of the station so we relaxed a little and felt our trip across the bridge had gone well.

We walked inside and got a drink of water then went back outside. Right away we spotted a big truck load of watermelons parked across the highway and headed that way. There was an old man and a young boy sitting in the back of the truck and before long, we were introducing ourselves to a young kid named Norman and his grandpa, Mr. Silas.

Norman was also on summer break from school and would be helping his grandpa a few days. They were very nice so we climbed up on the truck and began talking. It was a flatbed with sideboards loaded to the cab with many big Texas grey and rattlesnake watermelons just waiting for someone to buy them.

Many folks stopped to check them out and a few big ones were sold. It was always a practice to plug a watermelon before paying so the customers would know if it was ripe enough. The melons that were plugged but not taken were left under a big oak tree next to the truck. Mr. Silas told us to help ourselves to the rejected melons, so we picked out one of the biggest and cut it open with our pocket knives and enjoyed it under the big shade tree.

With no idea where to go from there, we decided to head west and search for my family after eating our watermelon! We walked about a mile on Highway 80 and turned south on the first gravel road we came to. It wasn't long till we saw an old rundown farm house and decided to stop. On the front porch sitting in an old rocking chair was an elderly colored lady so we introduced ourselves. Her name was Lizzy. She was nearly blind but her hearing was very good and she wanted to know all about us and what we were doing in Louisiana without our folks. I told her we were from Vicksburg and was looking for relatives living on a farm somewhere around Mounds or Tallulah. I told her their name and she didn't know them, but she invited us to sit with her on the porch and wait till her son got home. At the end of the porch was a bucket of water and a dipper and she offered us a drink. We were thirsty and drank our fill. We then sat down in two old leatherback straight chairs and waited for her son.

It was an old, dilapidated, unpainted, shotgun house built out of cypress lumber and just about ready to fall down. All the doors and windows were wide open without screens and it appeared to be more than a hundred years old.

About that time a big tom cat walked out on the porch and climbed up in the chair with Lizzy. She called him Samson and we could hear him purring fifteen feet away. He was a beautiful calico and was rescued on Highway 80 when he was only a few weeks old. She told us how Samson kept the mice away over the past ten years and how he always slept at the foot of her bed. For

Lizzy, he was great company and it was easy to tell they loved each other.

A few yards from the house on one side was a cornfield and there was a field of cotton on the other. An old leaning barn sat out back and we heard a mule braying close by. Lizzy perked up and said it was her son, Curry, coming home for dinner and maybe he could help us find my family.

He was wet with sweat when he walked up on the porch and looked tired from plowing his ole mule all morning, but then he washed up and Lizzy told him about me and Elmo. His wife, Maggie, came to the door and invited us to eat with them so we accepted her invitation and took a seat at the table. Everything smelled and looked good. Lizzy said the blessing. First she thanked God for the food and then asked him to take care of me and Elmo and help us find my family. They were very kind and treated us like their own kids.

The food was good so Elmo and I thanked them for their hospitality and kindness and went out on the porch with Lizzy and Curry while Maggie cleaned the kitchen.

Curry was a big strong man and spoke with a deep voice. He wanted to know all about my family and when I saw them last. I told him they were cotton farmers and I had visited them with my family several times but I didn't know where they lived. He had to go to town that afternoon for supplies and wanted Elmo and me to tag along; maybe someone there could help us.

Again we thanked Lizzy and Maggie for a great dinner and a fun visit. Ole Samson walked over and rubbed up against my leg and began to purr. I petted him while Curry said goodbye to Maggie and Lizzy, then we headed for town. It didn't take long till we were back at the truck stop and we followed Curry over to a grist mill. The miller was an elderly colored man who Curry called Moses and began telling him who we were and why we were there. A big grin came on Moses' face and we knew right away he had the information we needed.

He finished grinding the corn, then shut down the mill and walked over to where we were waiting. Curry was very happy but had to go back to work so he shook our hands and headed for home.

Moses asked all kinds of questions and said he knew my family and where they lived. We walked out to the highway and he pointed in the direction where they lived, telling us it was two miles south of the highway. We thanked him and headed out.

In less than thirty minutes we came to an old farm house I recognized from my past visits. No one was outside, so we walked up on the porch and knocked on the door. There was no answer so we pounded several more times but still no one came to the door. We walked out to the barn too, but no one was to be found. It was already close to two o'clock and we had to leave by seven to make it home before dark.

We decided to wait on the porch and found two chairs on the shady side of the house. We took a seat, figuring that someone would show up. It was hot even in the shade but a breeze helped keep us cool, so we leaned back and soon dozed off.

We hadn't been sleeping much more than ten minutes when a barking dog woke us up. We sat up in our chairs and were surprised to see a big bluetick hound a few feet away. It scared us both and we didn't know what else to do but sit still. We didn't make a sound, hoping he would calm down or go away. But then out in the edge of the field we saw someone walking through the tall rows of corn. Right away they saw us and called out to their dog. He jumped off the porch and we felt much better.

We waited for them but they didn't know who we were. They looked familiar to me so I told them who I was and introduced my friend Elmo. After hearing I was Rufus Conrad's grandson, they remembered our visits in the past! The man of the house was Wallace Conrad, Grandpa Conrad's first cousin and Mama's second cousin. He was surprised to see us and wanted to know where the rest of the family was.

At first I was a little hesitant about what to say but we did tell Wallace how we made the trip and how we were able to find their house. He thought we were foolish kids at first but glad we made it across the bridge without any trouble. We went inside and met his son, Ralph, and his wife, Martha. She made a big pitcher of lemonade and served it with homemade sugar cookies. We took a seat at the dining room table and finished our treats. Then Ralph took us out to the barn, saddled up his horse and put a bridle on his ole plow mule.

Ralph rode the horse and Elmo and I rode bareback on the ole mule and followed him to a swim hole not far from his house. Soon we heard other kids having a good time cooling off in the creek and were ready to join them.

In a few minutes, Elmo and I were tying our mule to a shade tree and Ralph tied up his horse and removed the saddle.

135

In seconds, we were doing cannonballs in the water and joining in the fun with all the others. Ralph and his friends were great to us, but after cooling off they all wanted to know about our adventure crossing the Mississippi River on a trailer load of cotton bales.

We told them all about it, which raised the question of how we would get back across the bridge to Vicksburg. Up till then we hadn't given it much thought, but since there wasn't a toll booth or inspection station at the west entrance, we would have to figure out a way to hitch a ride without being seen. The only place where trucks would be stopping was at the Rose Oil truck stop, but only a few trucks would be getting gas before heading across the bridge!

Now we were concerned and thought it best to start back earlier just in case there was a problem. So far our adventure had been fun but was now coming to an end. We went back to Ralph's house to see his family before leaving.

After nearly an hour in the swim hole, Ralph saddled his horse and we climbed back on the old mule. Soon we were turning them loose in the corral.

Right away we went in the house and asked Wallace if he could take us across the bridge, but he didn't own a vehicle. He suggested we go back to the truck stop and instead of hiding out, it would be best to ask one of the drivers for a ride to Vicksburg. We knew it was the right thing to do.

Martha gave us a glass of lemonade, a sandwich to eat right then, and a few of her sugar cookies for the way home. We said goodbye, thanked them for everything and headed out. Soon we were back at the truck stop and saw several truckers going in and out of the restrooms. We began asking for a ride but all their answers were no. We found out it was against the law for them to pick-up passengers. One driver wanted to let us ride along but he took us out to his truck and showed us the sign in his window that said No Riders Allowed.

This went on for an hour and since we had no way to get in touch with our folks, we knew they would be worried if we didn't make it home by sundown.

In front of the truck stop, we sat down on a bench and kept asking for a ride without any luck. Then an old beat up pick-up truck loaded with a family of colored folks pulled up for gas. Three young kids riding in the back jumped out and went to the colored restroom. When they came out we asked for a ride across the bridge and the oldest asked his daddy. It was okay with them, so we climbed aboard. After paying for the gas the old truck headed for Vicksburg and we were happy knowing we would make it home on time.

Within fifteen minutes we were stopping at the Mississippi toll booth so we jumped out and thanked them for the ride. From there, we made our way north on Washington Street toward home. There would be plenty of time before dark so we walked through town and soon made it to Elmo's houseboat. Like always, we made it back on time!

Elmo and I said goodbye and I headed north on Highway 61. In fifteen minutes I was climbing Givens Hill and walking in the front door.

Mama was home from work and Grandma was putting

137

food on the table. We all took a seat and Mama said the blessing. Yet again we enjoyed another meal prepared by Grandma Stephenson.

We kids began sharing our activities for the day and I thought it best to tell Mama where I had been. At first she was a little upset but then she wanted to know all about our trip to Louisiana and how the family was doing. She did tell me not to cross the bridge again without an adult and for me and Elmo to be careful on our adventures. Mama always had faith in God to watch over her kids but also knew Elmo and I were pretty savvy about taking care of ourselves.

From day to day, my adventures with Elmo were different and a new one was just a plan away!

I did visit Louisiana several more times with family but the trip with Elmo stands out in my mind the most. We had many fun times and our days together were always exciting, without a dull moment. Our faith in God, along with the faith and trust our parents had, would keep us protected from all the dangers we faced. There were many close calls along the way but we always came through with only a few broken bones, a few cuts, and bruises. Nothing that our folks or Dr. Pettit couldn't take care of.

That was the end of an exciting summer for me and my good friend, Elmo. We would attend Redwood School for three more years and our adventures were many before I moved from Waltersville with my family, three months after my 13th birthday. On September 9th 1951, after a friendship of more than three years, my mom was remarried and our family joined our stepdad, his three sons and a daughter, on a sharecrop cotton farm in the small farm community of Clem, Mississippi. She and her new husband, Monroe Heggins, were married late that evening by Andrew Griffith, a justice of the peace in Jeff Davis county. We were now living 90 miles south of the only home we had ever known, but the five Stephenson kids and four Heggins kids would soon became known as the Heggins Clan. We all worked the farm as a family for Mr. Ralph Ramsey.

I would return to Vicksburg once again in May of 1953 when my Grandma Conrad passed away. I stayed three days but never got a chance to visit my friend, Elmo. I never saw him again, but the memories we made were many and I've never forgotten any of them.

Grandma Lela Mae Conrad

Grandpa and Grandma Conrad with their youngest daughter, Agnes

Grandpa and Grandma Conrad

Aunt Aggie and the Stephenson kids

Grandma Stephenson

Great-Great Grandma Ophelia Conrad

Great Grandma Mary Elizabeth Hartley

Great Grandpa Conrad

141

Our church family. Kennie and Rufus are wearing suits.

Mom and her siblings. From left, Agnes, Betty, George, Lela, Ashford, Marie, Roy, Louise, and Estus.

Kennie and Rufus

My dad's retirement day

Ray, Dad, and Rufus

Step Grandma Gladys and Grandpa Conrad

Mom and her kids. Mom with Ray; front from left to right: Rufus, Mae, and Kennie

145

BOWIE

This creek and swamp created by God
Millions of years ago
Provided a home for animals and birds
And fish in the waters below.

Man came along and survived very well
On what God made for him,
Building a home and raising a family
But he never swung from a limb.

Blessed I was with memories.
Many fun things I was taught
Fishing and swimming in Bowie Creek
And hunting wild game in the swamp.

Those memories I made were many,
While exploring a world I never knew,
Wearing a shirt and worn out jeans
And rarely, if ever, with shoes.

My brothers and I were always close
And did everything together,

We worked the fields six days a week
But the fun never got any better.

Bowie Swamp and Creek was my playground beginning in the fall of 1951 when I was 13 years old. I spent much of my free time fishing and swimming there with my brother, Kennie, and stepbrothers, Hiawatha and Roosevelt. To put extra food on the table, we hunted wild game. It was an adventure from the first day and never did it cease to be a fun place for me and my brothers. This creek and swamp provided food for our family and along with much excitement when we explored places we had never seen before. Growing up around Vicksburg in my younger years was great, but moving to the community of Clem, Mississippi was fun too. I enjoyed the swamp and explored it throughout my teenage years. Even with all the hard times and a life of poverty, Bowie Swamp and Creek transported me to a different world when I was there.

FIRST BALE OF

COTTON

On August 20th of fifty-two,
Cotton bolls bursting in the heat,
Seventeen acres was ready to pick
And half was ours to keep.

On a sharecrop farm our family lived,
Ralph Ramsey owned the land.
It was our first year to ever raise cotton
And we were known as the Heggins clan.

In fifty-one, two families became one,
Seven boys and two pretty girls.
Our folks got married on September 9th.
We lived in a different world.

From three to fourteen were our ages,
The Stephenson kids numbered five,
Four boys and a girl from five to fourteen.
As city slickers, we'd all survived.

149

The Heggins kids were three boys and a girl,
From fourteen down to just three,
Farmers, they had been all their lives
As the Stephensons had plans to be.

With cotton sack straps on our shoulders,
Each of us headed down a row,
The sun beamed down at a hundred degrees
And the first day of picking went slow.

Everyone picked as much as they could,
Twelve hundred pounds filled the truck.
When ginning was complete, out came a bale
Weighing five hundred pounds with good luck.

The market for cotton changed often;
A good price was forty cents a pound,
The cottonseed paid the cost of ginning
And soon we were heading for town.

Living on credit was always a must,
Buying necessities at the country store.
Profits that day would pay on the debt
But the bills left to pay were much more.

One bale per acre was average;
Seventeen bales would be picked!
A bountiful year for sharecrop farmers
But paying off the debt wasn't quick.

No money was left after paying off the bills,

To survive, we still had to charge.
Necessities were bought from month to month,
Most importantly flour and lard.

The garden supplied most all of our food,
But a big need was the flour and lard.
Biscuits and gravy was always our breakfast
And feeding nine kids came hard.

Fishing and hunting put meat on the table
When the garden came to an end.
Life was tough through the winter months
And credit was needed again.

Life for our family never got better,
Year after year was the same.
Tough, it was, but we did our very best
Though living like this was a shame.

A good education was hard to get,
Attending when the work was caught up.
Hard, it was, to keep up with our class
So staying in school was tough.

Who do you blame for such a tragedy?
A few other families lived this way.
Pointing a finger would never be right
So we lived our life day by day.

God, I'm sure, let it happen,
A lesson was taught to many folks.
If life was without a few struggles

151

Would you value that nice, warm coat?

We never took anything for granted,
Our lives remained always the same.
Hard work fed and clothed our family,
But what, or who, do you blame?

On our sharecrop farm, we raised cotton,
A lifestyle other families knew.
There were three meals a day and a roof over our heads,
Clothes on our backs, and a pair of shoes.

We accepted our fate and were thankful,
Life could have surely been worse.
God and good health were all we had
But often we thought we were cursed.

We managed to survive and left the farm,
Found jobs and began a new life,
Leaving behind the good and bad memories.
But in California I found a great wife.

Often I look back on the roads I've traveled;
I was blessed to find my way.
It's hard sometimes to forget about the past
But thank God I survived every day

FEEDING THE

CHICKENS

I shuck the corn and shell it,
To the gristmill I will go,
Today will take much longer
'Cause I'll be walking slow!

On my shoulder is a burlap sack,
With hybrid corn, it's filled.
Two pecks is what I carry
And a small toll pays the bill.

Into the hopper, the corn is poured
But soon it turns to chops,
It only takes five minutes
And then the grinding stops!

The miller pours it in my bag
And then I head for home.
Most trips I ride my ole plow mule

153

But this time I walk alone.

Along the way I'll stop and rest
But soon I'm on my way,
The chickens love to eat fresh chops
So I hope more eggs they'll lay.

The laying hens have all slowed down
But maybe this will change.
Fresh corn sometimes will perk them up
And help them do their thing!

I'm soon back home and in my yard
Then I reach into the bag.
Upon the ground I'll scatter chops
And watch the chickens lag.

They cluck and sing while eating
But soon their craws are full.
Inside the barn, I'll store the chops
And watch out for the Boss Man's bull.

As kids, my brother Kennie, my stepbrother Hiawatha, my stepbrother Roosevelt and I took turns each week going to the gristmill. Most of the corn was ground into chicken feed and the rest would be ground into grits and cornmeal. The purpose of going each week was to use up the grits and cornmeal before the weevils hatched out. With hot humid weather, sometimes they hatched in about 10 days after the corn was ground. We were never concerned about weevils getting in the chicken feed but letting them get into the grits and cornmeal was a no-no.

Most trips were made on the back of an ole plow mule but we sometimes walked and this took much longer. We made the trip each Saturday morning and many of our friends did the same. We often visited with them before heading home. During the summer months the old gristmill and cotton gin were very busy but in the winter we always made a fast trip over and back. Going each Saturday was always a must and on cold, rainy mornings we made the trip as fast as we could. The round trip was less than four miles but on nice days it always took a couple of hours to get everything taken care of and spend time visiting with our friends.

For each peck of corn to be ground, the miller took a small toll and this was the only pay he needed.

The chickens loved fresh corn-chops! Our chickens were never in cages; they always ran free. When feeding time came and chops were scattered on the ground, they all came running to get their share.

Our family loved grits for breakfast and cornbread was always prepared for dinner and supper. Without corn, our table would have been bare sometimes and there certainly wouldn't have been any chickens or eggs.

AN OLD WOOD STOVE

Mama cooked on an old wood stove,
Three meals she prepared each day.
A fire was built at 4:00 am
To get breakfast on its way.

Her four oldest sons took their turns;
For a week, they each built fires.
Rising and shining before sun-up,
No matter how sleepy or tired.

Pine knots were used to start the fire,
Red oak fueled the heat.
Two minutes later her stove was hot
And soon it was time to eat.

Two extra fires burned in winter,
One in each of the fireplaces.

157

When the house warmed up and the chill was driven out
Eight more kids showed their faces.

It was early to bed and early to rise,
Each day started this way.
Mama cooked breakfast on her old wood stove,
Before sun-up every day!

Food was scarce in the winter,
The season determined what we ate.
Happy, we were, when the garden grew
But sometimes harvests were late.

For breakfast, it was biscuits and gravy,
Corn grits we often ate,
To drink there was water from the well
And we finished every bite on our plate!

For dinner and supper there were vegetables,
Sometimes four or five kinds,
Green beans and tomatoes were favorites,
Always fresh off the vines.

Cornbread was served two times a day,
Hot and fresh from the oven.
Everything prepared was mama's best
Made with a whole lot of lovin'!

Sometimes there were chicken and dumplings,
Squirrel stew if we killed six or eight,
Rabbit, fish, or blackbird stew

We were not very choosy what we ate.

If profits were down at harvest time,
Our food would run out fast,
It was back to turnips and cornbread;
We prayed all the staples would last!

Flour and lard were at the top of the list,
Coffee and sugar were next.
These staples were needed to feed our family
But mama always did her best.

A water reservoir sat on the side of the stove,
A warming cabinet over the top.
A big fire box furnished the heat
And her old wood stove was always hot.

Three meals a day, seven days a week,
Three special holiday meals.
One more purpose that old stove served:
It took away the morning chill!

Mama's old stove was a blessing,
It heated the kitchen and cooked our food.
A place to warm up on a cold winter day,
After splitting a cord of firewood.

For our family there were many memories,
At the dining room table we made a few,
Nine young kids shared their stories
And *most* of them were true!

159

Mama, thanks for always being there,
Hard times for you never changed.
You cared for our family and did your best.
Never did we hear you complain.

You cooked our meals and washed our clothes,
You worked hard every day.
God blessed you and our family
And you always found time to pray.

POOR FOLKS' FOOD

Cracklin' bread and sweet taters,
Pint jars filled with milk,
Nothing better on a winter day
To fill you to the hilt!

Turnips and cornbread are eaten year round,
Taking your hunger away.
To your ribs they stuck and filled you up
But you ate 'em sometimes for days!

Dried beans and peas with salt pork,
Sliced sweet onions on a plate,
Homemade, green tomato chow chow
You ate till your belly ached.

Biscuits and gravy for breakfast,
With tomatoes, it's always the best.
Most times it was just plain toodlum,
But any kind passed the test.

Homemade butter was a special treat,
Great on biscuits and cornbread.

161

Buttermilk from an old stone churn
Helped keep all the family fed!

Fresh English peas and dumplings,
In a cast iron pot they were cooked,
A springtime favorite for everyone
But the recipe was not in a book!

Wild Polk salad was a springtime green,
Next to fences and barns, it grew,
It was gathered and cooked by country folks
But city slickers liked it too.

Of Red squirrel stew, in the early fall,
Most families ate their share,
Cooked with dumplings and pepper,
It was a blessing when cupboards were bare!

Rabbit, always a lifesaver,
Hoover hogs, known to many folks.
For those who survived the depression,
Eating rabbit was always a joke.

Greasy ole possum with sweet taters,
Cooked in a big baking pan,
It was never a favorite but it took away hunger,
These critters from Bowie Swamp land!

Coons were hunted with hound dogs,
Two or three fed our family of eleven,
Baked by Mama in her wood stove oven,

And made possible by God in heaven!

A big mess of catfish from Bowie Creek,
In pure lard cooked golden brown,
Eaten with catsup and hot cornbread,
But cool water washed it all down!

Blackberries picked on the hillsides,
Were always a special treat.
A cobbler was baked in Mama's ole oven,
A desert that couldn't be beat!

Blackbirds and robins made a tasty stew,
In early fall many were cooked.
Hundreds were caught beneath Chinaberry trees.
But that recipe was not in a book!

Yellow corn grits, a breakfast treat,
Eaten with butter while hot.
Cooked on a stove until creamy smooth,
It always hit the right spot!

Coco was bought when there was extra cash,
Chocolate syrup was made in a pot.
Served over biscuits, this special treat,
Was best if you ate it hot!

Head cheese was a family favorite.
Once or twice each year,
We fried it in a skillet or ate it cold,
Made fresh from hog heads and ears!

163

Wild green onions were a tasty treat,
On hillsides, they grew in the spring.
Gathered and cooked with scrambled eggs
We were thankful for anything!

Fresh green beans and new potatoes,
From the garden, they tasted great.
A springtime treat that couldn't be beat
But too many made your belly ache.

Field corn raised for the animals,
The farmer and his family ate their share,
There was no such thing as fancy sweet corn
But shoepeg was always there.

Thankful, we were, for anything
But our table was sometimes bare,
Mama was a lot like Jesus,
And for family, she always cared.

CORNBREAD AND

BEANS

Hot cornbread from the oven,
Fresh churned butter in a bowl,
Navy beans in a cast iron pot,
Good for the stomach and the soul!

A piece of onion and hot sauce,
Sliced tomatoes on a plate.
Pint jars filled with sweet iced tea
Quenched a thirst while you ate!

A typical meal for poor folks,
If we were lucky there might be more.
Sharecrop families ate what they grew
And always knew they were poor.

Most families always struggled
Living from day to day,
Thanking God for all they had

When bowing their heads to pray!

DRUNK BIRD STEW

As a kid growing up in Mississippi, chinaberry trees could be found all over the state. Many grew across the hills and hollows but some were in yards and around old barns and abandoned buildings. They had beautiful flowers in the spring and because of their shape, some folks called them "umbrella trees".

Some grew to be 40 feet tall with a heavy growth of leaves and thousands of small berries. They were said to be poisonous but some folks gave them to their kids to get rid of worms. I heard that it worked without making anyone sick but I never found out if the story was true or false.

My friends and I used the berries in our pop guns to shoot targets but sometimes we shot them at each other. This tree is native to China and India but has grown throughout the south for many years.

Throughout the summer, chinaberries are green in color but they turn yellow in the fall and smell of poop. Hundreds of robins and blackbirds would gather in the treetops and gorge themselves. Some would fall to the ground and appear to be dead, but what a sight it was seeing dozens on the ground unable to fly! Drunk, they were, from eating fermented chinaberries and they lay there until they sobered up.

167

If it happened to be a bad year of farming, as it was after we first moved to Clem in the fall of 1951, food could sometimes be scarce and anything Mama put on the table was very much appreciated. These drunk birds were easy pickings so we gathered up what Mama needed for a pot of stew and left the others to sober up and fly away. If they lay around too long, an ole tomcat or a file-tailed rat would make a meal out of them.

We would gather twenty-five or thirty for Mama to cook in her big cast iron pot and they were served for our supper! They were prepared with spicy dumplings or baked in a big roasting pan with cornbread dressing. These blackbirds and robins were always in danger of becoming a meal for the Heggins clan.

Later in the fall when the chinaberries were gone, we would make a bird trap from a six-by-eight-foot wooden barn door. It was propped up on one end with a two-by-four and a rope was tied to the bottom. Ground up corn was then scattered under the door and we took the other end of the rope and hid in the barn until the birds showed up. Soon they would gather under the old door and the two-by-four was pulled out and the door came crashing down. Each time we caught a dozen or more robins and blackbirds that supplied food for our hungry family.

Where there's a will there's always a way, but God helps those who help themselves. There's an old saying that beggars can't be choosers so we took one day at a time, never knowing what the next would bring. We always prayed for food and God always made a way to keep us from going hungry. Thank you, Mama, for never failing to keep our family fed. We love you.

A GIANT TURNIP

When springtime came on the Ramsey farm,
Nine kids worked the land.
Mama and Daddy were always in charge
Of the hard-working Heggins clan.

Plows were pulled by long-eared mules,
The crops were cotton and corn.
We were always living from day to day
As we had since the day we were born.

Most of our food came from the garden,
There were vegetables of many kinds.
Turnips were always our favorite
And we ate them most all the time.

The soil was rich and crops grew well
If Mother Nature treated them right.
Rain was needed and lots of sunshine
And short, hot, humid nights.

Turnips were planted in early spring

And were always the first prepared.
With a long-eared mule, the rows were plowed
But the bounty from the garden wasn't shared.

The only crops divided with the owner
Were half of the cotton and corn;
Everything else was kept for ourselves,
A rule since sharecropping was born.

Furnished was our rundown farmhouse,
Our water came from a well.
We had a barn, a corn crib and a chicken house
But everything was junky as hell.

Out back was a two-seat outhouse,
There was no modern plumbing at all.
Well water was carried a hundred yards
And brought whenever Mama called.

Planted each spring were turnips.
The rows were a hundred feet long!
They were always planted by Mama
As she hummed and sang her songs.

A thin layer of dirt covered the seed,
Breaking through the ground in five days.
Ten days later it was ready to thin;
Turnips were always planted this way.

The thinned-out plants were discarded,
Allowing the others to grow fast.

170

It was ready to eat in less than three weeks
But a pot full of turnips wouldn't last.

One day while Mama worked her garden,
The two youngest boys were helping out.
Marshall was older by nearly two years
And they both were out and about.

Shocked, she was, after looking back:
Johnny was having a good time.
He had pulled up three feet of turnips,
In the middle he had left one behind.

At the supper table Mama told the family
And everyone had a good laugh.
Over the summer, it grew big and healthy
But keeping it protected was a task.

Soon all the turnips were harvested,
All but the one left behind,
It continued to grow and became a monster
It was the biggest ever grown of its kind!

This giant was harvested in September,
Weighed and measured on the spot.
Thirteen pounds and eleven inches in diameter
It filled Mama's old cast iron pot.

*Our family garden was a few yards behind the house and the
most important piece of land we farmed. Most of our food was grown
there and our livelihood depended on it. For our family of nine kids,
Mama worked in the garden each day and kept vegetables on the table*

171

*from early spring through late fall. This story about Johnnie Cecil and his mischief was one our family never forgot, but because of what he did, the largest purple-top white globe turnip ever grown in Jeff Davis County came from **our** garden. Turnips were a lifesaver for many and not only survived the cool weather of spring and fall, but also the heat of summer. Turnips kept food on our table when nothing else was growing in the garden and with Mama's cornbread and a glass of water you never went hungry.*

SQUIRREL STEW

Squirrel season opened in October,
A license, few people would buy.
Reds and greys were plentiful
And I thought I'd give it a try!

A twenty-two rifle was my favorite,
These critters lived high in the trees.
Quiet, I had to be, and use eagle eyes
'Cause they blended right in with the leaves!

Oak, hickory, and beech trees were best,
Where these critters were feeding at sun-up.
A twenty-two rifle was all I needed.
I shot 'em in the head not the gut.

About mid-morning, if lucky,
In my bag, I had eight or ten.
I then headed home, put away my gun
And soon had 'em gutted and skinned!

Washed up, cut up, and ready to cook
Then Mama poured water in a pot.

On an old wood stove, she brought it to a boil
And squirrels filled it right to the top.

It was then set aside after cooking an hour,
A big batch of dumplings rolled out,
Cut into squares and dropped in the pot
And her stew was the best in the South!

Seasoned with salt and black pepper,
Mama said the blessing before we ate.
Supper was now on the table
And everyone filled up their plate!

Squirrel season opened in October and the swamp and hillsides had many reds and grays. Some folks called the reds "fox squirrels" and the greys were known by many as "cat squirrels". Everybody in the county looked forward to opening day but few licenses were ever bought. That didn't keep folks from hunting. Their favorite weapons were 22 rifles and 410 shotguns. The woods were full of hunters but there were always enough squirrels for everyone to get their limit. Oak, hickory, and beech were the best trees to find them in and these trees grew all over the hills and swamp. To feed our family of nine kids and two adults would take eight to ten squirrels. Mama always made a big cast iron pot of stew with dumplings seasoned with lots of black pepper. This was a favorite meal for our family and the season would last till the end of the year. If Mama had enough flour, and we didn't run out of ammunition, she would prepare many pots of stew throughout the fall and winter months. Without wild game in the winter, our family would have gone hungry. So, we were never picky about what we ate and Bowie Swamp and the hillsides provided all the fish and wild game we needed.

TATER PATCH

Sweet taters were planted in early spring
But always a special way:
Plants were taken from a tater bed
And planting would take all day.

In the fall, they began in a shallow bed,
Six to eight inches deep,
Twenty feet long and six feet wide
Made a bed for taters to sleep.

Side by side on a layer of straw,
Hundreds of culls were placed.
A layer of dirt would cover them up
And another layer of straw was laced.

This same process was repeated again,
Our tater bed nearly complete,
Capped off again with three inches of dirt
And they rested all winter in peace.

When spring time came, new life appeared,

These new plants were then set out,
Watered and covered with fertile soil
Soon they were putting on sprouts.

The vines grew fast and covered the rows,
Sweet taters grew underground.
Harvest time came in the early fall
And our crop was the best in town.

Each fall after sweet potatoes were harvested, the best of the crop was put in the barn for eating and the culls were placed in a bed that supplied all the plants needed for the following spring planting.

These culls were first placed on a bed of straw in a six-by-ten-foot wood frame. They were then covered with a thin layer of dirt and another layer of straw was applied. A final layer of dirt was added and this kept them protected from the winter cold.

When warm spring rain arrived in April, it didn't take long till the culls would sprout and soon break through the ground and supply all the plants needed for our spring planting.

When the new plants reached a height of six inches, they were pulled from the bed and set out in rows and watered. Within three to five days, these new plants were putting on leaves and in three weeks they covered the ground with beautiful vines.

They continued to grow over the spring and summer months and produced many bushels of taters.

In early October a pair of mules was hooked to a middle buster plow and the taters were plowed up, sorted in piles and stored in the barn.

Our sweet tater patch was one half acre and produced about 50 bushels, which was kept for our family needs and not shared with the landowner.

They were used to make pies and some were fried in a skillet, but most were baked in an old wood stove oven with cracklins, which was our family favorite. A sweet tater patch was a necessary crop for poor folks and supplied a big part of our winter food.

A FISH STORY

In Bowie Creek, we fished all year
And caught catfish and eel.
The eel was hung up by its head,
With pliers, the skin was peeled.

The catfish dipped in boiling water,
With knives, the skin was scraped,
Then cut up in small pieces
And placed on a battering plate!

Seasoned well and rolled in flour,
Dropped in boiling grease,
Cooked till it was golden brown
And the kids all got a piece.

Other fish in Bowie Creek
Were also cooked this way.
Some had many tiny bones
And for kids they weren't okay!

They were always eaten with hot cornbread
So the bones would not get stuck,

But if they did and you choked on them
You may run out of luck.

I was always told to not drink milk
When fish was in your meal;
If you did, you may get very sick
And sometimes it could kill.

I found out later when I grew up,
This story was often told.
It was just a way to save on milk
But was believed by young and old!

The fish we ate was always good
And sometimes folks got choked,
Milk and fish never killed no one
Yet it fooled most all the folks!

Mama wouldn't allow our family to drink milk when fish was served, believing it could cause sickness and sometimes even death. We didn't drink much milk but neither had we ever heard of anyone getting sick or dying from drinking and eating the two together. Yet the fear was always there!

COTTON PICKER

Early to bed, early to rise,
Ready to pick all day,
Fingers get sore and sometimes bleed
But you'll earn a few bucks this way!

A nine-foot sack holds what I pick,
My body has aches and pains.
Two hundred pounds, I'll pick in a day
But I hope and pray it don't rain.

My back gets tired so I pick on my knees,
No relief for fingers or hands!
Both legs hurt and so do my knees
From crawling in hot dirt and sand.

Hot August days of a hundred degrees,
Humidity is often the same.
An ole straw hat will help keep me cool
But I hope and pray it don't rain!

At noon I'll climb in the back of a truck,
And ride to an old country store.
Soda pop, bread and lunchmeat I'll buy
But I just can't afford any more!

With no other means to earn money,
Cotton picking is the only way.
Two hundred pounds will pay four bucks
But it takes me nearly all day!

In five hot days, I'll earn twenty bucks,
Happy to finish out the week.
On Saturday I'll wear my very best
With a pocket full of money for treats!

In Prentiss, I'll watch two movies with friends,
And enjoy some favorite treats.
I made it to town by hitching a ride
But my weekend is hard to beat.

After a fun day with friends in Prentiss,
I'll walk to the east end of town,
Stick out my thumb and hitch a ride home
But I'll leave when the sun goes down!

Sometimes it takes me an hour
Before I can make it back home,
With friends, I've made this trip many times
But it's lonesome when I'm traveling alone.

I'll earn a few bucks as a picker,

But soon it comes to an end.
When picking time comes on our cotton farm,
I'll never get paid again!

My days of earning money as a picker
Will last no more than two weeks,
But it sure was great to earn a few bucks...
Especially when it's mine to keep!

Leaving Vicksburg and moving nearly 100 miles south to the small community of Clem, Mississippi was a sad time for the Stephenson family.

Our mom worked at Kress's department store in Vicksburg and we lived in a three-room shotgun shack in the community of Waltersville. There was mom and us five kids along with Grandma Stephenson living in a house much too small for our family.

Times were hard but with what Mama made from her job and help from our family and church, we managed to survive. Our dad had left us and never came around again and from that day on, life would always be a struggle for Mama and her kids. We did without and lived in two of the worst places Waltersville had to offer.

Our little community was made up mostly of Negro families and was known to many as Nigger Town. We lived next to the railroad tracks and Anderson Tully sawmill and many of our friends were colored.

Together, we played baseball, went fishing and swam in local lakes and the Mississippi River. On most Saturday mornings we rode the city bus to Vicksburg and saw our favorite cowboy movies at the Strand or Singer Theater.

The colored kids sat in the back of the bus while the whites rode in front and when we got to the theater, the colored kids sat in the balcony and the whites set in the lower level.

This was normal and we never thought anything about it. We always had a great time. When the movie was over, we rode the bus home with Mom and everyone went to their own home.

We tried to make it a weekly outing if everyone had a quarter. A movie ticket was a dime and a box of popcorn was the same but a small drink was only a nickel. But if we had an extra nickel, we could afford a candy bar. But everything about our life in Vicksburg would soon come to an end on the 9th day of September, 1951.

We had lived close to Grandma and Grandpa Conrad most of our lives and attended church and school with our family and friends. The colored kids had their own schools and churches and this was a way of life we had always known.

The two races kept their distances and very few ever crossed the line liked we did. We all played together and developed great friendships that would last right up until we moved away. We also had white friends and leaving everyone behind was very sad.

Saturday morning came and the big truck showed up. By noon everything we owned had been loaded and we were on our way south to *our new home in Clem. We would now be sharecrop cotton farmers and our new life would be very different from what we had known before.*

We would be starting the year off in a new school and the only person in town we knew was our stepdad, Monroe Heggins. We had never met his nine kids or any of his family and this was a stressful time for us. At the time only four of his kids were living at home.

Grandma Stephenson was left behind in Vicksburg and would be staying with Grandpa and Grandma Conrad until her son, Alton, picked her up at Thanksgiving and take her to live with him in California.

Soon we arrived at our new home, which was in the country not far from Bowie Swamp. Our closest neighbor was a mile away.

We arrived on Saturday evening and over the weekend we got everything set up in the house. We were ready for school on Monday morning. All but the two youngest boys (Johnny Cecil Heggins and Joseph Marshall Stephenson) would be attending the little country school of Clem, which was a four-mile ride in a 12-passenger school bus driven by Burnice Roberts.

Our first day was strange and meeting everyone was very awkward for the Stephenson kids. The Clem community had always been home for our new family and being with them made it a little easier. They had always attended Clem and so had their older siblings who were no longer living at home.

Over the next few weeks and months we adjusted to our new family and made friends. Since the farm work wouldn't start until the following spring, we were able to attend school through the winter months. But in the spring when the time came to start farming, the four oldest boys would not be able to attend all the time.

My brother Kennie, my stepbrother Hiawatha, my stepbrother Roosevelt and I would attend only two or three days a week right up until school was out in May. School was only eight months long and that first year was hard. We barely passed to the next grade.

We did survive that first year and had a good crop of cotton and corn. The garden kept food on the table and wild game was available from the hills and Bowie Swamp, along with fish from Bowie Creek.

On August 20th, 1952, we picked our first bale of cotton and took it to the gin. It had been a long, hot summer and it took many long hours of work, but it was a prosperous year for first-time sharecrop farmers.

Mr. Ralph Ramsey would receive half of what the cotton sold for and we got the rest. Cotton at that time was forty cents a pound and after the seed was removed and the cotton baled up, it would weigh around 500 pounds. This meant our profit would be around $100.00 and the cottonseed was used to pay the ginning cost. Give or take a few bucks, we left the gin that day with a hundred dollars but over the next month, 16 more bales would be picked. At the end of the year our profits were about $1,700.00 but it didn't take long till everything was gone after paying off the bills and buying clothes and shoes for the family.

We had lived on credit most of the first year and by the time all the bills were paid and everyone got shoes and clothes, there was nothing left. But the credit would start all over again and this was the life of a sharecrop cotton farmer. It never changed.

Our stepdad worked for the county road department right after he and Mama got married and earned a hundred dollars a month. His work week was six 10-hour days, starting in September of 1951 and continuing through January of 1952.

Without a garden and no other means of support, this was how we survived the winter until our garden began to produce in the spring. We did hunt and fish that first winter and that kept us from going hungry.

The clothes and shoes bought after harvest consisted of a pair of shoes for each of us along with a flannel shirt and a pair of jeans for the boys and a dress for each of the girls. We each got winter coats and the shoes for the boys were high-top, unpolished leather brogans that had to be treated with tallow to make them waterproof. This method of waterproofing caused our shoes to have an awful, rancid smell in a heated classroom. The girls got socks and black-and-white oxfords and a few other necessities.

Any other clothes we got came from donations made to our Aunt Mae and Uncle Tom Marshall's church. These were brought to us once a year from Vicksburg. Mama would sort out everything, and if we were lucky, a few items may fit each of us kids. After all there were nine kids and two adults to clothe.

All the flour and fertilizer sacks were saved and Mama made the boys' summer shirts and boxer shorts from the fertilizer sacks. Dresses for the girls were made from flour sacks. Everything Mama made was dyed with Rit dye and we each got two pair of socks to be worn in the winter with our brogan shoes.

187

From the time school was out until we started back in the fall, the boys never wore shoes and went without shirts. We wore old cut-off jeans and straw hats most of the time unless we went to town.

Sometimes we got a chance to pick cotton for the local farmers until ours was ready. This paid two cents a pound. We were able to go to Prentiss with what we earned and see a movie and buy a few treats for ourselves. We also bought combs, hair oil and toothbrushes. We used baking soda to brush our teeth and the four oldest boys bathed in Bowie Creek.

Life was a constant struggle and it never got any better. We just accepted the fact that life would continue this way and we had to make the best of a bad situation.

Poverty and lack of education was the culprit and many families were plagued with them. But pointing a finger would never solve the problem. Our only hope was to do our best and pray that someday each of us would leave the farm and go out in the world to make a better life for ourselves.

For me, this way of life would continue for six years, but after harvesting my last crop in 1956, I left home in October at the age of 18. I went to Vicksburg for a few months and then out to California in January of 1957. In Bandini, California I met my wife, Neoma Joyce Huitt 21 months later. We were married on November 24th, 1958.

My years of growing up in Mississippi were tough but they taught me much about life and have always been a benefit for me. It has made me appreciate everything I've accomplished in life and my wife and family have always been a blessing to me. As I write this, Joyce and I will be celebrating our 57th anniversary on November 24th 2015, God

188

willing. We have four daughters, 13 grandchildren and 8 great-grandchildren. I'm very thankful that life gave me a struggle but would never wish it on anyone. As I've said in the past, I wouldn't take a million dollars for all the memories I made throughout my childhood, but you couldn't give me a million dollars to go through it again. Thank you God for giving me the strength to handle all the ups and downs and I pray for many more good years before leaving it all behind.

FROM RAGS TO

RICHES

A toothbrush, rarely did I have,
Toothpaste was seldom bought.
In Bowie Creek I took a bath
And I hoped I didn't get caught.

With baking soda, I cleaned my teeth
With a brush or a piece of cloth.
I made the best of what I had
But necessities only were bought.

Clothes and shoes were hand-me-downs,
Or the cheapest money could buy.
Shirts and shorts were from fertilizer sacks
And colored with store-bought dye.

Never did I visit the barber shop,

191

My hair was cut at home.
Hand-squeezed clippers did the job
But they scalped me to the bone.

Hair oil I bought with money I earned,
Rose was the cheapest kind.
Red and yellow were the colors
But it slicked my hair down fine.

Never was there hair shampoo,
No shaving soap or blades.
When it was time for me to shave,
I let it grow like Abe.

The greasy look I always had
Helped keep me in my class.
'Cause I was poor as worn-out dirt
And sometimes called "white trash".

To school, I went, and tried to learn,
A chore most all the time,
Confidence, I remember praying for
But it was always hard to find.

There were other kids just like me
But our pain never went away.
I sometimes felt the urge cry;
I felt that way most days.

The shield I tried to hide behind,
Helped cover up my pain,

In my disguise, I tried my best
But nothing seemed to change.

Hard times were always on my mind
And I never understood,
Why God blessed other kids in school
But me, he rarely would.

My family struggled from day to day
But prayed for better times.
It never happened while I grew up
And life was not too kind.

My prayers seldom got results,
A reason, I'm sure God had.
Answers, I never got for years
And life was always sad.

In fifty-nine, I became an adult,
So much had changed my life.
Married, I was, for six short months
To Joyce, my beautiful wife.

Never the same after meeting her,
God blessed us both each day.
Married, we were in three short months
And for us, God made a way.

Life was great from that first day,
Bad memories soon went away.
Never again did I look back
And I thanked God for every day.

193

He brought me out of the miry clay,
Gave meaning to my life,
A new goal now with answered prayer
And my beautiful sunshine wife.

A miracle happened to both of us;
God blessed us from the start.
The promises we made would last forever
With love of God in our hearts.

The lessons I learned in 21 years
Have taught me many things,
But most important was: never give up!
And have faith in Christ the King.

Back in the '50s, times were rough, but many sharecrop cotton farmers already had the deck stacked against them from the very start. Most were uneducated and born into poverty and many couples with large families had to survive on someone else's farm and try to scratch out a living by raising a few acres of cotton and corn. Sharecrop farming was the only way for many and this lifestyle gave them a roof over their heads, a place to plant a garden and a few bucks each year at harvest time. Sharecrop farmers were a lot like coal miners and they too never got ahead. Like the old song says, another day older and deeper in debt. A husband and wife with a large family could barely survive and nothing came easy. Most were born into poverty and died there. Their only escape was an education, which was always hard to get. Ignorance was the biggest setback and the downfall of many. Poverty is still around today but sharecrop family cotton farming has gone by the wayside. The memories have never been forgotten by those who survived it. Many youngsters left the farm and ventured out in the world and made a good life for themselves and their families, leaving poverty and ignorance behind.

SLOPPING HOGS

The pen is full of big fat hogs,
Four sows and a boar.
I fill a bucket up with slop
And open up the door.

In water, the food had soaked for hours
In a bucket overnight,
But now it's time to feed them
And what a dirty sight!

At the very first smell, they begin to squeal
And gather around the trough,
I pour it in and then stand back
Just like I had been taught!

They carry on with squeals but eat their share
While standing in the slop,
And when it's gone they still want more.
They don't know when to stop.

197

They wander around inside the pen
Searching for more to eat,
But when they see there's nothing left
They all lie down and sleep.

Q: Why do pigs eat so much?
A: They're trying to make hogs out of themselves!

Very seldom did we have extra money to buy pigs but we did purchase a few over the years and raised them to be full-grown hogs. They were always fed and watered each day and kept in pens. They were then butchered in the fall. Hog killing time was around Thanksgiving and it was always nice to have fresh pork. The fat was rendered out for lard and the leftovers were called cracklins. Cracklins were used in cornbread or baked in a pan of sweet potatoes. The intestines were processed and cleaned for chitlins and all the organ meat was eaten right away. The hair on the entire hog was removed and the head was boiled and processed into head cheese. The feet and tails were removed and made into stew but the rest was cut up and salt cured or sealed off in small barrels covered with lard. With no refrigeration, this was the only way poor folks had to keep meat from spoiling. Fresh meat without refrigeration was always eaten during the winter months but this ended when the temperature began to rise.

BLACKSMITH SHOP

Our blacksmith shop was falling down,
Wind blew through the cracks.
It served a purpose on our cotton farm
And work, it never lacked.

The plows were heated and pounded sharp,
A hand forge fueled the heat.
An anvil was attached to a block of wood
Where plows and tools were beat.

Hot, they were, right out of the fire,
Cherry red, they had to be.
A two-pound hammer beat them sharp
Then they were used by my brothers and me!

Our daddy was Monroe Heggins;
He ran the blacksmith shop.
He kept all the tools in tip-top shape
And the farm work never stopped!

His job was very important;
Without him, nothing could be done,

199

In charge of a sharecrop cotton farm,
Repairing farm tools for his sons!

With mules, the red clay fields were plowed,
There was cotton and many other crops,
An acre of land grew all our food
But on Sunday the farm work stopped.

Life wasn't easy for any of us
But God always made a way,
With a roof over our heads and food to eat
And rest at the end of each day.

Lessons were learned and we grew up fast,
Each of us doing our part.
We farmed the land and earned our keep
With faith of God in our hearts!

Over the years, we left the farm,
Found jobs and learned other skills.
God blessed us all in many ways
And good lives, we all tried to live.

Kennie and Roosevelt were the oldest,
Hiawatha and Rufus a year behind.
We worked that farm six days a week
And tried to have a good time!

On September 9th 1951, Louise Elizabeth Conrad Stephenson
and Monroe Lavelle Heggins were married by Andrew Griffith. He was

a justice of the peace in the Clem farm community of Jeff Davis County, Mississippi. Louise had five kids and Monroe had four; between them were seven boys and two girls ranging from age three to fourteen! Roosevelt, Monroe's oldest son was fourteen and his second son, Hiawatha, was twelve, turning thirteen two days after the wedding. Kennie, Louise's oldest son, was fourteen and her second son, Rufus, was thirteen. These four boys bonded and became hard working farmers. School for the Heggins clan began the following Monday, which was the eleventh day of September and Hiawatha's 13th birthday. Kennie would turn fifteen in October and Roosevelt turned fifteen in November. These four teenage boys became a great working team in the spring of 1952.

Hiawatha and Roosevelt had grown up on a cotton farm, but Kennie and Rufus had no knowledge of farm life. This family of nine kids had moved to a sharecrop cotton farm owned by Mr. Ralph Ramsey, who would furnish them with a house, the farm land and plow tools, along with a barn and four mules. There was also an old dilapidated blacksmith shop used to make repairs to all the tools needed to keep the farm going. The equipment was old and was the same that had been used in the past century, but it still did the job when properly maintained by our daddy. The fall and winter of 1951-52 soon came to an end and farming began. Come spring, these four teenage boys and their daddy had a big job ahead of them. Rufus and Kennie had much to learn, but their new brothers were already seasoned farm kids and plow jockeys. It was a hard life but was an experience never to be forgotten. They all grew into men and left the farm with an ability to go out on their own and make a life for themselves. They grew up fast but the lessons learned would help them throughout their lives. The best education doesn't

201

always come from books; you can also learn a lot from the school of hard knocks and tough times. Sharecrop farming produced four adults who never expected a free handout and appreciated everything they got out of life.

RUFUS AND HIS

MULE

Pulling a plough was taught to the mule,
Rufus learned how to plow.
Four commands were used to direct every move
And it didn't take long to learn how.

Working a farm with long-eared mules,
Was an ongoing practice for years.
Hard work, it was, for Rufus and his mule
But sometimes it brought him to tears!

This animal was ornery, stubborn and mean
And she worked twelve hours a day,
From sun-up till sundown following commands
But this ornery ole mule led the way!

"Gee" was *right* and "Haw" was *left*,
Spoken many times every day.
"Giddy-up" was *go* and "Whoa" was *stop*,

These four simple words lead the way.

Smarter than a horse but twice as strong,
Like Rufus, she never wore shoes.
Rubbed down and brushed at the end of each day,
It was a treat for a hard-working mule!

Bits in her mouth and reins on the bridle,
A big leather collar round her neck,
A back band and hames and two trace chains
Would keep her always in check!

Geared up each morning before leaving the barn
Her harness was removed at noon.
It was time now to eat and rest for a spell;
Returning to work too soon!

An old Georgia stock was the antique plow,
Used for cultivating the crops.
The rows were long and fields were wide,
But twelve hours later they stopped.

Just before sundown his mule was unhitched
From the plow she had pulled all day,
Then up on her back Rufus would climb
And "giddy-up" was all he had to say.

His mule took a drink when they got to the creek,
Rufus took time out to swim.
In Bowie, the water was crystal clear
And mighty refreshing to them!

204

To the barn they headed before it got dark,
The harness again was removed.
That sweaty ole mule was hungry and tired
But free from her harness and tools.

Her bridle was removed and she lay on the ground
Then rolled over two or three times,
An indication of value for each turn she made.
A mule like her was hard to find!

Rufus worked hard six days each week
From sun-up till sundown every day,
Plowing the fields of cotton and corn
But never did he get any pay!

Three meals a day and a roof over his head
But sometimes he couldn't help but cry.
The plowing was finished on the 3rd of July
When the cotton and corn was laid by!

His faithful ole mule was put out to pasture,
They both had six weeks of rest.
Rufus went fishing and swimming in Bowie Creek
Since summer was now at its best!

Seven days a week there were chores to be done
But no more twelve-hour days,
There were cows to be milked and water to fetch
But they both had it made in the shade.

Cotton picking began in the middle of August,

Fingers and back were in pain,
But soon it was time to harvest the corn
And finish before winter came!

Farm work was over by Thanksgiving.
Winter wasn't too far away.
Christmas was close and the year nearly over.
They both had longed for this day.

Thanksgiving was all about family,
Bounty from the harvest was prepared,
For dinner there was never a turkey
But good Southern cookin' was there.

Money was scarce and there never was waste,
Presents for the family were few,
A tree was cut down on the boss man's land
And gifts were only clothing and shoes.

A big Christmas dinner was prepared by Mama
Along with her great cakes and pies,
Chicken and dumplings and many tasty vittles
And sometimes a special surprise.

Thankful, he was, for his food and shelter
And a bed to lie down and rest,
Hard times were many and he had his share
But he'd always done his very best!

His mule was then put out to pasture,
Freedom for her at its best.

206

She had performed so well for another year
And again had passed all the tests.

She was brought back to the barn in February
When farming was getting under way.
Her hooves were trimmed and her hair was groomed.
She was not very happy that day!

A half-day of school was attended by Rufus,
For many, it happened this way.
From the middle of February till school was out,
He walked home at noon every day.

Young boys had plowed mules for generations,
The picture was always the same.
Without these kids there would've been no farming
And life for them rarely ever changed.

A tough row to hoe but Rufus became a man,
His lessons in life were learned well.
Now he was ready to do other things
And let sharecrop farming go to hell.

His ole mule retired in the '50s
And was put out to pasture for good.
Rufus packed his duds and left at eighteen
And applied for every job that he could!

After working three months in Vicksburg,
On a Greyhound bus, he rode away
In search of the end of his rainbow,
California was definitely the way.

A TRIP TO THE

GRISTMILL

I shuck a bushel of hybrid corn
And put it in a can.
With a twist, I shell each ear
Just with my own two hands.

I pour the corn into a sack,
I twist and tie the ends.
I put a bridle on my mule;
To the gristmill we head again.

It don't take long until I'm there
But the miller takes his toll,
He grinds the rest into corn meal
And does just what he's told.

My mule don't have a saddle
But I climb upon her back.
My sack of corn is now corn meal

And I head for the sharecrop shack.

Soon I'm back at home again,
My mule set free to roam.
I give my Mama a sack of meal
And for me, she bakes cornpone.

BUCKY THE BEAVER

I was given a trap at age fifteen;
Catching a beaver was my goal.
Trapping I knew very little about
But the thought consumed my soul.

In Bowie Swamp, I met an old trapper,
Some tips he shared with me.
But soon I discovered a beaver slide
That was hidden behind an oak tree!

At the bottom, I set my rusty ole trap
With a twenty-foot chain attached.
In the creek bed, I drove a five-foot rod
With hopes that a beaver I would catch.

To the rod, a rusty ole chain was attached,
But the trap didn't need any bait.
The beaver would slide down his slippery slide
And so would meet his fate.

Once in the trap, he headed for his dam,

But soon ran out of chain;
Around the rod, he continued to swim
And in minutes, the end for him came.

Early one morning while I was at school,
It was recess and 9 a.m.,
In front of the gym, my stepdad drove up.
I could hardly believe it was him.

His name was Monroe and he was all alone
With a beaver in the back of his truck,
He had a big smile from ear to ear.
He'd come just to show off my luck!

Many of my friends gathered around,
This beaver, I had pursued a long time,
Permission was given for me to leave school
With my trophy that was one of a kind.

With Unlucky Bucky, we headed for home.
Down a gravel road, we drove for a mile.
Proud of my catch, and thrilled to the bone
I too had an ear-to-ear smile!

I removed Bucky's skin and cut up the meat,
Cleaned up the mess I had made!
Mama made stew in her cast iron pot
From a beaver that nearly got away.

Over a grapevine, I stretched his skin,
To cure it would take three weeks.

I then placed his hide next to my bedside
And it sure felt good on my feet.

Bucky, the beaver, took hunger away.
For my family, there was two tasty meals.
Feeding nine kids and my mom and dad
Was the reason I hunted and killed.

Trapping was something I had never done before I was 15 years old, when I was given 36 traps by my cousin in Vicksburg. I used them to catch beaver, possum, coon, and skunk and made a few bucks selling their pelts. I also enjoyed many hours in Bowie Swamp. When the Davy Crockett television program began in the '50s, coonskin caps were popular and many young boys wanted one. The coon population began to thin out but before the popularity waned, a few folks tried their luck at trapping. This beaver I caught weighed 37 pounds and added to my great memories of my teen years fishing, hunting, and trapping in Bowie Swamp.

BILLY THE KID

The year was 1953 and the Heggins clan was leaving the Ralph Ramsey sharecrop cotton farm after working his land for two years. We had farmed seventeen acres of cotton and twenty acres of corn each year without ever earning enough money to support our family.

Arrangements had been made to move one mile east of Clem School to another sharecrop cotton farm owned by Everett Magee. There we would have thirty-seven acres of cotton and thirty acres of corn, which was much more work but had the potential to earn more money. It was still not enough to supply all the needs of a family with nine kids and two adults.

The farming conditions were the same; we would continue to get half the cotton and corn and a milk cow was furnished from time to time when a new calf was born. We could also raise a few watermelons and cantaloupe and have a big garden, which supplied most of our food. We didn't have to share the garden vegetables and could earn a few extra dollars from the sale of melons, which would be ours to keep.

Our new house and farm was less than a quarter mile from

215

Bowie Creek and we still had access to all the hunting and fishing we desired. We had the same privileges we had while living on the Ramsey farm but this location would later become a playground for all the boys, who would continue to fish and hunt for much of our food.

Eight kids were now in school and the bus picked us up each morning at 7:00 am. We arrived in less than five minutes. Rufus, Kennie, Roosevelt and Hiawatha seldom rode the bus and often had to walk, because if there was lots of farm work, we either attended a half day or not at all. We missed far too much school because the farm work always came first.

The house was old and rundown and the interior walls and ceilings were not finished. There was a tin roof that leaked every time it rained. There were no windows or door screens and no indoor plumbing. Out back was a two-hole outhouse about a hundred feet from the back door. The wood floors and walls had cracks between the boards and daylight could be seen after sun-up. There were no standard door locks; instead ropes and wood latches were used to open and close the doors. The old house sat about two feet above the ground and the space underneath was used for storage. It also gave the dogs and chickens a place to get out of bad weather.

Our dilapidated old sharecrop shack sat on a hilltop about twenty feet above the level of Bowie Swamp. When heavy rains came in the winter and early spring, the creek overflowed and water came within two hundred yards of the house.

216

There were many times when Bowie Creek got out of its banks, and overnight the flood waters came close but they went down just as fast when the rain stopped. When this happened, many fish were trapped in low-lying areas of the pasture. These were gathered up and taken home for our food.

Mr. Everett had close to eighty brush goats that ate most all the briars and unwanted weeds on his property. Cattle also roamed free on the land and sometimes hay had to be hauled during the winter months to keep them fed. He always took one of us boys along to help but whoever went would earn at least twenty-five cents for working an hour. These small jobs were the only way to earn money during the winter and one of us four always accepted the work when asked.

When feeding time came, the goats always showed up with the cows and ate their share. Off the back of a pick-up truck I scattered hay as Mr. Everett drove and all the animals followed behind. Between the cows and goats there were many animals to feed and the mooing and baaing was always loud. The goats sometimes even tried to jump on the truck, but I kept them off.

One day after I had finished unloading the hay, Mr. Everett saw three big dogs chasing his goats. He quickly turned around and began to blow his horn, hoping they would leave, but before their attack was stopped, three of his best goats had been killed and several were injured.

He was very angry. He got out his shotgun and fired a few

217

shots as they ran toward the woods! Not one of them were hit so
we went back and loaded the three dead animals on the back of
the truck. As we were closing the tailgate, I heard sounds in the
thick brush and was surprised to see a baby goat running toward
us. Its mother had been killed. It was too little to be left alone so I
reached down and began to pet the little fellow. Mr. Everett asked
if I wanted to take him home for a pet and I liked the idea so I
picked him up. We climbed on the back of the truck and we
headed for home.

Mr. Everett thought he knew who owned the dogs and
would be going past his house on our way home. Before leaving
the pasture, I had to get off the truck and open a gate, so I put my
goat in the front seat with Mr. Everett until the gate was closed.
He wasn't too thrilled about having a smelly goat in his truck but
I took him out and we got in the back of the truck.

Within ten minutes Mr. Everett pulled up in front of an old
farm house. On the front porch was an elderly colored man
sitting in his rocking chair. In the front yard were three big dogs
and we knew right away they were the ones that killed his goats.

I held on to my little goat and stayed on the truck while
Mr. Everett got out with his shotgun, walked up to the gate, and
began talking to the old man. After a few choice words of
warning and threatening to kill his dogs if they ever came on his
property again, he got back in the truck and we headed home.

We stopped off at Polk's grocery store and got a Coke,

then several folks gathered around the truck and checked out the dead goats. They didn't have much to say about them or my baby goat; Everett told them what happened and who owned the dogs. He gave a few words of advice and we left.

In less than fifteen minutes, we were crossing over the cattle gap and parking in front of the house. I was still holding tight to my new pet and was anxious to show him off to my family. Right away I went inside and asked Mom and Dad if I could keep him. I was surprised when they said it was okay.

I ran outside and told Mr. Everett and he was happy with the news. My little friend was acting a little strange so I took him down to the well and gave him a drink of water and this perked him up. The kids wanted to play with him but I thought it best they left him alone for a while and let him calm down.

He was already weaned from his mother and able to drink and eat grass but we would have to keep an eye on him until he got a little older. It didn't take long till the little fellow settled down. He was enjoying the attention and the kids were having a good time.

Now it was time to give him a name and since he was a male, we decided to call him Billy the Kid. We couldn't leave him alone except at night when he was put in the barn. During the day someone had to keep an eye on him all the time.

From that first day, he was seldom out of sight and never without food and water. It was exciting to have a pet goat around the house and our days were never boring again. Billy the Kid never let any of us rest; everyone spent time playing with him and feeding him.

Because of the heat, our doors and windows were always left open, and with no screens, he often made his way inside the house. This upset Mom. She was always chasing him with her broom and telling us to keep a better eye on Billy the Kid.

Slowly, he became a troublemaker and climbed on everything above ground. The hood of our old 1949 Ford pick-up truck was his favorite. Dad didn't like it and threatened to shoot him if he didn't stay off.

The weeks and months went by fast and before we knew it, Billy the Kid was growing horns. He loved to butt the kids and chase all the hound dogs. He became a full-fledged nuisance by the time he was a year old and ceased to be much fun, so Dad said we had to get rid of him. We knew he was gradually becoming a problem but we had wanted to keep him as long as we could. In the end, Dad said he would have to go.

Billy the Kid continued to sneak in and out of the house and was always jumping on the kitchen table and benches. When friends stopped by for a visit, he climbed all over their cars. He also disturbed the chickens and was way too rough with little kids.

The time had finally come to get rid of Billy the Kid! He was no longer a kid, but was in fact a full grown billy goat with whiskers and horns.

We talked about other ways to get rid of him and our best idea was he might fit in with Mr. Everett's goats since he was once part of the herd. Dad thought it was worth a try so we dropped him off in the herd. Unfortunately, he made it back home before the sun went down.

After several unsuccessful attempts to set him free, Dad thought it best to butcher and eat Billy the Kid. The kids didn't like the idea and thought it was an awful thing to do; we wanted to try something else but nothing seemed to work. And Dad wouldn't change his mind.

Soon it was time to shoot our ornery ole goat. We caught him by his horns and led him to the barn. Dad came out with his rifle. He opened the door and walked inside and there was Billy the Kid, standing tall in the feed trough looking straight down the barrel of the gun that would soon take his life. Dad said Billy the Kid began to slowly back up but went too far and fell off the end of the feed trough. Dad was very surprised when the goat never moved or made any sound. He knew something was wrong so he reached down to see what had happened. Billy the Kid had died from a broken neck or a heart attack.

Us kids were waiting outside expecting to hear a gunshot but when dad came out to tell us what happened, we were all sad and nearly in tears. Billy the Kid was then taken outside and butchered and the meat was placed in three large, galvanized buckets. His hide was nailed to the barn as a reminder.

That evening, Mama cooked a hind quarter for supper and the rest was left to soak in salt water. It was enough for two more meals.

We were always thankful for our food but Billy the Kid had left a bad taste in our mouths. Never again did we eat goat without thinking about our once loveable little friend.

By now you may think this story is a tall tale but I assure you, it's true and really happened to the Heggins clan. It was late spring of 1954 on the Everett Magee sharecrop cotton farm in the Clem community of Jeff Davis County, Mississippi.

ERNIE THE PIG

While living on the Everett Magee sharecrop cotton farm, Mr. And Mrs. Holloway and their two sons, Pender and L.C., were our closest neighbors. They were colored and lived in an old rundown sharecrop shack. We all worked on the same farm. Like us, Pender and L.C. were in their teens and my three brothers and I had many good times with them.

They lived at the top of a hill about three hundred yards south of us. Pender played guitar and L.C. played the harmonica. They worked all week in the fields like us but we all got together sometimes on Saturday evening and sang ole time gospel songs on their front porch.

The Holloway family were very talented and had a 30-minute gospel radio program every Sunday morning in Jackson, MS. They were a good Christian family and known and liked by many folks both black and white.

They were poor like many colored and white folks and spent many of their hot summer evenings sitting on the front porch trying to stay cool. With temperatures in the 90s and often above a hundred, the best place was on a shady porch or under a big tree; but for the youngsters, a swim in Bowie Creek did the job.

The Heggins and Stephenson boys, along with Pender and L.C., hunted and fished throughout the year and enjoyed cooling off in Bowie Creek every chance we got.

In the spring and summer months when the gardens were producing, we often shared fresh vegetables with each other and tried to reach out and be good neighbors.

One Saturday after a fun afternoon of singing with Pender and L.C., they took us behind their house and showed off an ole sow and her twelve newborn pigs. They were still very small but they offered us one when they were weaned from their mother. We thought it was kind of them and we accepted this special gift.

It would take several weeks before the litter was big enough to separate from their mother so we had to wait for when the time was right. With a dozen to choose from, we were sure to find one we all liked! We continued our visits from time to time, and finally one day Mr. Holloway said it was time to take our pick. All the pigs were much bigger now and also much louder and harder to handle.

We had the first pick of the litter and after looking them over, we chose a black and white spotted male. He was a chubby little fellow and we had a hard time catching him but we soon had him in a burlap sack and were on our way home. We had been waiting over a month and had given much thought to names. We decided to call him Ernie.

When we first learned that we would be getting a baby pig, a pen was built and plans were made for his food and water. With four teenage boys in charge, each of us would take care of Ernie for a week at a time and this would give us a three-week break before our next turn. The weeks went by fast and Ernie ate everything we put before him. He sure did try hard to make a hog out of himself.

His pen wasn't very big and all he ever did was eat, sleep, and roll around in the mud trying to stay cool. He loved having his belly scratched; he always rolled over on his side for us and never wanted us to quit.

The weeks and months went by fast and Ernie slowly turned into a full-grown hog. We kept increasing his food and guessed his weight to be over a hundred pounds by the time he was six months old.

The well was a few yards up the hill from his pen so we carried buckets of water on hot summer days and cooled him off. This also added to his mud wallow and he loved it.

At the edge of the swamp not far from the pen grew many wild hog weeds and we often fed these to Ernie. They were his favorite wild green but he also got the leftover watermelon and cantaloupe rinds along with his regular food. He loved corn and turnips. In fact there wasn't much he didn't like.

Now our dad had his eyes on Ernie. He planned on butchering him around Christmas, but first he had to gain more weight.

Alton Ray, Marshall and Johnnie Cecil, our three youngest brothers, visited Ernie often but our sisters, Margie and Mae, didn't like the smell and rarely came around. The few visits they did make were quick and they soon retreated back to the house.

Ernie continued to grow and weighed over 200 pounds by the end of November. He was gaining more each day. Without a place to weigh him, we were still guessing but would get the correct weight after he was slaughtered.

Only shelled corn and water was fed to Ernie the last thirty days. This cleaned out his intestinal tract and made it easier to process the chitlins. This would also help remove excess fat and make him more solid.

Slaughtering day soon came and Ernie was taken out of his pen and cool water from the well was used to wash off the mud. He was then left to dry in the warm sun. This was the first time he was clean and he was now a sleek-looking hog. Dad soon came out with his gun and got ready to finish the job.

While Ernie stood still, he was shot in the head with a .22 rifle and his throat was cut. He was then hung up by his hind legs. He weighed 220 pounds on a pair of cotton scales. All this was necessary, even though the weak at heart couldn't watch without getting a little queasy.

A barrel of boiling water had been prepared to dip him and then he was placed on a large table where his hair was scraped off.

When this phase of butchering was finished, his stomach was opened and the internal organs were removed and placed in a tub. His head was then removed, placed in a pot of boiling water, and cooked until it was ready to process for head cheese.

The hams, shoulders and ribs were processed and the fat removed and rendered for lard. The feet and tail were also removed and set aside for stew.

The liver, heart, and other internal organs were cut into small pieces and made into a special dish called hashlet. It was served that day with iced tea and cornbread for the dinner meal. Everyone enjoyed it.

After the fat had been rendered and poured into gallon cans, all that was left were the cracklins, which were used in many ways but were best when baked in cornbread or cooked in a pan of baked sweet potatoes. They were also good with a big, fat possum!

Mom, Margie and Mae removed all the meat from the head and added special spices and other ingredients. It was then put in large stone crocks. Heavy weights were placed on top and it was left to age for two days before eating.

The intestines were then cleaned. Some were used for

making sausage but most were boiled and fried in a skillet and eaten.

Hog-killing days were always in the late fall or between Thanksgiving and Christmas. The reason being, there was no refrigeration and the meat would spoil if it got too hot. Much of the meat was salt cured but some was put in small barrels and sealed off with melted lard. The meat had to be eaten fast or it would begin to smell and taste rancid and then spoil.

With our big family, rarely did this happen because everything would be gone before the weather turned warm. Hog killing was not a yearly thing for our family but when it happened, everyone was thrilled to have fresh pork.

RUFUS AND JOE

Joe was a big ole black-and-tan hound
And spent his time in the woods
Chasing coons and possums all night long
Just doing what a hound dog should.

Up a red oak tree, he chased a big coon
But he climbed out on a limb,
Joe made sure he didn't get away
And never took his eyes off him!

Barking and howling till his master came
With a gun and carbide light,
A shot rang out and down he came
But never did he put up a fight!

By the neck, Joe shook him two or three times,
By the tree he laid him on the ground.
Rufus reached down and put him in a sack
And Joe never made another sound!

To the sharecrop shack they headed
But Joe got excited again.

229

He ran toward a grove of persimmon trees
And saw a possum looking down at him!

Rufus laid his burlap sack on the ground
And shined his light in the tree,
But instead of seeing one ugly possum
He discovered they numbered three!

They were grinning and eating persimmons,
Six eyes that glowed in the dark,
A shot rang out and a big one fell
But Joe just stood there and barked!

Shots echoed across Bowie Swamp,
And two more possums fell.
Rufus reached down and put 'em in his sack
While Joe stood by and raised hell!

With a sack full of game, they headed for home,
Ole Joe finally calmed down.
Soon they walked through the backyard gate
Trying not to make any sound!

The lights were out and the house was quiet.
The family was fast asleep.
Rufus had to clean three possums and a coon
'Cause overnight the meat wouldn't keep!

To the barn, he headed and took out his knife.
In no time he had 'em all skinned.
In salt water, the meat was left to soak

And Joe was locked in his pen!

Rufus washed up and headed for bed,
The meat would soak overnight.
For supper, the next day, it was ready to cook
And his family would enjoy every bite.

In the oven, it was baked with sweet taters,
Grease was collected in the pan,
His mama cooked possum and coon many times
And Joe was his favorite black-and-tan.

A FOX HUNT

It's Saturday night in Jeff Davis County,
A fox hunt is ready to begin!
Hunters gather in Bowie Swamp
All anxious to see who wins.

In pick-up trucks, the dogs arrive,
A fox, they're ready to chase.
It may be a red or a skinny ole grey
But both will put up a good race.

Fast is the lead dog, hot on the trail
Of a red or grey on the run.
More dogs are released and join the chase
Without ever a need for a gun.

A bushy-tail red will run for hours,
The grey puts up a good race.
The hunt may last throughout the night
But the lucky ole fox escapes.

Over the hills and through the swamp,

Muddy waters, brush and briars,
The dogs slow down but never give up
And the fox never seems to tire.

The lead dog is always identified,
From the bark, his master can tell,
In Jeff Davis County, ten dogs run a race
And a sly ole fox catches hell.

When time comes for him to run down a hole,
Or up a tree to climb,
The dogs catch up and so do their masters
But the fox is always left behind.

If an escape is made up a leaning tree,
Ten lights shine up on him.
The dogs are taken to pick-up trucks
And a party for the hunters begins.

The life of these critters are always spared
To live and run another day,
Time after time they make their escape!
Fox hunting was always this way.

All tipsy on White Lightning;
They've sampled a jug through the night.
It's time now to build a roaring campfire
While everyone gets high as a kite.

These nights were always special
For the farmers and their ole fox hounds.

234

They worked all week but then get together
To listen to their favorite sounds.

To their ears, the dogs are music,
Much better than an ole radio.
They might listen to the Grand Ole Opry
But there's nothing quite like June or Joe.

As a teenager growing up in the Clem community of Jeff Davis County, Mississippi, I spent a few Saturday nights in Bowie Swamp hunting with my stepdad and his friends. They enjoyed fox hunting and each of them had a special dog they used to chase red or grey foxes. Walker hounds were their favorite breed and my stepdad had one that was very special to him named June. He had purchased her as an eight-week-old pup from the Bluegrass Kennels of Kentucky. She arrived by train in Prentiss and Monroe picked her up at the railroad station and took her home. She was a playful little pup but serious training began the very next day.

She was well trained by the age of two and was considered by most fox hunters to be one of the best in the county. Monroe had a special talent for training fox hounds and everyone in the county knew that any dog owned by Monroe Heggins was the best there was. His dogs were always in demand and brought top dollar when sold.

Over the years, June had many litters of pups that were always promised before they were born. She was the best there was and could jump a fox quicker than any other dog. She was always the first in the pack to be released and it didn't take long till she had a red or grey on the run. After chasing ten or fifteen minutes by herself, one by one the other dogs were released and the fox hunt was on.

I had never been on a fox hunt until the fall after my mom and stepdad were married, but it never thrilled me quite like it did the old-timers. It was fun enough during late summer or early fall when the nights were cool. If and when I did tag along, I always stayed close to everyone and made sure I didn't get lost in Bowie Swamp; carbide lights were used and they always brightly lit the path ahead of the hunters. I was 13 on my first outing and for me this was an exciting, new experience. Sometimes I got tired just before the sun came up.

The chase could last for hours but rarely did the dogs ever get out of hearing range. After everyone got tired, we found a dry place to sit and rest and listened to a pack of hounds chase an ole fox. I do admit it was quite an experience and never did I ever forget those sounds as they echoed across the swamp.

I couldn't tell one dog's bark from the others but the owners always knew what position their dog was running. Sometimes the chase would last till sun-up but most were only three or four hours. A red fox was the fastest and could run much longer while the greys tired quicker and were likely to climb up a tree or down in a hole.

The fox was never killed and was left to run another day. The old-timers knew where to find him when it was time to hunt again and when they did, they would release their best dog and soon the chase was on. In many cases, the fox had a name and the place where he could be found was well-known, as was the running path he would take and how long the chase would last.

Popular names for male dogs were Jake and Joe. Females were June, Annie, or just about any name you could think of. My cousin once had a Walker hound called Lightning, but some folks gave their dogs names like Star, Moon, and Willie. One old man had a pair he called Skeeter and Chigger. One thing is for certain: An owner could always tell if his dog was in the lead. I never knew how they were so sure because I couldn't tell one from the other.

No matter how many men came out for the hunt, there was always lots of moonshine and by the time it was over, everybody was a little tipsy. The fox always went up a sloping tree to get away from the dogs or found a hole in the ground to escape. When this happened, it didn't take long till the dogs caught up and soon everyone showed up with carbide lights. If the fox went in a hole, the dogs were called off and taken back to the truck but if he went up a tree, all the lights were soon shining on him and the dogs just stood by and raised hell. The fox was never harmed. After everyone got a good look, the dogs were called off and taken back to the trucks and fed.

They were all wiped out by now and lay down to take a rest. Now it was time to build a big campfire and enjoy each other's company. The flames were soon leaping high in the night and everyone sat around the fire getting high on moonshine and telling stories. This was the highlight of the hunt and would sometimes last two or three hours or until the sun came up.

Soon everyone was saying goodbye and heading for home. The dogs slept all the way back and were put in their pen until the next hunt. These dogs were valuable and always had the best of care and shelter from the hot sun and rain.

Litters of pups were born each year and many were sold but some were traded for other dogs. Fox hunting was a great sport for the old-timers, with the second favorite being coon and possum hunting. Walker hounds were the best fox dogs but black-and-tans, blue tics, and red bones were the best for hunting coon and possum. Beagles were good pets and rabbit dogs. They all played an important role for folks living and hunting in Jeff Davis County. I don't want to forget the good squirrel dogs because they help put food on the tables for many families.

Hunting and fishing were always fun for many and kept food on the table when times were hard. There was nothing better than a big plate of catfish caught out of Bowie Creek, or maybe a pot of squirrel stew, or sometimes a big ole coon or possum and sweet taters. Another favorite was Cottontail and Canecutter rabbits, which were always plentiful in the swamps and across the hillsides.

With a big garden and all the fish you could catch out of Bowie Creek, along with wild game, there was no reason for anyone to go hungry. Where there's a will, there's a way. God gave folks the will and provided a way for families to survive even though it was a struggle. He was only a prayer away and like the old hymn says, he was there all the time. Without his help, life would have been much worse for many.

For me, those years will never be forgotten and I thank God for all the memories. Without the tough times, I would have never been able to enjoy the good times I've had with my family and friends.

Fox hunting never put food on the table but did provide many fun Saturday nights for a bunch of ole farmers and their dogs. I guess a few drinks of moonshine lifted their spirits and sharing their stories and tall tales was always fun. The dogs must have had a great time chasing *the fox but the ole red or grey must have got a kick out of always winning the race and outwitting the dogs too, time after time in Bowie Swamp.*

After the dogs and the fox rested for a week or two, they were ready to do it all over again. The ole farmers got out their bottles of moonshine and cleaned and polished their carbide lights; then loaded up the dogs in their pick-up trucks and headed out for another Saturday night of fun and music courtesy of their favorite ole fox hounds

A NUT CASE

He rolled a tire down gravel roads,
Made sounds like a car.
Wherever he was at dinner time
A farm house couldn't be far.

He made his way to the first he saw
And walked up on the porch,
Inviting himself to eat with them
And the answer was always, "of course".

At the table, he found a place to sit,
Joined in with all the others.
His manners were bad and they always showed
Since he ate like a starving brother.

After eating his meal, he disappeared
And retrieved his worn out tire.
Rolling it out to the gravel road
He took off like a streak of fire.

He never stayed long after eating
But continued on down the road,
Later in the evening before sundown
He was starving again and it showed.

Off at a distance when he saw a house,
Food was always on his mind.
Seven hours had passed since eating last
And he devoured all he could find.

When supper was over, he didn't move on
But planned on spending the night,
Inviting himself to rest for a spell
And he soon was out like a light!

He had found a place to lay his head
And it was time for him to sleep.
He expected eight hours of rest in a bed
But for breakfast he was ready to eat.

Awful, he smelled most of the time,
Sweating from too many clothes.
Never did he shave or wash his hands;
He was dirty right down to his toes!

Somewhere in the county he had a family
But for him nobody really cared,
It was plain to see, he was touched in the head
And survived because good folks shared!

His teeth were rotten and he never combed his hair,

Always sleeping in his clothes.
Barefoot, he was, most of the time
And had half-inch nails on his toes!

If you happened to live by a county road,
One day he could be your guest.
Few ever escaped this wandering man
'Cause your luck ran out like the rest!

No need for excuses or to get upset
If he knocked on your front door,
The best thing to do was invite him in
'Cause he knew there was room for one more.

After taking a seat, he was ready to eat
But everyone better eat fast,
Just fill up your plate and do it quick
'Cause nothing on the table would last!

He could eat much more than two grown men,
Drink a gallon of sweet iced tea!
He was the hungriest little man in the county
And it was best if you just let him be.

Known by many and few escaped
He expected you to accommodate him,
With food and shelter and a gallon of tea
Though some wanted to hang him from a limb!

He traveled the roads twelve months of the year
Surprising many folks all the time.
With no invitation, he could be your guest,

This vagrant who was one-of-a-kind!

THE WATERMELON

MAN

In 1952, I was told this story about a man who grew a record-breaking black diamond watermelon in the great state of Mississippi. He was a poor farmer and had lived and worked his entire life on the family farm.

Born in 1890, not far from the Alabama state line, he and his wife, Annie, had been married over twenty years. They lived on the same farm where he had been born and raised.

A tall, gangly fellow, some folks thought he was a little strange but a great father and husband. He and his family lived from day to day, always struggling just to survive.

The Great Depression had left him high and dry like so many others. Money was scarce and he would do anything to earn extra money for his family.

Each year on the 4th of July, a celebration was held and everyone in the community enjoyed the festivities. A contest was always held for the largest watermelon and he had participated several times without winning.

The ladies showed off canned vegetables from their

gardens and fresh fruit and vegetables were sold or traded for anything of value.

In the spring of 1930, at a local country grocery store, the watermelon man encountered a few old timers and wanted to bet that he could grow the largest watermelon in the county and win first prize. He went on to say that if he won, he and his family would eat the entire melon and he would crawl through the rind before the sun went down.

Everybody laughed but a few took him up on his bet. Some thought he was a little touched in the head for making such a crazy wager.

The contest would be held at the local fairgrounds. A three-dollar entry fee had to be paid in advance. He was always short on funds and had to pinch pennies just to pay the fee!

None of this discouraged him. This meant if he fulfilled his promise, they would have to pay him a dollar for a dollar but if he failed, then he had to pay the same to everyone who made a bet. There was a minimum bet of one dollar and a maximum of five, but only a few wanted to wager more than a dollar. A little book was used to record the bets. After leaving the store, the list of names was less than he had hoped for.

Over the next few days he found a special place to plant his prize seed, which he purchased from a New Orleans seed catalog. The company guaranteed the biggest and sweetest melons if the directions were followed. He wanted to prove to himself that he could beat out Wally Eastbrook, who had won in 1928 and 1929. For him, growing the largest watermelon had been a dream and he felt this would be his lucky year.

Leon Winters was his name. His special seed was soon planted on a small piece of ground a hundred yards south of his rundown old farm house. He protected these special plants with a six-foot chicken wire fence and also covered the top with wire to keep out birds and wild animals.

He arrived at the gate five days later and was surprised to see the plants struggling to break through the crusty, rich, black, sandy soil.

First, he cut down all the weeds and grass around the delicate plants and watered them. This took about thirty minutes and he went back to plowing his cotton field. Now Leon was excited and looked forward to checking them each morning!

This was a family project so his wife, Annie, and their twelve kids were always there to help. For him, this project was as important as all the other chores on the farm; he looked forward to winning the one-hundred-dollar prize and having his picture published in the local paper. He would also receive an achievement award from the seed catalog in New Orleans, but first he had to win.

His twelve kids were very excited about the contest. Their ages were three through eighteen and the oldest was his daughter, Reba.

The three plants were up and standing tall on the eighth day. They looked better on each visit. Every morning the birds were seen flying over or sitting on the fence when he arrived and rabbit tracks could be seen, but none of the plants had been disturbed.

They continued to grow and were soon covering the ground inside his special melon patch. He brought cool water from the well each day and kept the ground moist. He also kept the weeds and grass cut.

The hot, humid days and nights helped the plants grow and soon Leon had to enlarge the fenced area so the plants would have room to spread.

His melon patch was less than fifty yards from a gravel

road and folks often stopped for a better view. This made him happy, knowing the neighbors were impressed with what he was doing; it gave him the incentive to work harder as he prepared for the big event.

The plants grew fast and were soon blooming. Five days later, tiny melons began to appear on the vines.

Never did he skimp on water and he added fertilizer when necessary. The plants grew faster than he or anyone had ever seen and Leon was soon the talk of the county.

Memorial Day was only a week away and his goal was to break the record by the fourth of July. Folks were beginning to believe Ole Leon may achieve his goal and would produce the prize-winning watermelon for 1930.

Luck was on his side and the weather had been great. The animals and birds had caused no damage to his melon patch. A few coons and rabbits had tried digging under the fence but never made it through.

Now he was much more relaxed and everything was going great, but one morning after a heavy rain, he found a large hole washed out under the fence. Inside, he discovered two big coons and an ugly ole possum eating away at one of his prize melons. This upset him so he went home and got his gun and shot all three varmints. He then repaired the hole under the fence.

Since there was always a need for extra food, he took all three varmints home and his family ate well for several days. He couldn't help but be upset over his loss but kept a closer watch on his melon patch.

It was hot and humid, with summer over three weeks away, but there was still enough time to grow his record breaker before the special event.

A few days later he had an idea to tie Charlie, his ole

bluetick coonhound, to the gate post, leaving enough rope for him to move around the watermelon patch. Having Charlie on guard would take away the worry of coons and possums eating more melons! Before dark each evening ole Charlie was taken down to the melon patch and tied to the gate post.

Leon listened closely the first night for any disturbance but never heard any barking. He thought his plan was working. He was now much more relaxed and could sleep better knowing Ole Charlie would keep the varmints away.

Over the next few weeks, he and his family, along with his ole bluetick hound kept watch without any more problems and the melons grew bigger each day.

Five melons were now the total number on the vines. Hopefully they would grow big enough for the contest; the biggest and best had to be decided the day before.

The days went by fast and it was soon time to weigh his melons. The only scale available was in his barn so he and his daughter, Reba, loaded it on the wagon and his two ole mules pulled it down to the melon patch.

It was an awkward job to weigh them but he soon found the heaviest and largest in diameter. He was hoping he would fit through the rind after it had been eaten. A monster it was at 97 pounds! But it was perfect in shape and Leon was very confident that it was a winner.

Annie had prepared supper the night before the contest, consisting of several vegetables from the garden. To drink there was cool water from the well. Having a light meal would prepare them for eating a 97-pound watermelon the next day if they were lucky enough to be the winners. The family was now much more excited and looking forward to a fun day, but they thought they should go to bed early.

Fun plans had been made for a special holiday but they

were also looking forward to celebrating the Hillbilly Olympics for the first time. A long list of games and activities had been planned and many folks would be enjoying this special day.

It would also be a fundraising event for the local Baptist church. The pastor and his deacons would judge activities for the men while members of the Ladies Aid Society would judge the women.

For the men 21 and older, there would be a fart contest, and there would be a burping contest for the women over 21. There was also an underarm farting contest for the boys 16 and younger and a spitting contest for anyone over 21 who chewed tobacco or dipped snuff.

To prepare for the events, cabbage and beans would be available at five cents a bowl and baking soda was furnished to the women competing in the burping contest. All the men furnished their own chewing tobacco and snuff but bars of soap would be furnished for the young boys while competing against each other in the underarm farting contest. The women were also invited to compete in all events but most felt it best to just compete against their lady friends.

Boiled cabbage and beans were also available at the same price to anyone who was hungry. These vegetables would take away hunger pangs but also provided fuel for the ladies to burp and the men to show off their special talents.

The baking soda was available for the ladies in case they needed help in generating power for their burping, but beans and cabbage was a back-up that guaranteed extra power from both ends.

It looked like a fun way to start their first Hillbilly Olympics. This special holiday celebration would leave a mark on the entire community never to be forgotten, while raising much-needed funds for the church.

The ladies and young girls would wear their very best and the men and boys wore overalls and a starched and ironed shirt. None of the kids would be wearing shoes and some of the adults removed theirs since it was so hot.

The night before the big event went by slowly and everyone could hardly wait to meet with their family and friends to celebrate.

It was early when Leon and his family got out of bed. They had decided the night before to skip breakfast and got dressed and ready for the big day.

The mules were hooked to the wagon and everyone climbed aboard. In less than ten minutes they were loading the champion watermelon on the wagon and were soon on their way to the fairground.

With twelve kids and two adults, along with the giant watermelon and other items, the ole mules would be pulling a heavy load and the three-mile trip would take an hour.

They soon arrived and went straight to their assigned location, where all contestants would line up in alphabetical order by their last name.

Leon was surprised to see that many had already arrived but the number was increasing by the minute. He checked all the watermelons as they arrived but never thought any of them were bigger than his.

The display area was set up under tall shade trees so Leon and Reba took five bales of hay from the wagon and placed them on the ground for the family to sit on.

It didn't take long till the wagon was unloaded and everything was in place, along with an extra bale of hay for the mules.

It was already after 9:00 am but folks were still coming and many booths and tables were occupied. Great smells of popcorn, cotton candy, and fresh baked pies were in the air and everyone was anxious to get the celebration started. With nearly two hours left, Leon visited the other contestants and checked out all their watermelons.

Local bands had gathered on the stages; instruments were being tuned and songs rehearsed. The stars and stripes had been raised across the fairgrounds and Mississippi state flags were flying by their side.

The watermelon contest was first on the agenda and was still on for 11:00 am. There was nothing left to do so the kids played games while Leon and Annie visited with all the contestants.

Annie had baked oatmeal cookies, and before the contest got underway, they each had two with a glass of water. A 25-gallon wooden keg filled with spring water had been brought along and everyone had been drinking their share because of the heat.

Leon and the kids would eat lightly just in case their 97-pound melon was the winner. The estimated weight of the rind was about 27 pounds, leaving 70 pounds of watermelon to be eaten by Leon, Annie and their twelve kids. That would be five pounds each but he planned on keeping his promise. This meant that he and Annie and the older kids would have to eat much more than the others.

With just minutes left before the first weigh in, all the contestants took their places in alphabetical order and the first melon was weighed. The names were written on a chalkboard and the weight recorder in big numbers.

One by one, the judges weighed them and the race was close. Most of the entries were in the upper 80s and lower 90s but this had Leon nervous.

With his name being Winters, he was the last contestant; but so far he had everyone beat if his scales were right. With three more to weigh, he was keeping a close watch as the numbers were recorded.

The next one weighed 93 pounds, and then 89. At least there was one more left. Leon was worried because it looked close, but it only weighed 96 pounds.

Leon hoped his old cotton scales had been correct. The judges put his watermelon on the scales and Leon was surprised to see it weighed 98 pounds. He was declared the winner!

Everyone began applauding and Leon went to the podium with Annie and their kids. They accepted the blue ribbon and the one-hundred-dollar cash prize.

In the audience a chant could be heard: Eat, eat, eat your watermelon! The crowds began to gather. The ends of the giant watermelon were cut off and the smallest kid ate what was ripe. The rind was laid aside.

Leon began to scoop out the ripe red melon and passed it around to Annie and the kids and they began to eat. There was no time limit so they never got in a hurry but the spectators were laughing and applauding as the melon began to disappear.

The four smallest kids were the first to fall behind. Leon kept encouraging them to eat slower but they soon had to stop, which left much more to be eaten by the others.

There were still eight kids along with Leon and Annie. After more than half had been eaten, they decided to take a 15-minute rest. After a bathroom break they began eating again.

A bigger crowd had gathered and Leon was determined to carry out the promise he had made. The melon was slowly disappearing and the kids were dropping out one by one. Soon there was just Leon, Annie, Reba, and the twins, Ruthie and

Robin.

There was laughter throughout the crowd but after more than two hours, the watermelon was all gone. Now the part that everyone had been waiting for was about to happen.

The shell of the winning melon was brought to the judges' platform. Leon removed his shirt and shoes and lay down beside it. Slowly, he began to crawl through the rind. He was very careful not to split it and after ten minutes of tedious work, he slipped through and got loud applause and a standing ovation.

Annie and the kids were thrilled that Leon was the winner and were happy that the entire family had fulfilled the promise that was made.

Leon walked down to the creek and cleaned up then returned to his family. Together they attended all the festivities throughout the afternoon and evening.

They stayed clear of the fart and belching contestants but were close enough to hear all the sounds and laughter. They did stop by the spitting contest and watched a few old-timers show off their talents. The underarm farting contest with the young boys was another place they visited and they had a few laughs. In all, they did have a good day and Annie sold or exchanged a few of her canned vegetables and fruit.

Throughout the day, Leon often stopped and talked with a few farmers. Annie noticed that money was being exchanged and asked what was going on. Leon was a little hesitant at first but he said he was collecting bets he had made with them.

After a fun day with friends and neighbors, the wagon was loaded and they headed home. The kids were tired and soon fell asleep but Annie and Leon talked about their fun day and winning the watermelon contest.

When they got home, the wagon was unloaded and the

mules were unhitched and taken to the barn and fed.

The kids went straight to bed and Leon and Annie sat down at the kitchen table. He then reached in his pockets and surprised her when he laid out a handful of dollar bills. One by one they were counted and the total was $49.00.

It had been a profitable day for the family: Leon had won a blue ribbon for the biggest watermelon and the $100.00 prize, along with $49.00, since the family was able to eat the big melon and he was able to crawl through the rind.

Now he would be anxiously waiting for a letter from the seed catalog and would also get his picture published in the local paper.

Leon's dream had finally come true! He would now be preparing for the next contest with hopes of winning again.

THE FUNNY FARM

Have you ever been to the funny farm?
If not, you'd have lots of fun,
The birds and animals living there
Will thrill you when you come!

You'll meet them on your visit:
There's the old red rooster, Chester,
Maud is a snow-white Canadian goose
And there's a handsome duck named Lester.

There's Thunder, a big, brown Roman-nose mule,
A tom cat called Leroy,
Sooner, a black-and-tan hound dog,
And a workhorse known as Big Boy.

A flying guinea they call Big Mouth,
A billy goat named Ole Stink,
A milk cow who answers to Bessie
And all the food is healthy to eat!

Ralphie is a bushy tailed bandit raccoon,

257

An ugly ole possum is named Spook.
There's a squirrel that flies like Superman
And a tiny chipmunk called Luke.

A 300-pound hog answers to Chubby;
There are dozens of pigs for sale.
They're always content in a muddy pig pen
And they all have short, curly tails.

Thirty-seven geese roam a red clay field
Where acres of cotton once grew.
They eat the grass but leave all the weeds
And they sometimes make good stew!

Beneath the barn lives a big kingsnake,
He eats other snakes and rats.
Leroy helps out with his brother, Sam,
Along with many other cats!

Willard, the skunk, is a favorite,
With him, you'll have a great time.
A black-and-white streamlined kitty cat
Who no longer has fluid drive!

There's an old Brahman bull named Charlie,
His horns and ears are long.
Cowboys once rode him in rodeos
When he was much younger and strong.

Charlie is now a lazy old bull;
Under an oak tree, he spends his days.

Eating and drinking when he desires
While watching all the children play.

Long-eared rabbits play in the grass,
They'll eat right out of your hand.
Black and white and many other colors
They're happy on funny farm land.

Sheep roam freely throughout the year,
In the spring, the baby lambs play;
Their mamas and papas will lose their wool
But for them, it happens every May.

All the turkeys strut their stuff,
Ole Tom is in charge of the flock.
In the fall each year, folks run a race
And it's called the Ole Turkey Trot!

Throughout the day, you'll see pigeons,
In the barn, they roost every night.
When the sun comes up, they all fly away
And sometimes they block out the light.

Watermelon is served on the 4th of July.
Some weigh more than fifty pounds.
An eating contest is held every year
And folks compete from all around.

Everyone loves the funny farm,
Tourists come from far and near,
With family and friends, you'll have a good time

So please come visit this year!

MILKING A COW

Saw cow, back your leg,
Give me some milk to make my bread!
Please don't hit me with your tail,
When you swing it hits my head.

To your leg I'll tie your tail
While sitting on my stool,
I'll wash your bag with lukewarm water;
It's so much better than cool.

From a trough you'll eat while being milked,
Your wheat shorts and cottonseed meal,
The milk you give will feed our family
And everyone will be thrilled.

So thank you, Bessie, for all the milk
You give us from your udder,
There's always plenty to go around
And cream to make our butter.

Your milk turns sour if not drunk fast.

261

Weeds sometimes make it bitter.
That don't happen all the time
But it tastes much better when sweeter.

KENNIE, ME, AND

TUBBY LEE

High miles and old described it well,
The first car we ever owned.
A fifty-dollar bill was all it cost
And it thrilled us to the bone!

Our four-door sedan was forest green
With scrapes and several dents.
It sure ran great, our Ford V-8.
It was worth every hard-earned cent!

In fifty-three an agreement was made
With the owner who'd bought it new.
We picked his cotton for two cents a pound
And paid every dollar that was due!

It was kept in his barn all summer
Till the last pound of cotton was picked.
Then we drove away on a September day

And it never misfired a lick!

The gauge showed empty and we couldn't go far
So we headed to Polk's Country Store.
Five gallons were bought with a dollar bill.
That paid for the gas and more!

Kennie was older by seventeen months
And was the first of us to drive.
We took our turns behind the wheel
But God kept us safe and alive!

The paint and chrome polished up nice,
Shining and sparkling in the sun.
The white-walled tires were worn and bald
But that never interfered with our fun!

There were many close calls but no one got hurt
While driving those crooked gravel roads,
Slipping and sliding (sometimes in the ditch)!
With our friends, there was always a load.

Sometimes a flat tire slowed us down
But out came the jack and a spare.
We were delayed for a while but drove off with smiles
Without any worries or cares!

The starter was bad and it had to be pushed
Every time we needed a start,
As the speed increased, the clutch was released
And engine sounds thrilled our hearts!

We had no licenses, insurance, or plates
But that never kept us off the road.
The constable and his deputy were friends of ours;
If caught, our stepdad was told.

We got no tickets but we got chewed out
Which hurt down deep in our souls.
"Park that piece of junk!" was the most we heard
So we kept on driving gravel roads!

Sometimes we were brave and drove to school,
For us it was always a thrill.
We were the first in our school to own an old car
But our friends helped pay the gas bill.

After a year of fun and many close calls,
We sold our Ford to our friend, Tubby Lee.
It was time now to buy another old car
But we were sad when we gave up the key!

He worked for his dad, saved his money
And bought it for a hundred-dollar bill,
That old Ford sedan was no longer ours
But our friend, Tubby Lee, was thrilled!

The first repair made was the starter
And the engine fired up right away,
Restoring the old Ford would take a long time
But Tubby was counting each day.

After hours of work and hundreds of bucks,

That old Ford sedan looked new.
The scrapes and dents soon disappeared
And it was painted a midnight blue!

The interior was upholstered in white Naugahyde,
All four tires were replaced.
That old Ford sedan was the talk of the town
And put smiles on everyone's face.

We rode many miles with our friend, Tubby Lee
But so did most of our friends,
In Jeff Davis County he was king of the road
And the title was his till the end.

This was written for my brother, James Kennie Stephenson and
my friend, Burnice (Tubby) Lee! They both went to be with the Lord at
an early age, leaving us way too soon. I am blessed with many memories
of them and will always miss them. One day on the other side, we'll
meet again, and maybe, just maybe, we'll get a chance to drive that old
1936 Ford again. We don't know what God has in store, but with him,
anything is possible! Who knows, they may still be driving that old Ford
sedan but on streets of gold rather than gravel roads. May God bless us
all and continue to watch over the families of Kennie and Tubby.

CARTOAD

An apprentice I was, on the railroad,
Learning the mechanical trade.
To earn my diploma as a carman
Would take over a thousand days!

Eight hours of school each Monday,
On-the-job training four days.
Beginning in March of fifty-seven
I was learning the cartoad ways!

Inspecting and repairing railcars,
Learning the mechanical skills,
Earning a paycheck twice each month
That was used to pay all my bills.

Right out of school I began my career,
My dad would help pave the way.
At the age of 18 when I first began
I was earning $12.72 a day!

Hard work, it was, from the beginning
And I always did my best.

267

I studied and worked five days a week
But on weekends had two days of rest.

A dangerous job, it sometimes could be
But safety was always on my mind.
Changing brake shoes and making air tests
And getting the trains out on time!

Arc welding and using the acetylene torch,
Floor decking and truck overhaul,
Draft gears, couplers and knuckles, I changed;
In time I learned to do it all.

Changing out wheels and truck sides,
Three months of caboose overhaul.
Replacing linoleum on all the floors!
The list of repairs was long.

A year on the heavy and light repair tracks,
Six months of air brake school.
The list of jobs were many
While obeying the FRA rules.

Graded each month for performance
When the foreman made out his report,
My fate was determined the first 60 days
If the railroad would keep me or abort.

A vacation I earned after working two years
But qualified for only five days.
I had holiday pay from the very first day

And all of my insurance was paid.

AAR billing for passenger and freight,
Testing air brakes on each car,
Repacking bearings with waste or pads
And sealing off journals with tar.

Cab carpenter repairs to diesel engines,
Replacing floors and the glass.
Other repairs were made when defects were found.
I did my best to learn fast!

Reading blueprints and drafting,
Drawing all parts of the car.
With passenger and freight, the list was long
But learning these jobs was required.

Milling the lumber for floor decks and walls,
Replacing the heavy plug doors,
Heating and bucking and driving rivets
And yet the list of jobs was much more!

A thousand and thirty-three days to complete
And soon with kids and a wife,
On September 29th of 1962
This career I had chosen changed my life.

Schooling and training came to an end
But I often look back on that day,
Proud, I was, of what I accomplished
And I thank God for making a way.

269

To Yermo I was sent on my first job,
There were times when I worked all alone.
No more instructors to guide me each day
So the decisions I made were my own.

Responsibility and knowledge, I trained for,
But I was frightened sometimes of my choice.
In time I became a good carman
And like all railroaders, had a voice.

My confidence and skills got better with age
As I worked over forty-three years.
Traveling cross-country to four different states
My moves sometimes brought me fears.

My years were divided with five railroads,
There was Santa Fe and Union Pacific Lines,
The Colorado and Southern & Burlington Northern
But the BNSF merged in time.

My job sometimes was hectic
But thank God, I handled it well.
An adventure it was for me and my wife
And Yermo was our own living hell.

To Denver, we moved in 1965,
The next ten years would be rough.
After gaining seniority on the roster,
No longer was my job ever tough.

In 1982, I was the fifth oldest man

And most jobs I wanted could be mine.
I worked the day shift for 18 more years
With my weekends free all the time.

I retired in 2000 at the age of 62,
In seniority, the second oldest man.
Retirement came the first day of May
And I was the happiest cartoad in the land!

There were never regrets and I loved my job,
The men I worked with were great.
An old-timer, I was, when time came to leave
But I retired while still in good shape!

*A carman was often referred to as a "cartoad" or "car-knocker,"
taking 1033 days to complete a four-year apprenticeship program. It
required eight hours of school on Monday and 32 hours of on-the-job
training each week. We were trained to inspect and repair the interior
and exterior of all passenger and freight cars and were also taught the
skills of drafting and blueprint reading.*

*Prior to working with the Union Pacific, I had begun an
apprentice program in the same department with the Santa Fe railroad
on March 7th, 1957. Unfortunately, I was laid off right after the
Christmas holiday of 1957.*

*I applied right away with the Union Pacific and was hired on as
an apprentice but my time with the AT& SF was never honored. I had to
start all over again. I was now 19 and was very disappointed but I had
to abide by the rules. I began my employment with the Union Pacific in
January of 1958 and Dad was helpful again with getting me the job.*

Dad was a four-year journeyman carman but also a heavy repair track foreman and always kept his eye on me. If I did something wrong, no matter what job I was working, he was the first to know and always set me straight. His intentions were good and I'm sure I had it coming. Dad was a great carman but also a good foreman and knew the craft as well, if not better, than most men in the mechanical department. He was a perfectionist on and off the job and expected me to be the same so I tried very hard not to disappoint him. He was my best teacher and because of him I became a railroader. I learned a lot from Dad and right up until he passed away. We never ran out of things to talk about and the subject was mostly about our career of railroading.

HOBO HOTEL

A gathering place for hobos,
There was always room for lost souls.
In the C&S yard they gathered at night
To escape the rain, snow and cold.

Six blocks west of downtown Denver,
They came for shelter and food.
Close to a fire, they slept on the ground
And shared their food and their booze.

This hobo hotel was a basement;
By the C&S it was owned.
Abandoned and razed many years before,
Everything above ground was gone.

The walls and ceiling were made of concrete;
The only original structure that was left,
It looked like a WWII German bunker
And sat all alone by itself.

In the Colorado and Southern rail yard,
This shelter to many was known.

273

For the hobos traveling through Denver
This hotel was used as their home.

Everything they owned was in backpacks,
Their favorite booze was brought along,
They ate and slept in this hobo hotel
And lived the life of a song.

A favorite spot it was for many years,
But one day it all was torn down.
Six Flags bought it for an amusement park
And the hobos had to move uptown.

Kennie and Rufus

Gene and Mae with Rufus and Joyce, Central City, 1966

Cousin Charles, friend Charlie, and Rufus

Joyce, Shelly, Connie, Mitzie, and Rufus in 1968

Joyce on the phone

Aunt Estus

Welcome to Vicksburg!

Dad and Mom

Rufus, Joyce, and Joyce's family

Rufus and Joyce in the 1970s

278

Joyce with her best friends, Jeanie and Mary Lou

Joyce

Joyce, Rufus, and Mom at Connie's wedding

279

Joyce's mom and dad

A family portrait

Mae, Rufus, Ray, and Marshall

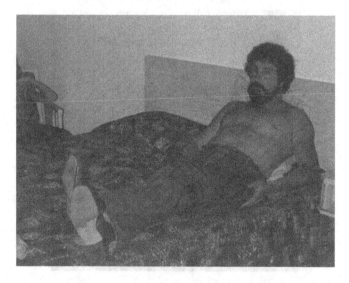

Rufus's centerfold

281

Joyce's centerfold

Aunt Mary and Mildred

The Stephenson Family

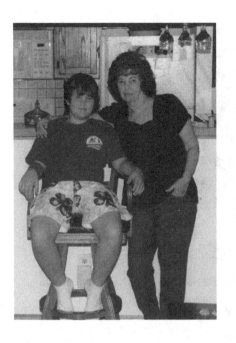

Charles and Joyce

Connie and Jim in 1994

Eric, Anthony, Chris, and Brandon

Eric, Shelly, and Brandon

Etta, Joyce, Larry, and Mildred

Eric, Shelly, and Brandon

Joy and Mitzie in 1998

Gene, Mae, and Rufus

285

Joyce and Kim

Shelly and Rufus

Rufus and Joyce

Joyce and Mitzie in 1998

287

Joyce and Rufus

Joyce and Rufus

Joyce and Rufus

Joyce in the autumn of 1996

289

Rufus in the autumn of 1996

Rufus and his bounty

Joyce, Etta, and Mildred in 1998

Joyce and Rufus with granddaughter, Emily

Joyce, Shelly, Mitzie, and Kim

Joyce and her siblings in 1999

Rufus and Marshall

Joyce

Joyce

293

Mitzie, Shelly, and Kim in 1997

My mother and daughters with the first four grandkids

Kayla in 1997

The Stephenson Family

Lance and Kim going to prom

Kayla, Megan, and Chris

Golden railroad crew at my retirement party

Megan, Emily, Joy, and Kayla

Our family

Joyce with her brother, Roy, and sister, Etta

297

Rufus and Charles

Rufus and Emily

Rufus and Joyce

Rufus with youngest grandson, Charles

A CHRISTMAS

ANGEL

On the Tuesday after Labor Day 1965, we moved with our three daughters to Golden, Colorado from Salt Lake City, Utah. We arrived late that evening after several car repairs along the way. Since our trailer was small, we had to leave several pieces of furniture behind but planned to replace them when we got to Colorado.

Our trip had been much delayed, but at last we arrived at Joyce's parents' house in Golden. The next day, we began looking for a house to rent, planning to stay with Joyce's parents until we found one. We did find one and moved in the following Saturday morning.

After paying two months' rent, buying food, and enrolling our oldest daughter, Connie, in school, our funds were getting low. We still had to replace the furniture left behind in Salt Lake along with other expenses.

Knowing by the middle of November that we wouldn't be caught up for Christmas, Joyce's mother suggested we order gifts for the girls on her Spiegel catalog account.

Joyce placed an order in late November, but by the middle of December, no packages had arrived. Joyce was worried and began calling the Golden post office since there were three deliveries each day. She called often, but the answer was always that there were no packages for the Stephenson family.

On Christmas Eve, nothing had been delivered and we were very upset knowing the girls would have very few presents under the tree from Santa. On Christmas morning, we were up early and the girls were excited even though they had very few gifts under the tree. Unprepared for this, we told them that Santa hadn't left everything yet, but would soon return with the rest of their gifts.

Little did we know it would be so soon! At 8:30, while we were eating breakfast, we heard a knock and when Joyce opened the door, to her surprise, there was a postal employee with several packages. Joyce could hardly contain herself, but thanked him and began crying tears of joy. She was so excited and forgot to ask his name but we've always called him our Christmas angel.

Our girls, Connie, Shelly, and Mitzie, ages five, three, and two, received the rest of their gifts along with new red velvet dresses and black patent leather shoes. That was nearly 50 years ago and it was the best Christmas we've ever had. Thank you, Christmas angel for that special delivery. We'll never forget you.

We believed in Santa of course, but that was the first time we saw him dressed in a blue postal uniform. Yes, there is a Santa Claus, and our faith and belief in him has been stronger ever since that special Colorado Christmas of 1965 in Golden.

A NEW LIFE

The 20th century had ended,
The twenty-first then began.
Retirement came on the 1st of May
And the hard work now would end.

Over forty-three years on the railroad
And the good times had finally come.
Moving to Branson had been our dream
And had always been number one.

In Colorado, we lived for 35 years,
But moving was now our plan.
Our dream was to move to a mountain top
Somewhere in Ozark land.

A brand new car was promised to Joyce
Before we moved away.
A Hyundai Elantra would be her choice
And we bought it from John Elway.

303

With fancy wheels and a sunroof,
A spoiler on the trunk,
Loaded, it was, with everything
And it had lots of style and spunk.

White, it was, and top-of-the-line
Of all the Hyundai cars.
It was the last one on the showroom floor
And Joyce's shining star.

THE GHOST OF

ROARK RIDGE

Head 'Em Up, Move 'Em Out

It was one o'clock in the afternoon on Saturday, August 23rd 2000. In the driveway was a 30-foot Budget rental truck loaded with everything we owned. Joyce's new 2000 Hyundai Elantra was securely tied down on a flatbed car hauler and hitched behind the truck. Our family and friends had come by early that morning to help load the truck, but now it was time to say goodbye.

After living and working in Colorado for more than 35 years, we had sold our home and were moving to Branson, Missouri with plans to buy our dream home and a few acres of land somewhere high on an Ozark Mountaintop.

At the Thousand Hills Golf Course and Resort in Branson, we had made reservations for as long as it took to find a home once we arrived. It would be an exciting adventure. Surely,

305

somewhere in the Ozark Mountains was a home that would fit our needs!

For us, it was a happy time but we were also sad to be leaving everyone behind. There were many hugs and tears, but we soon climbed up in the truck and fastened our seatbelts. I started the engine and everyone stood in the yard as we pulled out on Lamar Street and headed south toward Interstate 70. There were more tears as we looked into the rearview mirror and saw them waving goodbye. We were following a dream that we had envisioned for most of our married life and it was now coming true.

Driving to Junction City, Kansas was our plan for the day but we would arrive late. It would be a short night and we got very little sleep because we wanted to get an early start Sunday morning. Sunday's plan was to arrive in Branson before midnight.

We had motel reservations and arrangements had also been made for us to meet two men on Monday morning at a storage shed in Hollister. They were a father-and-son team I hired through an employment agency to unload. After that, I would still have to drive to Springdale, Arkansas to return the truck before six o'clock. It would be another long, busy day, but God would surely help us meet our deadline.

Retirement had finally come for me on May 1st, 2000, after more than 43 years on the railroad. It took more than three months before our house sold after a busy summer of weekend garage sales, trying to lighten the load of things we didn't plan on taking. Over the years, much had been accumulated so we sold what we could and donated the rest to charity.

We would be celebrating our 42nd wedding anniversary on November 24th and we hoped to be in our new home by then. Branson wasn't new to us; we had been vacationing there since 1980. We knew the town and countryside very well but would be starting out with no family or friends living there.

Over the years, we had taken most of our vacations in October but we did visit a few times in early spring. We had fallen in love with Branson and the Ozark Mountains on our first visit and knew it was the place we wanted to retire to. The time had finally come to fulfill our longtime dream and our prayers had now been answered.

It was a beautiful day and we were anxious to leave, but also sad to be saying goodbye. For many years, we had planned this move, but we had failed on two prior attempts. Everything was now going our way.

In less than 15 minutes, we were on Interstate 70 heading east. It took nearly an hour to get across Denver but traffic was much lighter as we continued east. I set the cruise control and was much more relaxed and able to talk about how God had prepared the way for us. He had blessed us with a great family and nearly 42 years of marriage. He was now allowing our dream to come true.

In less than three hours, we arrived in Limon, Colorado. We had driven over 100 miles and thought it best to fill up with gas and check everything out. Our rental truck was a 1996 Ford with high miles and a rating of 8 mpg, but after filling the tank and doing the figures, it was much closer to 5 mpg because of the heavy load and towing a car and trailer.

We were thirsty and also needed a bathroom break, so I pulled away from the gas pump and parked out by the road and went inside. In less than 15 minutes we were back on the freeway heading east! With such a heavy load, I kept the cruise control set at 50 mph. Ahead of us was mostly flat prairie with an occasional hill, but the high crosswinds could sometimes be very dangerous!

The ride wasn't smooth and the old truck didn't seem to have the power I expected. It rattled every time I hit a rough spot in the road. After driving 20 miles, I began to look for a place to pull over and check out the problem. The noise I was most concerned about was coming from the roof and it seemed to get worse by the minute.

Soon I came to an overpass. I pulled up close to a concrete wall and was able to climb on the roof and check it out. The traffic was light, and being in the shade made it much cooler. Right away, I found the problem and was glad I stopped when I did. The front section of the roof had lost many sheet metal screws and was slowly coming off.

I climbed off the roof and found everything I needed behind the seat! I put a hand full of screws in my pocket and grabbed a screwdriver, a hammer and a punch and the problem was solved in less than an hour. I put my tools away and after checking the tires and making sure the car was securely tied down on the trailer, we continued on to Branson.

There was no longer a noise from the roof and the other sounds didn't seem as bad, so we decided to drive on to Salina and have a late dinner at the Cracker Barrel there. This was one of our favorite restaurants. We knew there would be plenty of room to park and the food was always great.

With no more problems over the next four hours, it was much more relaxing but sundown was less than an hour away. We were seeing less open prairie and more trees but we were now entering the east Kansas hill country and I was having problems maintaining my speed up the long hills.

It wasn't long till I saw the Cracker Barrel exit and we were soon parked. We went in and gave our name but a few folks were already in line so we went to the restrooms. Our name was soon called. After a good meal and some rest, we drove on to Junction City, Kansas and stopped for the night.

It had been a long day and we were looking forward to a shower and a few hours' sleep! We had done well our first day but we would have to get to sleep fast. Hopefully, without any more trouble, would arrive in Branson late Sunday night.

We were up early the next morning and back on the road by eight o'clock with over 400 miles left to drive. We were now halfway there, but the hills were slowing us down and our speed had been reduced sometimes to 10 mph. It was another long, hot day and we arrived at our motel just before midnight. That old truck could hardly make it up the hill.

We grabbed our luggage and were in bed by half past midnight. I requested a wakeup call for five thirty and we both were out like a light when our heads hit the pillows. It seemed like only minutes had passed when the phone rang! We were startled and still very tired, but we were ready to leave in an hour. It was less than 20 miles to the storage unit and mostly on level roads, so we made it with five minutes to spare.

Our two helpers were standing out by the roadside waving when we arrived. I pulled over and disconnected the car hauler and backed up to the storage shed. Three hours later, everything was unloaded. It was still 150 miles to Springdale, Arkansas and we had to return the truck by six o'clock.

From Branson to Springdale, Arkansas

The employment agency had paid my helpers in advance but I gave them a tip for finishing so fast. Joyce and I then drove over to the condo and unloaded the car. Now the truck was empty and so was the car, so with a much lighter load, the ole truck had more power as we continued south on Highway 65. It was 37 miles to Harrison but from there, the roads were crooked with lots of hills. Traveling was now much slower than it was crossing Kansas, but we still had enough time to meet our six o'clock deadline.

I didn't know it at the time, but the old truck was on its last leg. Even with a much lighter load, it was slow going. Still, we arrived in Springdale at around three o'clock.

We spent extra time searching for our drop-off location but soon spotted the Budget rental station. We passed it by and had to turn around and go back. I turned off on the first street but didn't see a dead end sign. We only realized after driving two blocks that there was a problem. It was a residential neighborhood, but thank God there were no cars parked along the street. There was no need trying to back up so I spent 30 minutes with Joyce giving signals and we soon got turned around. In less than five minutes, we were parked in front of Budget rental on Highway 71. We were thankful to have made it without more problems.

We went inside and I began to complain about all the trouble we had traveling from Denver, then gave them a copy of the rental agreement. The man at the desk checked it and that's when we learned our truck had already been taken out of service in Wheat Ridge, Colorado; it was no longer to be used for local or cross-country hauling. In other words, it was ready for the junkyard but rented to us by mistake. We were lucky to have made it without breaking down, but God kept it together for us until we reached our destination.

After voicing our complaints, we were refunded half the cost of the truck but we still had to pay full price for the car hauler. We had driven a thousand miles in a defective vehicle and spent more on gas than we should have. Not to mention that our safety had been in jeopardy for two days! We wanted a full refund on the truck and to just pay for the car hauler but they didn't see it our way. A check would be mailed once the bill had been reviewed but it would take over a month before we received payment.

I drove Joyce's car off the trailer and we were soon ready to head back to Branson. We were disappointed about the refund but thrilled to be going home. We arrived safe at our condo by seven o'clock.

Branson, and most of Missouri, was having a heat wave and the temperature when we arrived was over a hundred degrees. It had been this way for several days and more hot weather was forecast for the next week.

We went to our condo and took a shower and got ready for dinner. On the way to the restaurant, I drove through a car wash and cleaned off the dirt and bugs, but we were soon having dinner at one of our favorite Branson restaurants. It had been a long three-day trip and we were very thankful to be in a place we would now be calling home.

Looking for a Home

Our condo had one bedroom, one bath, a kitchen, dining room, and living room combined, along with a utility closet with a washer and drier. There was also a screened in porch overlooking the golf course. We had paid the first month in advance but would rent by the day if it took longer for us to find our dream home.

After a night of rest, our realtor picked us up Tuesday morning at nine o'clock and drove us 12 miles west on Highway 248 to a house located three miles east of Reeds Spring Junction.

With all the crooked roads, it took 30 minutes but we were soon parked in front of a beautiful home. We hadn't discussed the price yet, but our initial thought was that there was no way we could afford a home like this. It had five huge bedrooms, three baths, a walk-out basement with a 20-foot patio, a 30-foot front porch and a one-car paved parking space on the lower east end. There was a three-car garage attached to the main level off the kitchen and a 20-foot screened and glassed-in sunroom on the south upper level off the master bedroom. It had 12-foot cathedral ceilings in the living room, a beautiful earth stove and six-foot windows in all the bedrooms and living room. There was central heat and air and all the appliances came with the house. There were 8.7 acres; two were in lawn and the rest had hundreds of huge oak and hickory trees along with dozens of dogwoods and redbuds. One thousand and thirty-three feet behind the house was Roark Creek, which was the south side property line. There were huge protruding boulders, larger than a house, with overhangs that could provide shelter from a storm if needed. There were three apple and two pear trees, a 12 x 12 storage shed, and a 1000-foot gravel drive out to Highway 248. The house was seven years old and had been custom built by the owners, but the husband had recently passed away. There was also a handicapped son, and with the husband gone, there was no way they could take care of everything.

The husband had been a retired professor at the University of Missouri and his wife was a retired school teacher. Many years before, they had purchased 40 acres on top of Roark Ridge with plans to build their retirement home at a later date. They had sold part of the land to their daughter and son-in-law and they had built a beautiful home on the east end of the ridge. Thirteen acres had been sold to another couple and they too had built a small cabin, but the remaining property was kept for their retirement home. This beautiful custom built home had 4200 square feet and was in immaculate condition.

A 720-foot community well that produced 20 gallons per minute provided water for all three homes! The cost of upkeep had to be shared but an electric meter kept track of the cost for operating the pump, which was less than $50.00 a year per family. There was enough water to supply all possible needs, including water for the lawns.

The maintenance to keep up the thousand-foot driveway was also shared, but everyone got together twice each year to make the repairs made necessary by rain and snow.

Now that we had all the information on this beautiful home and land, it was time to make a decision. We had spent over three hours checking it out but had to decide if we could afford it.

A home like this in Colorado would have cost a half million dollars, but with nearly nine acres of land as well, the price would have been much more. We didn't think we could afford a home like this, even in Missouri, and would keep looking.

We thanked the owner and said we liked her home but needed more time before making a decision. We got in the car and drove away but were shocked to learn the price was only $145,000.00! We were on a budget and had to stick with what we had planned on spending. We knew real estate was cheaper in Missouri but could hardly believe the price was less than the house we had sold in Colorado.

It was still more than we planned on spending and thought it would be a slap in the owner's face by offering less, so we chose to leave without making an offer. Our home in Colorado had 2600 square feet with four bedrooms and two baths on one third of an acre; it sold for $199,000.00. It was no comparison to what we had just looked at.

Over the next two hours, we toured two more houses but one was infested with termites and the other with mold. They were both beautiful homes and the prices were within our budget, but the cost of exterminating termites and getting rid of mold would be very expensive. We decided to pass them by.

Tuesday was coming to an end so we went back to the condo. The realtor would be checking back the next day with more places to see.

On Wednesday morning, we got a call from our realtor saying she would pick us up for an eleven o'clock showing. We rode out in the country and soon arrived in front of a beautiful home and went inside. She said it belonged to a Branson entertainer and asked if we could identify who we thought it might be.

As soon as we entered the living room it was easy to tell from the pictures on the walls that there was a connection with Mel Tilles. The owner happened to be his brother who had a comedy show in Branson which we had seen earlier while on a visit. It was a beautiful double-wide modular on a foundation, but it didn't look anything like a factory-built home. There were three acres with trees but the interest rates on a factory-built house were much higher than a standard-built home. The price was in our budget, but we decided to put it on the shelf and continue to look.

Over the next four days we toured 15 homes but none were what we wanted. Mold and termites were the main problems but some were in need of other repairs. I didn't want to take on another remodeling job. While living 35 years in Denver, we had bought and sold seven homes but always made a profit. Once we purchased a lot and had a new home built, and later we bought two more new homes. The other four were used, but with a little remodeling there was always a good profit made. We bought our last home in Colorado in 1991 and the profits would help buy our retirement home in Branson. It was the biggest remodeling job we had ever taken on and it kept me busy, but nine years later a great profit was made that allowed us to follow our dream to Branson.

After I had worked over 43 years on the railroad, we weren't in the mood to take on another project. We just wanted to enjoy our retirement. Finding that dream home wasn't easy and we never got discouraged, but we didn't want to get in a big hurry and have regrets later.

The first house we were shown kept entering our minds so we asked our realtor what she thought about offering $140,000. Without any hesitation, she thought it would be okay, and she said that the answer may be no, but it was worth a try.

We met with our realtor on Sunday morning and wrote a contract for $140,000,00. It was delivered, but we later got a call saying that two contracts had already been written and the owner would get back with us soon. Now it was a waiting game so we stayed by the phone praying our offer would be accepted. Without a cell phone, we couldn't leave, so we hoped that we would get an answer later that day or Monday.

Slowly, the weekend went by and Monday morning came without any news. I needed to wash the car so Joyce stayed home while I went down to the car wash, but I finished and was back home in thirty minutes. In the parking lot, I wiped down the car and went inside, only to be shocked when Joyce said our daughter, Michele, had called saying her husband, Ron, had passed away from a major heart attack. He was only 38 years old and we were both in shock, yet we had to be ready to leave for Denver in less than an hour.

We made a quick call and gave our realtor the bad news but said that we were willing to pay full price if needed. She still thought there was a good chance of getting it for the price we offered since we were pre-qualified and putting $50,000.00 down. This gave us hope and we promised to call along the way to see how things were going.

We made our first call from Kansas City, but no decision had been made. Later in the day, we called again but there was still no change; now we were getting a little discouraged, but we weren't giving up. After dinner, we called again but this time the news was good and our offer had been accepted.

Tragedy in Colorado

We were still in shock over losing our son-in-law, Ron, and very heartbroken, but the good news we had just received was an answer to our prayers. We continued on to Colorado, arriving at eight o'clock. We made it in twelve hours instead of thirteen like it usually took.

While in Colorado, Joyce's oldest brother, Roy, had been very sick and wanted us to stay with him at night so we did. The six days we were there were mostly spent with Michele and her kids during the day, but we also visited our other daughters, Kim and Mitzie. It was a stressful week, but we had to say goodbye shortly after the funeral and we left for home.

Roy had a heart condition and had a defibrillator installed prior to Ron's funeral. He seemed to be doing well when we left. We were on the run the whole time, but we managed to get through it all and returned to Branson on Sunday night.

After being back just seven days, Joyce received another call that her brother, Roy, had passed away and a memorial service would be held later in the month. Now we were in a bind and this created a big problem, so Joyce called her brother's family letting them know we wouldn't be able to attend under the circumstances, since we were closing on our house. Roy had donated his body to science and his ashes would be returned to his family in six months. We were thankful for the time we had spent with him and wanted to remember him that way. These tragedies had left us very sad and it would take time to get our life back to normal.

Moving into Our Dream Home

Over the next four weeks, we were shopping in Springfield for furniture but also taking care of other business. This would keep us busy right up to the closing, which was set for September 25th.

We did get permission to have the carpet cleaned before closing since Rowdy, the owner's dog, who we had agreed to take along with the house, had spent most of her life inside. Joyce was highly allergic to animals but our newly inherited pet would no longer be staying inside once we moved in. The owner had promised to have her trained to stay outside if we purchased the home but this I had to see. Right away, she had the doggie door removed from the kitchen but left one in the garage.

Two days after closing, I rented a U-Haul truck and hired a young man through an employment agency. After an early morning start, we had everything moved from the storage building and finished by six o'clock that evening.

He was a hard worker and I thought he deserved a little extra since he did such a great job. I gave him an extra twenty-five dollars, which he didn't want to take, but I insisted until he did. Before leaving, I got his phone number and used him on several other occasions. I always paid the same as the employment agency had charged me, knowing he was worth every penny.

It was now time to see how well Rowdy had been trained! I did notice she stayed outside while we moved everything in, but we didn't know how she would react once we were finished.

Later, I made an attempt to see what would happen when the door was left open, but was surprised when she wouldn't come in even when I coached her. Now we knew the problem was solved and Rowdy would be spending her nights in the garage.

Now it was time to spend our first night, but much work had to be done before it looked like our dream home. There were boxes stacked in every room but my helper and I had assembled the bed before he left. Later that evening, we went over to Reeds Spring for dinner then went home to bed. We were exhausted mentally and physically and needed a good night's sleep.

For the rest of the week, we unpacked boxes and the house slowly began to look like a home. We had sold most of our furniture before leaving Colorado with plans of buying what we needed for our new home. We had to furnish the formal dining room, the living room and two bedrooms, along with drapes and curtains for the entire house. Joyce would be shopping for two oak rockers for the sun porch, an Amish glider for the front porch and a big swing for the back patio.

Our new pet was a beautiful lab and Irish setter mix who had lived her entire life of seven years on Roark Ridge. Teddy, the next door neighbor's dog, had been friends with Rowdy for several years and when you saw one, the other wasn't far away. Teddy was a pit bull but was a very playful friend for Rowdy and they kept watch over the ridge.

They had the run of Roark Mountain and would chase deer and any other animal or varmint that crossed their path. We were in the country where every kind of animal and bird could be found. Once I spotted a small brown bear down the road from the driveway and deer and turkey could be seen most any day. There were coon and possum and the armadillos and skunks were always a nuisance. A pack of coyotes could be heard most evenings across the mountain and this drove Rowdy and Teddy crazy. The rattlesnakes and copperheads were all over the mountain and I had to be very careful when working in the yard.

One afternoon on our way home from shopping in Reeds Springs, Joyce spotted a beautiful, orange wildflower growing along the roadside so I stopped to check it out. It was just a few yards from our driveway so I took her home, grabbed a shovel and went back to dig it up. After a few shovels of dirt, I looked down and a rattlesnake was coiled up inches from my foot. I had on shorts and shoes without socks but kept my cool and stood very still as he continued to shake his rattlers. At first I thought he would crawl away but he stayed in one spot. I knew I had to do something fast or get bit, so with a swing of my shovel I cut off his head. My fear was gone so I finished digging the flower up and soon had it planted next to our mailbox as a reminder of the day I nearly got bit by a rattlesnake. At the time, I didn't know what kind of rattlesnake it was until my neighbor, Jeannie, looked it up. We then discovered it was a pygmy rattler, and like all snakes in Missouri, it was protected. I never went around looking for snakes to kill but in this situation it was either killing him or getting bit.

One early spring morning while raking leaves, I uncovered six baby copperheads that were about six inches long. They were just as poisonous as the adults, but since they were in my front yard, again, I had no problem putting them out of their misery. We had many copperheads, rattlers and bull snakes but most were always on the move. We left them alone and got out of their way.

With all the hickory and several different types of oak trees, there was an abundance of squirrels, but very few rabbits since Rowdy and Teddy kept them thinned out. The birds Joyce and I enjoyed most were the hummingbirds, cardinals and blue jays. We had every kind there was and always tried to keep my feeders filled.

While raking leaves shortly after moving in, I took my rake and began pulling leaves from under a juniper bush in front of the house. I looked down and to my surprise there was a dry land terrapin (turtle). He was nestled away in his shell and was about six inches in diameter. He was very much alive and after I picked him up, he poked his head out and looked around. I called Joyce and asked her to bring a bottle of her red fingernail polish. She was dumbfounded but she soon brought out a bottle of her bright red nail polish. I showed off my turtle and she thought he was cute but didn't want to hold him. We took a seat on the front porch and I painted the date and her name on the top part of the shell then turned him loose after it dried. It didn't take long till he disappeared under the juniper bush.

One year later, I got a call from our neighbor wanting to know if we were missing a pet turtle. I walked down to his house and there in his front yard was Joyce's turtle with her name and date still on his back. I took him back to the house and placed him under the same juniper bush but never saw him again.

As the days passed, Joyce enjoyed the many trips we made to Springfield while shopping for everything needed to furnish our new home. Over the years, she had decorated it many times in her mind but her talents would now be shown off to everyone who came to visit. She did a beautiful job inside while I took care of the outside and soon our dream home was no longer a dream. It had come true!

After we had been in our house two weeks, Etta and Mildred, Joyce's two sisters, came down for a visit. They lived in Colorado and had flown down to Springfield, where we picked them up. We went to Silver Dollar City and several shows in Branson, and many other fun places in the Ozarks. We also visited Eureka Springs, Arkansas and had a great time of shopping and sightseeing. It was sad for all of us too in a way, since Joyce's brother, Roy, had planned on making the trip but never made it. Soon it was time for Etta and Mildred to leave so we drove them back to Springfield and said goodbye. It had been a fun two weeks and we invited them to visit again.

Once I got a break from helping Joyce in the house, I began to work in the yard. Fall wasn't far away; the leaves were already changing and falling to the ground. Keeping them picked up was next to impossible and I tried with little success.

When we first looked at the property, getting down to the creek took over an hour so I had to do something about it. One Monday morning, I gathered my tools and began to clear a thousand-foot path down to the creek. It would be six feet wide and would twist and turn through many obstacles before reaching the bottom. My work days were ten to twelve hours long and resulted in many tick and chigger bites, and even a few contacts with more snakes and poison ivy. It was a tiring job, but one I enjoyed and the scenery was beautiful everywhere I looked.

Rowdy was never far from my side. When a rabbit was disturbed, she chased him a few yards but soon returned. She loved being outside in the woods and kept her eyes on me no matter where I went. It was like we had been together her entire life and not one time did she leave unless I was with her. There were times when her friend, Teddy, showed up and they ran and played but they never got out of sight. When Teddy decided to leave, he left alone and Rowdy found a shady spot from which to continue to watch me at work.

We did climb the mountain every few hours for a snack and water. There was an automatic feeder and water bottle in the garage. I also came up to let Joyce know everything was okay before I grabbed something to drink and a snack and headed back down the mountain. Before my project was finished, I bought a set of walkie-talkie radios so Joyce and I could be in contact at all times. This made us both feel better knowing we were just a call away.

After the first five days, I had completed a six-foot path over halfway down the mountain but the next five days were just as tough. By late Friday evening, I had reached the creek. The thousand-foot-plus climb back up the mountain would be much easier now with everything removed down to the dirt and rock. There was lots of stubble but from that day on, a weed eater was all I needed to keep it clear.

324

The creek nearly dried up during the hot summer months but was 15 feet wide most of the time and five feet deep in some places. There was very little sand along the creek bank but there was lots of small gravel and boulders as big as cars. Along the creek banks were huge cottonwood and sycamore trees that grew over 60 feet tall. In Reeds Springs each year, a local contest was held for the largest sycamore leaf but we never entered. The record was more than 13 inches wide.

In 2003 our friend, Jeannie, painted and framed a 10-inch sycamore leaf with two love birds in a nest and gave it to us for our 45th wedding anniversary. She was a local artist and sold her art at Silver Dollar City and local craft shops. Her work was rustic and very beautiful. She also painted large rocks that were used as doorstops, which was a big hit with many. She and her husband, Tom, were great neighbors and invited us to visit Sycamore Log Church.

New Friends and Sycamore Log Church

In 1930, a little one-room church, was built of sycamore logs and was attended by the locals for many years before being abandoned in the late '50s. In 1972, Pastor Erma Downs, her husband, Hansel, her sister, Chloe, Chloe's husband, Dick, and Willard Jones, a local rancher, had plans to resurrect the old landmark and start their own church. Weeks were spent cleaning and repairing the old building and the local community was invited to attend their first Sunday morning service. Pastor Erma was well known in the Ozarks through her 25-year Branson radio ministry.

For over a year, the pews rested on a dirt floor, but in time money was raised to build a rustic wood plank floor. Later, his and hers outhouses were built out back and electricity was brought in. Two ceiling lights and fans were installed and a big wood burning stove kept the congregation warm. There was no air conditioning but with hand held fans, two ceiling fans and the windows and door left open, everybody was able to stay cool. A black walnut tree trunk was made into a beautiful rustic pulpit and a long, wood bench sat against the front wall for special guests. An upright piano was brought in and some of the original pews were used but several more had to be built. This little church would seat about 50 if everyone squeezed together in the pews.

All the rough log interior walls were exposed, along with a log ceiling. It was like going back in time. There were two windows and one entry door that was never locked. A big guest book sat on the pulpit for visitors to sign after church services or when tourists stopped by for a visit. Over the years, many famous country singers signed the book. Johnny Cash and June Carter were among them, as were local Branson performers and other stars from the Grand Ole Opry.

Less than a half mile below the church was Roark Creek, with a pool deep enough to baptize new Christians. With the help of a board member, Pastor Erma baptized many while the congregation stood on the creek bank singing hymns. It was a sight very few people would ever see but one Joyce and I would never forget.

The first Sunday we attended, Pastor Erma and her sister, Chloe, played guitar, our neighbor, Jeannie, played the piano, and Ima Jean Isaacs played the tambourine. During the first 30 minutes, several members of the congregation volunteered to read poetry or sing special songs they had written. Also attending was Leroy New, a local Branson entertainer who always brought his five-string banjo and a guitar. He was introduced by Pastor Erma and came forward to play and sing with her and Chloe. This was a church service conducted like none we had never seen, but we thoroughly enjoyed it. Special music was always a big part of the service and poems were read or recited. Sometimes special speakers were present too. Out-of-state visitors often joined the congregation and after visiting once, they always came back on their next visit to Branson.

When everyone had sung their songs or read their poetry, Pastor Erma walked to the pulpit and said a prayer. You would have thought Jesus was standing by her side as she presented a message that touched the hearts of everyone. After closing her sermon, the congregation came forward and joined hands in a circle, requesting prayers for themselves or family members and friends. She then prayed for each need without ever forgetting a request. She dismissed everyone with prayer and the congregation visited awhile, until it all happened again the following Sunday.

Pastor Erma and her congregation treated us like family and it was easy to tell they were all great Christians who cared. We had never seen anything like it before and planned on coming back.

In the coming week, I bought a custom made set of musical spoons made out of Ozark Mountain ash that was crafted and sold at Silver Dollar City. The following Sunday, I began learning how to stay in rhythm with all the other instruments and what a fun time it was for me to play along with everyone. We continued to attend each week and we made great friends. We always enjoyed the Christian fellowship in this beautiful little Sycamore Log Church.

Each year, a Christmas program was always written, produced and directed by our neighbor, Jeannie, and the congregation made up the cast. The public was invited at no charge and the little church was filled from wall to wall with regular members and their family and friends. A big wood stove kept everyone warm but when it got too hot, a window or door had to be opened. Joyce and I always had a role in the programs and had a great time.

Inside the church, a beautiful tree was decorated each year and gifts were brought by the men, women and children, all deposited in separate boxes. When the program was over, everyone received a gift and refreshments were served. This was surely an old-time Ozark Mountain Christmas as love and happiness were shared with each other and the birth of Jesus was celebrated in a very special way. Pastor Erma and those who brought this old log church back to life in the '70s had provided a place of worship for many.

Behind the church were three graves! The lady who donated the land was buried in one at her request and next to her was an unidentified baby. A dog was also buried close by. Being inside this little church, or being on the grounds as a tourist, or attending a Sunday morning service, was like being on holy ground. God was always there and with the door open 24 hours a day, many people stopped by to pray. Very few times was anything missing and rarely was there vandalism.

Visitors during the week would leave written prayer requests, as well as checks and cash in a collection box. It was always a favorite place to take pictures or just visit.

Pastor Erma often got requests to perform weddings but she only did them if the couple agreed to meet for a council session. Rarely did they object and many wedding vows were said in the old Sycamore Log Church. For a fee, the church could be rented for the reception but no alcohol was allowed. This little log church was a blessing for many and God was always there for those who needed a helping hand.

I grew up in Vicksburg, Mississippi and attended a Missionary Bible Baptist church until I was 13 years old. Our congregation was small but Grandma and Grandpa Conrad also attended with their nine children. Grandpa was a deacon and song leader but also one of the ushers who passed the collection plate each Sunday. He and his family were always first to arrive for all events. He, along with other members of the congregation, kept the church in good repair, but Grandpa was pretty much in charge of everything that went on. He and Grandma were great Christians and always followed the Ten Commandments and all the other teachings in the Bible. At no time have I ever had any doubt that they were not in Heaven with Jesus.

Grandma Stephenson, along with Mama and us five kids, were grounded in the Baptist faith and I was saved under the ministry of Reverend Guy. He was blind and taught his congregation that women should never be ordained as ministers. According to Baptist doctrine, a woman was to be silent in the church, but using her as a Sunday school teacher or playing the piano or singing special music was okay.

This strike against women being ministers was what I had believed until moving to Branson, Missouri and meeting Pastor Erma Downs. Joyce and I then made a change in our thinking after seeing the effects of her teachings and hearing all about the people she had led to Jesus in her 25-year Ozark Mountain radio ministry. I wasn't a bible scholar, but knew all about the plan of salvation and what was required to become a child of God and to inherit the Kingdom of Heaven. This little Ozark Mountain lady presented a message that put most preachers to shame and told it just like it was. She preached about the sins of the world and taught the Ten Commandments, condemning the sinful lifestyles of the world.

Now I had second thoughts about who was appointed to present the plan of salvation and knew the job wasn't left up to just men. Women could also be the mouthpiece of Jesus and everyone was capable of delivering a message that would lead sinners to Christ. Pastor Erma Downs was doing what God appointed her to do and followed his teachings throughout her life. She was just a poor Ozark Mountain woman who received her calling one day to go out in the world and preach the gospel like the Bible said. She followed Jesus throughout her life. I believe women are just as capable of presenting the Word as any man; a woman's place is not to stand by in silence.

After attending Sycamore Log Church and getting to know Willard Jones, I discovered he had a favorite song. It was *The Little Brown Church in the Dale*. He often requested for it to be sung by the congregation and they always accommodated him. It was also a favorite of mine and one day I was asked to sing it with him as a Sunday morning special. I was happy to assist and with the help of Pastor Erma and Chloe playing their guitars, we sung his favorite hymn. But Willard always wanted to change "little brown church" to "little log church" and we sang it that way many times until his death in the fall of 2004.

He was a great Christian and available every time there was a need for a helping hand around the church. During the winter months, he arrived at the church an hour or more before the congregation and built a roaring fire in the old wood heater. By the time everyone arrived, it was warm and toasty and they always voiced their appreciation.

On several occasions throughout the year, Willard Jones and Cecil Isaacs caught dozens of sucker fish out of local lakes and rivers and put them in freezers to be cooked at a later date. Willard also caught catfish out of his small pond and they were frozen. When there was enough to feed the entire congregation along with their family and friends, a picnic was planned and all the members and their families were invited. This happened several times each year and everyone had a great time.

These cookouts were always on Saturday evening. Willard and Cecil cooked the fish in a deep fryer under a canopy and the ladies brought their favorite dishes along with great desserts. The tables were filled with some of the best food in the Ozarks and we had a feast fit for a king. There was always hot coffee and plenty of sweet iced tea, along with everyone's favorite pop. There were sometimes 60 people or more at these gatherings, because the church was open to the entire neighborhood. Everyone first gathered inside the church and songs were sung. Then Pastor Erma blessed the food and a great fellowship began. This feast started in the early evening and continued until dark, then it was time to clear off the tables, put away the fryer, and get ready to go home. A prayer was then said and everyone was dismissed with a satisfied appetite and happiness in their hearts.

While growing up in Mississippi, I remember these large gatherings at our church but they were known as "all-day singing and dinner on the ground". Being able to do it all over again in a different way brought back many memories of my early childhood. No church I had ever attended in my adult years had left a mark on me like the little Sycamore Log Church in Branson, Missouri. Joyce and I were blessed to have been a part of this church and its people for nearly five years. Each and every person left us with fond memories and someday we'll meet them in Heaven.

In 2002, Willard bought a new, ton-and-a-half, four-wheel drive, flatbed Ford truck. Each Sunday, he drove it to church and often brought fresh vegetables that were passed out to the congregation. As always, he was dressed in bib overalls, a flannel shirt and his ole favorite hat. He was definitely an old-time Ozark Mountain man, and a proud one at that. On his farm were many longhorn cattle, his favorite dog, a few mules and some goats, and a beautiful pond where he raised catfish. There were other animals but also a special garden growing a short distance from his house. This same garden spot had been used for over a hundred years, dating back to the mid-1800s. It produced many great vegetables. Willard always canned what he needed and the rest was either given away to the church congregation or sold from the back of his truck on Highway 248. Willard loved his garden and always tried to outdo his old friend, Cecil Isaacs. When turnips were ready in the spring, Willard and Cecil brought their best to church and gave them away. Joyce and I always took a few but their competition was on every year.

Joyce was always asked to pass judgement on which turnips were best but she never wanted to choose one over the other, so her answer was that she liked them both. It was always a battle between these two old-time mountain men but always a tie with Joyce. Willard and Cecil spent much of their time working in their gardens and their tomatoes, cucumbers and squash, along with onions and green beans; they were much better than those found in the supermarkets.

One Sunday after church, Joyce and I met Willard for a picnic under the church canopy. After everyone was gone, we spent a short time eating our lunch then left on a sightseeing tour of his farm. There were hundreds of acres to see but our first stop was his house. We then went out to his garden, which was beautiful. From there we visited his sawmill, where in the past he had milled cedar and other types of wood that were sold to Silver Dollar City and local folks in the craft business.

One thing that amazed me the most was a patch of peonies that had grown in the same location for over a hundred years. They had been planted by his grandmother back in the 1800s! We also visited his storm cellar, where he stored canned fruits and vegetables, and where hundreds of quarts and pint jars were stored. He asked Joyce to pick out something so she took two quarts of pickles and a pint of okra.

Then he had a special place to show us. We headed south on a dirt trail and soon came to a one-room schoolhouse. After parking, we got out and walked through tall grass and weeds to the front door. It was in need of repair, but was overall in pretty good condition, considering the age. Willard was now using it for storage but then said it had been his childhood school for six years. He had bought the building and land ten years before for sentimental reasons. We went inside and took a few pictures but as we were leaving, it was easy to see that it brought back memories. We could see tears in his eyes. He told stories about the old school and pointed out where he and his classmates had sat and all the good times he'd had.

We continued south and soon came to several old buildings that were the remains of an old town called Garber. He parked his truck and Joyce took our picture as Willard and I stood in the doorway of what had once been a post office. The old town had been abandoned 50 years before and was located a few miles east of Reeds Spring next to the railroad tracks.

From there we visited his catfish pond and a beautiful little cabin he had built for his family. It was small and rustic but well furnished, with sleeping arrangements and an old wood stove and table, along with a 40-foot ramp over the water. The lake covered about two acres and was stocked with thousands of catfish. On the porch was a 55-gallon barrel filled with fish food, so he filled up a gallon bucket and scattered it across the water. It was hard to believe that hundreds of fish came up to eat and in seconds they, along with all their food, disappeared.

At the Sycamore Log Church picnics, most of the fish came from Willard's pond, along with many suckers caught in local creeks and rivers by Cecil Isaacs and Willard Jones.

On November 24th, 2003, a special anniversary party was held for Joyce and me at the Sycamore Log Church. All the congregation attended but only a few members of our The Best Is Yet to Come singing group were invited since the church was so small.

Once after coming home from a two-week visit to Colorado, we were surprised with a large welcoming banner across the front of the church on our first Sunday back. It brought tears to our eyes. These Ozark Mountain folks were our family and we loved them. What's more, we always felt that we were loved by them. This was now our home and their friendship never faded. God had brought us to Branson and not only did He help us find a home, but He also gave us a church and a new family that we never forgot.

Our Friend Willard Jones

It was Tuesday morning when our neighbor, Jeannie, called to let me know that Willard was on his way over with a holly tree and asked if I would help plant it. I was happy to assist and would meet him in front of my house when he was ready.

In less than 10 minutes, he was parking his truck. Jeannie and I met him and together picked out a place to plant this special tree. The location was north of our Roark Ridge neighborhood gravel driveway that separated our properties and which could be seen from both the kitchen window and the front porch.

Willard and I took a shovel and pick axe from the back of his truck and began to dig. The soil was full of large rocks, making it difficult, but we finished in about an hour.

As a gift to Jeannie, Willard had dug up the tree that morning on his property and balled it with burlap to keep the dirt from falling off and avoid exposing the roots.

Five gallons of water were poured in the hole and dirt was added around the roots. The planting was now finished. Four metal stakes with tie-down ropes were used to secured it from the wind.

Jeannie expressed her appreciation and invited us to her cabin for coffee and donuts. We enjoyed her treats and visited a few minutes, but Willard had to get back to the farm. His plans for the rest of the day were to cut down cedar trees that would be sold to Silver Dollar City and local craft shops.

We thanked Jeannie for the treats and Willard left for home. From our front porch, the little holly tree could be seen and Joyce and I thought it was planted in a perfect location.

I had many chores to do but first the lawn had to be mowed. I still had time to do a few other things before taking a lunch break, but was back to work by one o'clock. There was enough work left to keep me busy most of the afternoon and evening, but I was done by six o'clock.

I took a shower and sat down at the dinner table but just then, I got a phone call from Jeannie saying that Willard hadn't showed up at home. His family had called him several times but never got an answer and were very concerned. Jeannie told them that Willard had left our place earlier that morning with plans of cutting down a few cedar trees when he got home.

They were more puzzled now and went over to his house. He was nowhere to be found. They did notice his off-road, four-wheel-drive scooter was missing and this frightened them even more! With several hundred rugged acres to check and with it nearly dark, it would be a guessing game where to look first. They began their search but several hours later with no sign of Willard, they decided to check one more place before calling off the search until daylight.

It was nearly midnight when Willard's son, Bob, and some others arrived at the location, but right away they spotted Willard's off road vehicle. They spread out and began searching through the trees. They found him lying on the ground. A large cedar tree he had cut down had fallen across his upper body. The chainsaw was lying beside him and he had died instantly from a broken neck.

It was a tragic accident and soon the news spread. Branson had been Willard's home for his entire life of 82 years, and most everyone knew him. His family lived close by and the little Sycamore Log Church was a short distance down the road from his farm.

Sadness and shock were felt by many as funeral arrangements were made. Pastor Erma Downs would preach the funeral and the local mortuary chapel would be filled with family and friends. Among those attending were the owners of Silver Dollar City, along with the entire congregation of Sycamore Log Church. Branson had lost one of its favorite sons, but God had brought one of His children home. The little Sycamore Log Church would now have an empty pew on Sunday morning but the spirit of our friend would live forever.

No longer would our special friend build a fire in the wood stove on cold winter mornings or be there to welcome everyone with a smile and a handshake. No longer would he and I sing *The Little "Log" Church in the Dale*, and fish fries would never be the same. We had lost a good friend but knew someday we would be together again where life would have no end. Thanks, Willard, for being everyone's friend. You will never be forgotten.

Our Early Visits to the Ozarks

For twenty years before retirement, Branson was our favorite place for a vacation. We visited mostly in October but sometimes April or May. The reason was that spring and fall were much cooler and Silver Dollar City was at its best then. Many bands performed throughout the park and your ticket covered everything other than food and gifts. This included all the rides and a free two-hour concert each night after the park closed.

We did visit Eureka Springs, Arkansas, as well and often stayed two or three days. The outdoor passion play was the number one attraction, but we also enjoyed the shopping, the many other attractions, and eating at our favorite restaurants.

On those visits, if possible, we stayed on the east end of town at the Rose Garden Motel on Highway 62. It was owned and operated by a Pentecostal minister and his wife, and their son-in-law played Jesus in the passion play. Over the years we got to know them very well and always enjoyed our stay.

Eureka Springs had three country music theaters and we attended each of them over the years. One of the largest statues of Jesus in the world is located on the grounds of the passion play, along with many shops and restaurants. There's also a miniature version of the Holy Land; I saw it under construction from the beginning till it was finished. Busloads of tourists came from all across the country and filled the 4000-seat outdoor theater each night, where 170 actors and many animals and birds were used in the production. It was open every day except Sunday, if weather permitted. Once in October, Joyce and I, along with our friends, Bill and Lill Murphy, attended and it just happened to be one of the coldest night of our lives, even with blankets. One other thing about the play that kept us amused that night was a pair of raccoons that kept running out on stage and stealing the show.

Another attraction was the Crescent Hotel and Spa built in 1868. It was said to be haunted but it was a favorite place for many. There was a beautiful dining room and gift shop and all the rooms had been restored. The outside gardens were beautiful and maintained to perfection.

Just a block away was the Victoria Sampler Tea Room, which was one of our favorites. It was purchased in 1984 and was restored by Jim and Ruth Spears and their daughter Lori. It had formerly been the home of Dr. C.F. Ellis and dated back to 1879. After the first year of operation, it became the number one restaurant and lace shop in Eureka Springs. Not once did we miss going for lunch or dinner on our visits.

In restored rail cars, the Eureka Springs and North Arkansas Railroad provided lunch and a scenic four-mile ride that we both enjoyed! The museum was interesting for me but not so much for Joyce, since she had heard all about railroads throughout our married life and her dad was also a railroader. Between him and me, she got an education on railroading her entire life.

The first thing we did on our visits to Eureka Springs was tour the old residential area and see what changes had been made since our last visit. When a home was sold, the new owner couldn't make any changes to the original exterior other than bringing it back to the original condition and putting on new paint. An approval by the city was necessary for any additions, which had to match the original structure.

Eureka Springs was a beautiful Ozark Mountain community and our first pick for retirement. We inquired about several homes and one commercial building before changing our minds to Branson. Even after moving to Branson, we visited Eureka Springs several times each year and we continued to enjoy our visits.

It was a town that attracted thousands of Christians and most all of the billboards and marquees advertising their businesses mentioned something about God, using scriptures from the Bible. During the time we visited, very few sales of alcoholic beverages could be seen. Something else we found to be much different in our favorite Ozark Mountain towns was that the people were much friendlier than any place we had ever been. You never saw anyone get bent out of shape while driving their car or while waiting in line. Purchasing tickets at the theaters or being in a checkout line at the grocery stores was always a place to get acquainted with other visitors like ourselves. Very seldom did you ever find folks in a big hurry or rude and impatient. I often got acquainted with strangers while sitting on benches at Silver Dollar City or while resting anywhere there was a place to sit.

People attracted to these two Ozark Mountain towns had a different view of life. They came with their families to enjoy a more laid back way of life that at one time was found everywhere you went. After spending a two weeks' vacation around these kinds of people, it was hard to go home and face the rat race of life.

Jammin' for Jesus and Barbara Fairchild

Jammin' for Jesus was a free, three-hour Saturday evening gospel music concert held once a month in local Branson theaters. Singers, mostly from the Branson area but with many from across the country, would entertain tourists and local residents. It was one of the great attractions in Branson.

Shortly after arriving in Branson, we attended our first concert and found it to be a great evening of entertainment. During intermission we met many folks but Bobbie and Art Stone were the first. They were local residents and great Christians who attended the Branson Baptist Church.

Art was Santa Claus to many children and adults but was loved and known all across the Branson community. He and his wife, Bobbie, were active in their church and volunteered for several Christian groups, but the one I most remember was The Best Is Yet to Come, headed up by D.K. and Sherrie Brewster.

After living in Branson less than a month, Joyce and I were introduced to The Best Is Yet to Come and found it to be a great Christian organization that played a big role in the Branson area. It had an outlet for talented writers and performers in the field of gospel music with a large following across Missouri and as far away as Florida. Entertainers would audition by sending CDs, and if they were found to be good enough, they were notified to perform on stage before a large audience.

342

Once a month there was a two-hour showcasing that allowed many to come and show off their talents. This monthly program was free and open to the general public where hundreds would attend. The ministry started small, but grew in leaps and bounds and soon became a popular Friday night program in Branson.

After attending our second gathering of their Senior Luncheon held at the Allan Edwards Showroom in the Golden Corral, we decided to volunteer and became active members.

D.K. Brewster and his wife Sherrie were no strangers to the music industry! Prior to starting their The Best Is Yet to Come ministry, D.K. traveled with George Jones and performed for several years.

Adventures

We found all the functions to be fun and our days and weeks were filled with many activities. From the first day we joined The Best Is Yet to Come ministry, there was never a boring moment; everything we did was an adventure.

We became involved with their 78-member choir and performed in several Branson theaters, local churches, and many fundraising events across Missouri. In 2002 and 2003, the choir participated in the Easter Spring Spectacular Concerts presented by the world-famous singer and pianist Dino Kartsonakis. The performances took place at the Lawrence Welk Theater with two shows each day. Each year, there was a three-day celebration which several thousand people attended.

The Christian dance team *Ballet Magnificat* from Jackson, Mississippi also took part. The group was owned and operated by Keith and Kathy Thibodeaux. Keith was once an actor and played both Little Ricky on *I love Lucy* and Johnny Paul on *The Andy Griffith Show*.

It was an elaborate production! All the choir members were dressed in beautiful robes, singing on stage behind the ballet dancers, and there were many numbers by Dino Kartsonakis, his wife Cheryl, and her brother, Gary McSpadden.

Randy Brooks played Jesus. He wore a harness under his robe and would descend from the ceiling down to the stage and then ascend back to heaven at the end. Randy and his brother, Bill, are cousins of Garth Brooks, and had a stage production in Branson called *The Promise*, which chronicled the life, crucifixion and resurrection of Jesus. With Randy playing Jesus, both shows sold out every day.

We performed in two shows in 2002 and three in 2003, and it was a great experience for everyone. We met many of the ballet dancers, along with Dino, Cheryl, and Gary McSpadden. Being able to participate in this production was one of the highlights of our time in Branson.

Again at the Lawrence Welk Theater, from January 2001 till the November presidential election, we attended a weekly Sunday morning campaign service for George W. Bush conducted by Barbara Fairchild and her husband, Roy. The program was held from 10:00am till noon, then everyone was invited for lunch in the theater dining room. We enjoyed great food and fellowship for more than an hour.

Barbara Fairchild is a well-known member of the Grand Ole Opry and has won many awards in the field of country music. At the Bush campaign services each Sunday, she and her husband, Roy Morris, performed gospel music favorites and spoke about the need to elect George W. Bush as our next president. There were other speakers each week along with an audience of hundreds.

In January of 2001, Barbara invited Joyce to a Mary Kay party! She had a beautiful home and Joyce and several other ladies had a fun evening that would last till midnight. She got to know Barbara and the other ladies and continued to attend the weekly campaign program until it ended.

Barbara and Roy were celebrities, but they befriended everyone they came in contact with. We found this very odd; they never shunned anyone. One of her big hits, *Teddy Bear*, sold millions of copies, but her popularity never kept her from mixing and mingling with her fans like family.

D.K. and Sherrie Brewster are well known in Branson, and The Best Is Yet to Come ministry was a big hit with many. Barbara was sometimes a special guest performer on The Best Is Yet to Come programs along with many other local Branson entertainers. The Platters were guests at our senior luncheon several times and Rooster, one of the originals, was always a fun character to be around. The Platters owned and performed in their theater seven days a week and were always a big hit with their fans.

In the early summer of 2001, D.K. Brewster and his family were honored with the Branson Love Award of the year, and Joyce and I, along with Randy Brooks, were asked to participate in making a short video about our friendship. For us, it was an honor to be involved with such a special occasion where hundreds of local residents and entertainers came out to honor this family.

The ministry was already a favorite attraction but over the weeks and months, it became much more popular. In 2002, a weekly, one-hour Sunday morning gospel television program, featuring solos, duets, and quartet performances, and The Best Is Yet to Come 78-member choir was broadcast out of Springfield, Missouri. There was an audience across the Ozarks that tuned in every Sunday morning from 10:00 till 11:00am.

Along with other volunteers, together we reached out to help make the ministry a success. I was the cameraman, greeter, and usher, but I was also the cashier for food sales. There were others, including myself, who helped set up the stage props and sound system. I was in charge of passing the collection plate at all the events. Joyce was Sherrie's assistant, and helped out in any other way she could.

346

D.K. and Sherrie became our best friends and we made many great memories together. Dining out was always fun since D.K. was often mistaken for Kennie Rogers. There were times when people stopped by our table and gave him CDs of their music, wanting him to listen and hoping he would respond. We always thought it was funny and D.K. simply heeded their requests and smiled. He just ate it up. He always dressed in black and most everyone agreed that he was a spitting image of Kennie Rogers.

Their son, Cody, took care of the soundboard and their young, but only daughter, Jaimee, never missed a chance to sing. She had a great voice from an early age and was loved by everyone. She was nine when we met and was always ready to sing on stage, whether there was an audience of 20 or 2000.

Another well-known singer in our circle was Gary S. Paxton! He wrote the big Halloween hits *Monster Mash* and *Ally-Oop*, along with many other songs in the fields of secular and gospel music. His biggest gospel hit, *He Was There All the Time* was recorded by dozens of well-known artists in many languages. Gary was a member of The Best Is Yet to Come ministry, and performed often on our programs.

After new members proved their ability to write and sing gospel music, they were offered a membership in The Best Is Yet to Come ministry and invited to perform on stage. If they had a desire to make demos of their music, D.K. and Sherrie made arrangements at a local recording studio which gave them a jump start with their career.

This was an opportunity many artists would have never gotten if not for The Best Is Yet to Come ministry. They were also connected to the Gaithers, who were, and still are, the most famous gospel performers in the world. The Best Is Yet to Come music productions always went through the Gaither production company.

In 2001, D.K. and Sherrie had written a song called *Party Time* and were nominated for a Dove Award as Writers of the Year. They couldn't attend the ceremony in Nashville so we invited them to watch on our big screen TV. Their song was recorded by Sherrie and Jeff Easter and they too were nominated for Song of the Year.

D.K., Sherrie, their daughter Jaimee, along with our friends, Dan and Pattie Elliot, arrived at our home early that evening with time to visit before the show got underway. The girls stayed upstairs while the men went downstairs and waited for the show to start. It was a great two-hour program with many stars performing between the awards. Song of the Year would be the last presentation and everyone was anxious to hear the results.

At 9:50 pm it was time to present the last award of the evening but Joyce, Sherrie, Jaimee, and Pattie were upstairs and missed hearing the winner announced. With D.K. and Sherrie not present to accept the award, someone else accepted it for them.

Right away D.K. shouted out, "We won! We won!" and everyone began to scream with glee. It was a joyous occasion but after all the excitement, the evening soon came to an end and we said goodbye to our friends.

D.K. would travel to Nashville the following week to pick up his Dove Award and could hardly wait to get back to Branson to show it off. He was walking on clouds and all his family and friends were happy for him.

Our friendship continued to grow and we became more involved each day with the music ministry. We began to visit a rest home each month and performed special music and other programs for all the holidays. The number of people participating in our visits had to be smaller, of course, for those performances, but there was always an audience of 20 or more.

A senior luncheon was held each month at the Allen Edwards Showroom, where a hundred or more would attend. Not just one, but sometimes two special guests from local theaters were invited along with regular performers from The Best Is Yet to Come ministry. The event started at 10:00am but everyone took a one-hour lunch break from noon till 1:00pm.

The Golden Corral restaurant gave our members a special rate of $8.00 and that included a beverage and all-you-can-eat lunch at the best buffet in town. The program ended around 2:00pm and everyone left except D.K., Sherrie, Joyce and me, along with a few others who helped take down the stage props and load up the sound equipment.

For us, everything was exciting no matter what it was. It never seemed like work. We were always having fun and made many friends while learning about the music industry. We got involved with things we never thought would be of interest to us, but found everything to be an adventure. We made many friends who we grew to love like family.

Once D.K. and the ministry were asked to do a fundraiser for a lady who lost her husband in a car accident. She didn't have funds to pay funeral costs, so The Best Is Yet to Come ministry volunteered to do a concert at a local church and donate everything to the wife and her three kids. The family needed $800, but over $1000 was raised. The church members did a potluck and the food was great! It was a cause we all felt good about but it was still very sad to see such a tragic accident taking the life of a young father and husband.

A permanent location for all the events was not always available. They were often held at the Allen Edwards Showroom, the Salvation Army chapel, the Denny's convention room, or local churches. We were never without a place for the events.

For one hour each month, choir practice was held at D.K. and Sherrie's home. There, our visit would continue till late in the evening. Coffee, pop, snacks, and my favorite, cheese and bread, were served and the fun would sometimes last till after 1:00am. Joyce and I rarely got home before 2:00am but 5 or 6 o'clock wasn't unusual. Retirement for us was great and we were enjoying every minute!

At a *Jammin' for Jesus* program shortly after arriving in Branson, we met George Bryant. He just happened to ask if he could sit next to us since the theater was nearly full. Joyce and I moved down; he took the seat next to the aisle and we introduced ourselves. I was surprised to discover he was a popular radio disc jockey from a Baptist college in Springfield, Missouri.

The theater was dark and his first words to me were, "I want to remain incognito for a while and keep a low profile until intermission."

We hit it off right away and enjoyed the first half of the program. He and everyone else took a break at intermission and he disappeared into the crowd. Joyce went to the ladies' room and I stayed behind to save our seats, but after she returned, I left for a few minutes. We were able to keep out seats and saved one for George in case he came back.

Since we had been sitting for more than an hour and a half, we decided to stand until the second half started. We could see an increasingly large group gathering up front next to the stage and was easy to see George was in the middle since he was 6 feet 6 inches tall. Soon the second half was ready to start and everyone made their way back to their seats.

Joyce and I took our seats but then saw the silhouette of a large man walking up the aisle. Then I realized it was George and he thanked us for saving him a seat. From that day on, we were friends and we saw him often on his visits to Branson.

George had a big family but his kids were grown and his wife had passed away a few years before. As a disc jockey, he played all the old gospel songs along with new hits. He reported the local news and weather and was well known across Missouri and the Ozarks. He had a large following and often played music recorded by members of The Best Is Yet to Come ministry. We could get his show in Branson and I always kept my radio set on his station. While traveling back from Colorado on Highway 13 through Clinton, Missouri, I could always pick him up and listen to him the rest of the way home.

He was a great minister, singer, and writer, and soon became a member of The Best Is Yet to Come. On weekends, and while away from his job, he traveled across Missouri, Arkansas, and Kansas preaching and singing in many churches. He was a great man and was loved by his family and those who knew him. George would later marry Ruth Pennick and would invite Joyce and me to their wedding. D.K. Brewster was his best man!

He and his new wife and her daughter, Carol, were active members of The Best Is Yet to Come and became friends with everyone. They put together a trio and began to write and sing, while George continued to preach.

At the Jim Stafford Theater, The Best Is Yet to Come choir was asked to provide music for the Tim Hill ministry and his

352

congregation. The service was held in the theater every Sunday morning and our choir would sing several songs before the worship service. It was a fun time for everyone and again we met many local Christians along with the band that provided the music. We sang for the Tim Hill ministry for over a year.

We had a different experience every week with the choir, and every one of them was a great time. Once in the early summer, we were asked to perform at a blackberry farm just outside Branson. People would come and pick their own berries since it was much cheaper than buying from a market. The owners asked D.K. to provide music for the pickers, so with a 45-passenger bus owned by the ministry, everyone traveled there and spent the day singing.

Another time, we took a busload of members and attended a program at a Pentecostal church in northern Missouri. The famous Crabb family provided the music and we were able to meet them all. They were already famous at the time, but later they became a household name in gospel music.

Once the ministry bus was provided for those wanting to attend a Gaither concert in St. Louis. Everyone made arrangements for their own lodging and Joyce and I rode up with our friends, Dan and Pattie Elliot. We arrived two hours before the bus so before checking into our rooms, we drove 50 miles north of St. Louis to an antique and classic auto sales garage. There were hundreds of beautiful cars on display inside a huge building and we were hoping to find a 1958 Chevy Impala there for Pattie.

It was raining and very cold, so we parked close by and went inside. There were many makes and models but after checking more than 50 classic and antique cars, we actually found a 1958 Chevrolet Impala. Pattie thought it was beautiful, but she experienced some sticker shock after learning the price was $25,000. Dan took a business card from a salesman and we loaded up and headed back to St. Louis.

There was heavy evening traffic and it was slow going all the way. When we arrived at our hotel, most of our friends had already arrived and were getting ready for dinner. We checked into our rooms and joined everyone at a local restaurant. After a great meal, we drove over to the college stadium and went to our assigned seats.

The stage was set up in the center of the arena with the audience sitting in chairs all around, but most of the crowd sat in bleachers on both sides. It was like a basketball arena. Yet, everyone had a good seat and enjoyed a two-hour concert put on by Bill and Gloria Gaither along with many other performers.

It was after 11 o'clock when we got back to the hotel so after a short visit in the lobby, everyone went to their rooms. On Sunday morning, we got together for a continental breakfast and then headed back to Branson. Everyone stopped along the way for lunch and got home in the late afternoon.

There was just always something going on! Between the

showcasing and praise gatherings held on the last Friday and Saturday of each month, along with the senior luncheon at the Allen Edwards Showroom and rest home visits, we were on the go all the time.

In September each year, the Branson Gospel Music Awards were held at the Chateau on the Lake Resort. This was a big event for those connected to The Best Is Yet to Come ministry. Everyone dressed in their best and attended a banquet where awards were handed out in all categories of music and to everyone who volunteered in the ministry. It was a fun evening and the local Branson newspaper and radio station were there to report the winners. Pictures were taken and were available to everyone. The turnout was always big. The beautiful Chateau on the Lake Resort and Hotel was the largest in Branson and reservations were made each year for this special occasion.

After the awards ceremony, a new year of music would begin and new members were added to the ministry. The outreach was all across the Ozark states, as well as Oklahoma, Texas, and as far away as Florida and Louisiana. It was a great ministry that provided help to those interested in writing and singing gospel music.

We become fascinated with the ministry and made many friends. We always enjoyed reaching out a helping hand in any way we could. Joyce and I had never thought that retirement could be this much fun!

I had always thought of writing a book, but I had to put that on hold till I had more time. I did write one song that was picked up by Randy Plummer, a local Branson artist. A group of writers and singers through The Best Is Yet to Come ministry made a 14-song CD called *A Big Hearted Trucker in a Good Lookin' Hat*. My song, *He Will Surely Shine His Light*, was on the CD and I was very excited to be a part of the team.

We did take yearly vacations as well, visiting California, Texas, Mississippi, and Pennsylvania, and of course we went back to Colorado each year for family visits.

The Ghost of Roark Ridge

In 2001, as we returned home from our first Easter visit to Colorado at around 10:00 in the evening, I took a walk through the house to see if everything was as we left it. Our neighbor, Jeannie, had been checking the house while we were away, but I noticed something strange on the basement floor. There were 13 acorns lined up in a row about three feet from the water softener. I called Joyce, and like me, she found it strange. We figured Jeannie was playing a trick on us and we decided to talk with her in the morning. The long drive had left us tired so we simply unpacked and went to bed.

The night went by fast and as I was eating breakfast, around 9:00am, I looked through the kitchen window and saw Jeannie walk past the house. I stepped out on the porch to let her know we were home and invited her for coffee. She came in and wanted to know all about our trip and to welcome us home. She and her husband, Tom, were great neighbors and always took care of our dog, Rowdy, and looked after the house when we were away.

After coffee and a short visit, I told her about the 13 acorns on the basement floor. She too was surprised and only laughed when I asked if she had played a trick on us. She hadn't. I thought it was strange and yet I had seen nothing else out of place the day we got home. I had left the acorns where I found them so we all went downstairs to look, but Jeannie swore she had nothing to do with it.

We were all puzzled because there was no explanation for the acorns. I couldn't get it out of my mind. I thought maybe the water softener man did it after delivering salt the day before we left. It also entered my mind that a pack rat may have gotten in the house and was the culprit. Whatever the case, it was a mystery and we tried to forget about it.

We continued with our activities and kept busy most of the time. We spent most of our daylight hours at home but were almost always out and about three or four nights a week into the wee hours of the morning.

Thursday was always house cleaning day and we usually finished up around 5:00pm. For dinner, Joyce always prepared our favorite hamburgers and French fries. By 6:30, we would kick back and watch TV till bedtime. We had a great routine that never changed.

On Fridays, I mowed and edged our two-acre lawn, an all day job! This was my day of exercise. I began at 6:00am, taking a 30-minute break for lunch and stopping often for water. The temperature got up in the 90s most days and the humidity was about the same. I wore a wide-brimmed hat, shorts, a light shirt, and shoes without socks. With ticks and chiggers to worry about, I had to spray often with repellant to keep these critters from eating me alive.

On the third Friday of each month, we had to be at the praise gathering by 7:00pm. We would arrive early and I helped set up the stage props and sound system while Joyce helped Sherrie with the evening line-up of performers. On all the other Fridays, if nothing was happening, we took in a show or went out to Silver Dollar City for dinner.

About two weeks after the acorn mystery, I was downstairs at my computer when Joyce came down and wanted to know what I had been doing upstairs. I had been at my computer for over two hours but she thought she heard me walking through the living room and out on the sunporch. She had called my name a couple of times but never got an answer.

Our house had 4200 square feet with a walkout basement. On the lower level were two bedrooms, a bathroom, and a huge family room and craft room. Upstairs was the living room, three bedrooms, two baths, the kitchen, a formal dining room, and a 30-

by-15-foot enclosed sunporch.

I brushed it off but insisted she heard someone walking across the living room and out on the sunporch. To make her feel better, I checked the entire house. Nothing was out of place so again we tried to forget about it.

Our daily routine rarely changed but one night the sound of someone walking through the living room woke me at 2:00am. I had heard footsteps on the carpet, which was a distinctive sound that changed when whoever it was reached the tiled sunporch floor.

Joyce often went out in the living room and slept in her recliner when her allergies were acting up but with the bathroom nightlight on, I could see she was still in bed. The noise had me concerned but I didn't know what to do other than lay still. After waiting a few minutes, I heard more sounds of footsteps walking across the sunporch, through the living room, and out to the front door. It stopped at the top of the stairs. The distance from our bedroom to the front door was about 40 feet, so I slowly got out of bed and stood still. I heard them continue down the stairs.

I kept a fiberglass ax handle under the bed so I picked it up and began walking toward the staircase. I could see okay since the outside security light was shining through the glass front entry door.

Shortly after we moved in, public service had mounted a mercury light on a pole that lit up the front yard and shined through the guest bedroom window. I peeked out and everything looked okay. Rowdy was still in the garage. With the ax handle in my hand, I began making my way down the stairs. I turned on the light but everything looked okay so I walked from room to room, turning on the lights and checking closets and doors. Nothing was out of place so I turned on the outside lights. Right away Rowdy showed up on the patio.

This was the third time something strange had happened and yet another unsolved mystery. I returned to bed and tried to push it out of my mind but I found it hard to get back to sleep.

The next morning during breakfast, we talked about what I had heard. Neither of us had ever experienced anything like this before, and we had always been skeptical about the stories we had read and heard of unexplained happenings. Slowly, our thoughts on the subject were beginning to change.

Our activities continued and The Best Is Yet to Come kept our minds off what was happening. The days and weeks went by and we rarely talked about our "ghost," hoping whatever it was would go away.

The only other people who knew about it were Jeannie and Tom, but even they only knew about the acorns. We had mentioned nothing about the other two episodes to anyone!

A few weeks later, I was sitting on the sunporch in my favorite rocking chair talking to my friend, Ed Jacobs, in Colorado. We talked for nearly two hours while my feet were propped up on a wood bench. The sunporch was on the southwest corner with six-foot sliding glass windows that allowed plenty of sunlight for Joyce's beautiful plants.

After my conversation with Ed, I hung up, went downstairs, and got on my computer. After checking my e-mail, I went back upstairs and Joyce wanted to know why I moved the rocking chair down to the east end of the sun room. I went out to see what she was talking about but she had moved it back to its proper place. I was sure I hadn't moved it, but she pointed to where she found it. It had been moved more than 20 feet and yet I was sure I hadn't put it there. Was my mind playing tricks on me? Or did we really have a ghost in our house? Joyce knew I would have known if I moved it, so she and I both began to think we had something strange going on.

We became more concerned but didn't know what to do! I did check with my friend Willard Jones and asked if he knew any history of Roark Ridge. He was 79 and had lived his entire life three miles east of us on his 1000-acre farm. His family had lived there since the early 1800s.

He had heard stories of an Indian village on top of Roark Ridge which was one of the highest points in Missouri. The elevation was nearly 1200 feet and Roark Creek was just over 1000 feet south of the house. The ridge was flat, about 600 yards long and more than 100 yards wide. It was high above the flood zone and it made sense that the Indians would choose a safe place like this to live. There were Indian relics to be found on the property, as well as signs that a whiskey still had once operated 100 yards south of the house. I had discovered the latter shortly after moving there while I was cleaning up the yard.

My first indications had been broken quart and gallon jugs while digging up a spot for a flower bed. I could tell the area had never been used for a garden but the deeper I dug, the more glass I found. I also found copper pipe and rusty remains of what looked like a whiskey still. With so much debris buried in the ground, I abandoned the project and let the grass grow.

I brought it to the attention of my neighbor, Tom, and after seeing what I dug-up, he too agreed it looked like the remains of a whiskey still. I removed enough glass and rusty metal, along with copper tubing, to fill the back of my old Chevy Luv pick-up and had to help the garbage man load it up. Whiskey stills were not uncommon in the Ozarks and there were many stories of moonshine operations across the mountains.

We had both heard stories of haunted houses. After hearing what Willard had to say, we wondered, could it be true that someone once operated a whiskey still on Roark Ridge? Could our house be haunted by an Indian, or maybe and old moonshiner?

There weren't many nights when we didn't hear sounds of footsteps and things seemed to be getting crazier by the week. But we never saw any damage, and though the sounds persisted, no more furniture was moved. So far, there had been no "sightings."

Then, one morning after doing her make-up and hair, Joyce walked out of her bathroom and stopped in front of the bedroom dresser. The sliding glass across the room was open out to the sunporch and she saw a reflection in the mirror of someone walking across the porch. Terrified, she ran to the living room where I was reading and told me all about it. She had seen the side view of a man with a dark complexion, dressed in black, with long, dark hair. I was frightened too, but again I checked the entire house and found nothing. Now we had another unsolved mystery on our hands but had evidence of what the ghost looked like. Over a few weeks and months, Joyce had several more sightings and we both continued to hear sounds of footsteps.

A few weeks later, Joyce was home alone reading in the living room and saw a bright red-and-green laser light move across the carpet and disappear. It had traveled a distance of four feet beside the ottoman in front of the couch where she was sitting. She thought it was strange but had accepted the fact that whatever was happening, nothing was there to harm us. That same evening, the TV came on by itself and changed channels on its own.

At the breakfast table, we often talked about what we had heard through the night! These sounds of footsteps continued, and eventually, I quit checking and just rolled over and went back to sleep whenever I heard them.

We did share our story with Pastor Erma and members of the Sycamore Log Church congregation. They shared a few strange tales about their own experiences and a lady visiting from Oklahoma even suggested we conduct an exorcism with members of the church. We never thought there was a need for that and felt it was nothing to be concerned about.

It wasn't long till all our Branson friends knew about the Roark Ridge Ghost. Because we had learned the previous owner's husband, Bob, had passed away in the house less than a year before we had moved in, we decided to name our ghost "Bob."

Our encounters continued. One night at 2:00am, a loud noise woke us up. I said to Joyce, "Did you hear that?" Her response was, "Oh, that was just Bob," so we turned over and went back to sleep. We were now used to having him around and any weird things that happened were forgotten and pushed out of our minds.

I got up the next morning and went to make coffee as usual. I walked over to the closet, opened the door, and was shocked by what I found! Joyce was awake but still in bed. I told her, "You won't believe what Bob did last night. Come see for yourself." This frightened her, but she slowly walked over to the closet and she too was shocked by what she saw.

The entire contents of this double-door, walk-in closet that took up an entire 14-foot wall were lying on the floor. And what a mess it was! All the rubber-coated, heavy-duty wire racks and shelves were pulled from the wall. There was nothing at all left attached, and this definitely got our attention. Had Bob become angry and decided to show us he was capable of doing something other than walking around the house and playing tricks on us?

We left everything on the floor and had coffee, then removed the mess to the bedroom.

All the brackets had been pulled from the wall, but luckily for us, nothing was broken. The shelves had to be reattached but first I had to go to Branson for new anchor bolts, brackets, and drywall mud. By the time I finished and had everything back in place, the day was over.

I was now tired, upset, and without a single answer as to why these crazy things were happening.

I went out to the garage and that's when I heard a radio news bulletin about an earthquake centered in northwest Arkansas. It was felt all the way to Springfield, with minor damage reported. What a relief it was knowing Bob wasn't responsible! For an entire day we had been upset with our ghost for something he hadn't done. We were very happy to learn the real cause. Bob continued to be a joke between Joyce and me, and the sounds of his strolls through the house continued.

In June of 2001, we went to Colorado on vacation and brought our three granddaughters back. They were on summer break from school and our daughter, Mitzie, and the rest of her family would be coming later. They lived in Arvada and were looking forward to a fun vacation in Missouri.

We never mentioned anything about Bob, but the girls thought it was spooky living way out in the country away from the city lights. That first night, Joyce put Megan and Kayla in an upstairs bedroom and Joy had her own room down the hall. They had a bathroom between them and they thought the arrangements were great.

It wasn't long till Kayla and Megan became frightened after hearing strange noises outside their bedroom window. They were both upset and went to Joy's room, wanting her to come check it out.

Together, they went back and sat quietly on the bed with the light off! It didn't take long till the sounds were heard again. Now they were all frightened and began whispering in the dark.

It didn't take long till Joyce heard them and went to see what was wrong. She tiptoed across the living room, and with a nightlight burning in the hallway, they soon saw Grammy coming to their rescue. They were all scared and told her about the strange noise outside their window!

It took a while but Joyce soon had them calmed down but then the strange sounds were heard again. Right away Joyce knew it was a whippoorwill and tried to explain there was nothing to be scared of, but stayed a while longer nonetheless.

Joy soon went back to bed and Grammy tucked Kayla and

Megan in bed. They weren't frightened anymore. Once she explained this strange night bird would whistle, "chip fell out of the white oak" until daylight, they actually thought the sounds of the whippoorwill were funny. They slept the night away without any more interruptions.

One week later, Mitzie and her husband, Loren, and their son, Chris, would join us for a week. Their trip down from Denver took a day and a half but they arrived early Sunday afternoon. Joyce prepared a great dinner that everyone enjoyed and visited the rest of the evening. We got to bed before midnight.

Monday morning came and the weather was beautiful! We all went out to Silver Dollar City and enjoyed lunch, dinner, and a fun day of water rides and shopping. We also stayed for the evening concert that began at 10:00pm and would last till midnight. It had been another exciting day and the kids were looking forward to the rest of their vacation.

Mitzie and Loren had a bedroom downstairs and Chris would be sleeping on the couch. In less than an hour, Mitzie woke up and heard what she thought was Chris crawling around on the floor, so she told him to go back to bed. Since it was a walk-out basement and it was very dark with all the drapes closed, it was hard to see anything.

The noise stopped and Mitzie thought Chris had gone back to bed. Then she heard it again, but this time, she turned on the lamp. No one was there. This caused concern and she went to check on Chris. With the nightlight on in the bathroom, she was able to see and found him sound asleep on the couch. She was frightened even more but did go back to bed and soon fell asleep.

She woke up at 9:00am and went upstairs, where everyone was eating breakfast. She told them what happened, asking Chris if he was in her room the night before. He said he never got up all night.

After breakfast, everyone took showers and got ready for another day of fun. Overnight, Mitzie had left her purse on the floor next to the bed and found a handful of acorns inside. We still hadn't told them about Bob and thought it best to keep quiet about that for a while. She still thought Chris was playing a trick on her and she laughed it off.

Since we had bought our tickets to Silver Dollar after 3:00pm on Monday, we were entitled to a free day on Tuesday and decided to go back. The kids were excited and looked forward to another fun day of water rides that would help keep them cool. The temperature was in the 90s, so another day at the park would make everyone happy. On Monday, they had especially enjoyed the water fights! In a large arena, many water cannons were set up where you could pick a station and defend it with your own personal water cannon. One was located all by itself in the corner and whoever manned it could battle as many as six at a time. I stood by and watched and found it funny seeing six against one.

After seeing this single cannon abandoned time after time, I thought it would be fun taking on my four grandkids and seeing how long I could last. From watching, I had learned a few tricks and took charge of this cannon the first chance I got. Chris, Joy, Megan, and Kayla would be my enemies and it wasn't long till the battle was on.

There was no time limit and I thought I could fight them off for a while before having to abandon my station. Next to my cannon was a pole that was five inches in diameter and wrapped with one-inch rope; this was my only protection. My cannon had great pressure but my face was the biggest worry. We did have eye protection. There were times when I had thoughts of giving up, but I kept the battle going.

I started out against four and when someone left their station, there was always someone waiting to take their place. This continued for more than an hour but soon they all gave up and Papa was declared the winner. It was fun but they were surprised I had held the fort and chased them all away.

We were all soaking wet but it felt great and we continued through the park. I rode all the rides with my grandkids except the loop-to-loop roller coaster. They tried to persuade me, but I had to pass!

The next day we stayed home and the kids played on a tire swing I had made for them. We also hiked down to the creek and showed them around our Roark Ridge property.

In the early afternoon, Kayla and Megan wanted to play computer games so I gave my permission with the understanding that they would share with each other. After an hour or more, I heard a door slam and another loud bang. The girls came running up the stairs, scared out of their minds.

According to them, they were arguing over the computer when the door to my office suddenly slammed and one of my favorite pictures showing all the Civil War battles in the state of Missouri fell to the floor.

My first thought was that they got angry with each other and one of them slammed the door, causing the picture to fall. But they swore they had nothing to do with it. The door had supposedly slammed on its own. I was surprised to find that nothing was broken. Needless to say, they didn't want to play on the computer or spend time in the basement any longer. It looked like Bob was at it again, but I didn't say anything about him.

Later in the week Joyce, Mitzie and the girls had a fun day of shopping in Branson and Loren, Chris, and I took in a country music show. It was another fun day and we later had dinner in town, arriving home late.

On Friday, we saw *The Promise*, which was a stage production about the life and death of Jesus. It was one of the most popular shows in Branson, in which our friend, Randy Brooks, played Jesus and another friend, Dow Escalante, played Peter. Randy and his brother, Bill, owned the rights to *The Promise* and Randy and Dow were members of The Best Is Yet to Come choir.

On Saturday, the day before Mitzie and her family left, we went to Table Rock Lake for a picnic and a day of swimming, during which most of us got bad sunburns.

The week soon came to an end and they left early Sunday morning, making it back to Denver that night. Our home was now empty and quiet and everything was back to our normal routine on Monday.

Taking care of my yard and the garden I had planted earlier that spring kept me busy and left very little time for me to loaf around, but I enjoyed it all.

There was rarely a day with nothing to do. Our fun activities were going to Silver Dollar City, taking in a show in Branson, or eating at our favorite restaurants. Joyce loved to shop too. In 2001, we bought season tickets to Silver Dollar City and we went 19 times. On many Sundays after church, we went there for lunch and spent the afternoon walking throughout the park and listening to music. The people we met on our visits were never like strangers; we met hundreds over the five years we lived in Branson.

Throughout the park were many water rides for the young and old as well as great places to eat. The fall theme was the late 1800s where you could watch log cabins being built, a working grist mill, steam-powered farm machinery in operation, wagon

371

wheels being built, and a fully operating blacksmith shop. There were endless numbers of arts and crafts along with stage and outdoor shows featuring all types of music. Country, gospel, and bluegrass were the favorites but after the park closed, everyone was invited to attend another free two-hour outdoor concert in Echo Hollow, an outdoor theater that holds 4000. There were always great performers participating each night and it was often full if weather permitted.

Silver Dollar City also had a large cave which was another favorite attraction and the smell of good food was never out of range.

When visiting with your family, there was never a worry about safety for young children. The park employees and visitors were considered to be great babysitters and Silver Dollar City claimed to have never lost a child.

Even before we moved to the Branson area, Joyce and I had visited Silver Dollar City every year from 1980 to 2000! The beauty of the Ozark Mountains and the great people filled a void in our lives until we moved there. For the next five years, it was a 42-year-old dream that came true. Our lives changed in a way we never thought possible.

Looking Back to Our Beginning

At the age of 13, I moved with my family from Vicksburg to a farm in Clem, Mississippi. There I lived with my mom, three brothers and a sister, along with a stepdad, his three sons and daughter, as sharecrop cotton farmers. In October 1956, at the age of 18, I left the farm and went back to Vicksburg. With the help of two aunts, I got a job at the local Westinghouse plant, but after working three months, I got laid off a week before Christmas. Jobs were hard to come by but lucky for me, an opportunity came up to go out west to California. I took advantage of it and left Vicksburg on January 4th, 1957, riding a Greyhound bus to San Francisco.

I would visit my Grandma Stephenson and Uncle Alton and his family for a short time, after which Uncle Alton drove me to Los Angeles. There, I met my dad for the first time since I was eight years old.

It was a strange reunion but I stayed with my dad and stepmother, Celia, and went to work for the Santa Fe Railroad on March 7th, 1957. After working nearly 10 months, I was laid off but in January 1958, Dad got me a job with the Union Pacific railroad doing the same as I was with the Santa Fe.

In March, I met another railroader who would one day become my father-in-law. His name was Dolphia Marion Huitt. We lived at the same apartment complex in Bandini, California and we became friends.

I would meet my wife, Neoma Joyce Huitt, the following August and it was love at first sight. Our dreams began on August 31st, 1958 which was the day I returned home from Camp Roberts, California after two weeks of basic training. Through my friendship with Mr. Huitt, I learned a lot about his daughter.

While I was in boot camp, she and her family had rented an upstairs apartment in the complex. She knew nothing about me, but I couldn't wait to meet her.

She was born in Longmont, Colorado but grew up in the little town of Arvada just 35 miles south. Her dad had been employed with the Union Pacific Railroad but lost his job in 1957 after working in Denver more than 20 years. He was transferred to east Los Angeles, California, living and working there until his family could join him.

One day while we were doing laundry, he had shown me a picture of his family and his beautiful daughter had caught my eye. She became a permanent picture in my mind. She was now my dream girl and I put everything on hold until we met seven months later, when Mr. Huitt decided his job was secure and he could move his family. Joyce, her mother and her brother Larry, had come out by train for a visit that Christmas.

Moving his family to California made him happy but it thrilled me for a different reason. The days, weeks, and months passed slowly, but thoughts of my sunshine girl kept me going. I never expressed my feelings to anyone, but the truth of it is from the very first day I saw her picture, I thought she would one day be my wife. That may sound crazy but that is how it happened. I didn't know what she would think of me but I prayed her feelings would someday be the same.

374

After a long seven-month wait, I had become much more excited about meeting my dream girl! It was Sunday afternoon, August 31st, 1958. I had traveled all day in a hot, canvas-covered, ton-and-a-half Studebaker troop hauler at speeds that never exceeded 30 mph. Even with a police escort through all the big towns, it was still slow-moving all the way from Camp Roberts back to my National Guard Armory in Montebello, California. During the two-week training mission, I had stood by anxiously waiting for my platoon to be dismissed.

By 3:00pm, I was making my way over to the motor pool and was soon behind the wheel of my 1948 Oldsmobile heading for home. I knew Joyce and her family were now living in the apartment complex where I lived so I was very excited. A drive that always took 30 minutes or more would take only 20 since I broke a few speed limits along the way.

When I got home, my brother Kennie told me where Joyce lived so I walked upstairs and knocked on the door. Her mother answered and said that Joyce had just walked down to the local market with her brother, Larry, and sister-in-law, Eleanor. I went back to my apartment and told Kennie where I was going but he wanted to ride along. We jumped in the car, made our way to the market, parked in front, and waited. Soon they came out, and there she was, looking just like her picture but even more beautiful than I had ever expected.

Since Kennie knew Mr. Huitt, and had already met the entire family he had told them I would be home that day. Joyce knew little about me but seeing Kennie in the car, she knew I had made it home. I asked if they wanted a ride so they got in the back seat and I took them home.

I parked in front of the apartment complex and visited for a few minutes but Joyce wanted me to come in and meet her mother. We went to her apartment and after a short visit, I asked if she would go with me to a drive-in theater that evening. Her answer was yes, but first she had to ask her mother! Her mother agreed to let her go if Eleanor went along, but that was fine with me.

I walked downstairs to my apartment and took a shower, and soon we were on our way to the drive-in. She had to be home by 10:00pm, so there was only enough time for one movie before we had to leave. All we did was talk but everything went just like I had prayed for. She was the answer to that prayer.

She had beautiful, long, black, curly hair down to her waist. She wore no makeup and had pearly white teeth and a great smile. She was 5 foot 4 and weighed 93 pounds. From the very first, she was my perfect sunshine girl.

We dated every Wednesday, Friday, and Saturday night and visited Disneyland and Knott's Berry Farm many times, along with countless other fun places across the city. She had to be home at 10:00pm on Wednesdays, but midnight on Friday and Saturday. When we were not on dates, I visited her every day, since she lived on the second floor and I was just below on the first. We didn't have telephones so we met in the hallway each morning before I left for work and before she left for school.

Two months after our first date, I ask her to marry me and she said yes. I then spoke with her dad, but he was hesitant at first. He finally gave his permission. Her mother liked me and thought I knew what I was doing, but she still thought Joyce was too young and wouldn't give her permission.

We wanted the blessings from her parents along with my dad and stepmother, Celia, in addition to my mother in Mississippi and my brother, Kennie. Mom was happy but everyone else thought we were making a mistake and were not very nice to us.

At the Los Angeles County Courthouse, we applied for a marriage license but ran into problems. It took a while to get everything in order since my mother lived in Mississippi. She and Joyce's dad had to submit notarized letters of permission and getting the forms back from Mississippi took two weeks. We also had to get permission from an L.A. County judge, another obstacle in our way.

Things finally came together and we were married in Maywood, California at the home of Rev. E.A. Worthy. It was on the 24th day of November, 1958, and no one in my family was present; Joyce's dad, Larry, and Eleanor were the only people to attend.

While waiting for the minister to arrive, we sat on a sofa

and watched an episode of *The Beverly Hillbillies*! I wore a grey suit and tie and Joyce had on a beautiful blue dress and heels. We received no cards or flowers and the only gift was an electric skillet from Joyce's cousin, Donna Maddox. This never caused us any sadness because it was a special day for us that we would never forget.

We did visit my dad and stepmother Celia and stopped by to see my brother, Kennie. They were not very nice and had nothing good to say! After a short visit, we left for our wedding supper of hamburgers, fries, and cokes. In Maywood, our new home would be a small duplex I had recently rented. We drove there and I carried my new bride over the threshold. Now we were husband and wife. It was a happy time for us and we looked forward to a long and happy life together. Dreams do come true and this was just the beginning.

Our conversations about moving to the Ozarks had begun shortly after our first meeting, but it took 42 years to come true. We never gave up but always knew it would happen if we kept our faith.

Following my railroad career became hectic at times! We moved often but Joyce handled it well, complaining only once when we moved from Los Angeles to Yermo, California. With two little girls, it was hard to leave the city life behind in exchange for the small Mohave desert town of Yermo. It was far away from everything we had always enjoyed. With my four-year apprenticeship program now completed, she knew what a railroader's life was all about since it was her dad's career too. We did the best we could and moved several more times before settling down in Colorado.

We arrived in Golden, Colorado on Labor Day of 1965 and I continued my job with the Union Pacific Railroad. Over the next four years I worked in the Denver Coach Yard and Union Station. My job was working passenger cars and running trains out of Union Station on the afternoon shift. We rented the first two years but bought a home in 1967 on Pearson Street in Wheat Ridge, Colorado. Life for us was improving, but since I needed extra money to provide for my wife and three little girls, I also got a part-time job as a painter. This allowed us to take vacations every year back to see my mom in Vicksburg, Mississippi as well as visits to my other family living in Utah and California.

Temptation and Disappointments

In 1966, an opportunity presented itself to those interested in going to Alaska and working for the Alaskan Railroad. It was a place many of us thought to be an exciting change in railroading, but only two men applied. They were accepted, given a one-year leave of absence, and headed north. The work would be hard and the winters cold, but at the end of the contract, they were happy to return to their old jobs in Denver.

It was tempting to me at first, but since my family and I had bounced around for nearly seven years, I passed up the opportunity and stayed where I was. Our oldest daughter, Connie, was six and I didn't want to disrupt her schooling or take our other two girls away from their family and friends.

Later, after hearing the horror stories from those who went to Alaska, I was happy about the choice I made. It proved something to me that I had heard all my life: The grass isn't greener on the other side.

The first move we made was not to a place of my choosing; it was brought on by the railroad. If I had not accepted the position in Yermo, I would have lost my job in 30 days. I had just completed my apprenticeship and facing a layoff sealed my fate. It was a place with horror stories associated with it and most everyone I knew had turned down the opportunity to go. My friend, Benny McGraw, his wife Karen, and their six kids had gone there one year before me for the same reason.

This little desert town was halfway between Los Angeles and Las Vegas and was a location where train crews made a turn around. The town was small but had been much larger in the '40s and '50s. The old timers living in town and the outlying area had moved there during and after World War II and took jobs at the local military base between Yermo and Daggett. The Yermo railroad shops had been much larger during the war, but slowly, jobs were depleted in all crafts. During my tenure there, we had less than 25 men. Barstow was the largest town where most families did their shopping.

It was a place no one wanted to live but a few families had moved there for relief from health problems. Living in Yermo proved to be our Hell on earth. I never quit dreaming about moving on to a better life for my wife and family.

From Yermo, we moved to Salt Lake City, Utah where we lived for two years. We then went on to Kansas City, Missouri in September of 1965. This job never materialized and I was sent to Denver, Colorado, where we would settle down and raise our family.

As the years passed, job offers came and went. One of them was an offer to work for a family member in his business located in Vicksburg. At first it sounded great, and it would mean a chance to return to my hometown where most of my family lived. Being close to my family again was something I always wanted, but the money and benefits were not like what I had on the railroad. I had to push those thoughts out of my mind and decided to keep my job in Colorado.

A few years later, my brother, Marshall, approached me with a job offer in Utah. He wanted me to join him in a business of management and maintenance for apartment complexes close to Hill Field Air Base. They were located north of Salt Lake and not far from Ogden, Utah. If I chose to accept, the plan was for me to transfer from my railroad job in Denver to Salt Lake on the Union Pacific Railroad and work the business together. There again, it generated an interest but I soon put it out of my mind and stayed where I was.

Life for me, my wife, and our four daughters was always

great. We lived in beautiful homes and drove nice cars and had everything we needed, along with a few of the finer things in life. We bought property 18 miles west of Denver in Jefferson County and hired a contractor to build our first new home. Eventually, we sold it and bought another new home less than a mile away. Over the next 10 years, we bought and sold two more new homes and three older homes.

As you can see, Joyce and I enjoyed moving, but there were no more cross-country moves. We never moved very far and our kids never changed schools. They were able to keep their friends and attended the same church until they finished high school.

We did have other hair-brained ideas! The one that nearly materialized was a railroad job in Shreveport, Louisiana. Our youngest daughter, Kim, was just three years old and this job was with the Missouri Pacific Railroad. Our plan was to buy a home in Hosten, Louisiana that was built in the late 1800s. It was located on Highway 71 in the northwest corner of the state, 15 miles south of the Arkansas state line. It was in need of repairs but was set on 25 acres with a five-acre lake. There was a six-stall carport plus a six-car garage and the lake was stocked with fish. The owner was a 90-year-old man who had lived there for 20 years. Everything was in need of repair, but only a few rooms had been lived in; the rest sat empty. It was a two-story house with an attic and over 4000 square feet. There was a thousand-gallon water tower that had been used since the house was built and a new well had been in use for over a year.

We thought this was an answer to our prayers but we were still living in the home we had built. I was in contact with the union representative and also the general car foreman and was promised a job as soon as I could make the move. Now our home was listed and sold fast. I then contacted the Missouri Pacific Railroad and gave them a date when I could be there. On that call, I got the shock of my life. I was told that an unexpected layoff had occurred and the position was no longer available.

We were now without a home and had to find one right away. Less than 24 hours later, we found one less than one mile away. It was a model for a community of homes and was the only one left. We liked what we saw and we were fortunate enough to be able to write a contract, get okayed for the loan, and close before the buyers of our home would be moving in. Since it was a model home, we bought all the drapes and curtains along with other wall decorations.

It was a brick tri-level with a basement, three bedrooms, two baths, and a single-car garage. The move that got our hopes up had just about turned into a disaster but it worked out great for us. The kids kept their friends and their school and would continue attending the same church.

This was another lesson well learned. Our temptations to move were about to come to an end. Our itchy feet were cured once and for all and we found Colorado to be the best place for us. We would now settle down and I would continue my railroad career until I retired.

Our Biggest Temptation Ever

In 1967, I met Don Gosnell. He hired on with the Union Pacific Railroad and took a job with me in the Denver Coach Yard. His previous job had been working for Kennecott Copper Mines, headquartered in Silver City, New Mexico. He had just completed an 18-month assignment in Lima, Peru, where he had worked as a supervisor in a tire recapping shop for heavy equipment.

Everything he talked about while living and working in Peru was interesting and it sounded like something I would enjoy. Don, his wife, and two kids would become our friends while living in Denver and working for the railroad.

About a year into our friendship, Don's brother contacted him with another offer to return to Lima on the job he left. The wages were still great and were much more than his railroad salary. He was also exempt from taxes. He asked if I would be interested if a job was available! I was but wanted to talk it over with Joyce and was surprised to find her very excited to go.

I got back with him a few days later and told him to check it out and if a position came up, I would consider it. Within a week, he came to work all excited and said a supervisor's position in charge of inspecting and maintaining railroad ore cars would soon be available. Since this was the trade I had gone to school for, I was willing to accept it. There was no physical work involved and all I had to do was supervise a repair shop crew that inspected and repaired railcars used to haul copper ore out of the mines.

Speaking Spanish wasn't required since there would be a translator working with me. At first, Don couldn't speak the language, but he'd had no problem communicating after working there for 18 months.

I contacted Don's brother and supplied him with a copy of my apprenticeship certificate along with my work history. The job was mine if I wanted it.

Kennecott would pay transportation for me and my family to Lima, plus our health insurance, housing, and private schooling for our kids. We would also be provided with a furnished, private home with maid and a gardener along with a vehicle. But to get these benefits, I would have to sign a contract to complete the entire 18 months. I would also have two weeks paid vacation every six months and free round-trip airfare for me and my family anywhere in the states.

Leaving the railroad wouldn't keep me from returning to my job in Denver because I would be taking a leave of absence and would lose only my pay and benefits until I returned.

Joyce and I were thrilled with this opportunity but first we had to make arrangements to store our furniture and vehicles. We were renting a house and not bound to a lease, which would make our move much easier.

Joyce's mother had lost her vision in 1964 and we had been helping her in every way we could. At the time we were making plans to leave, we were hoping someone in the family would help out during the time we were away. We spoke with them but no one was willing to take on the responsibility for 18 months. Joyce's dad was still working on the railroad and her mother needed someone to depend on at all times. This looked like a problem that may keep us from going to Peru, but we continued looking for a way.

Everything was soon in order except for shots required for the entire family before leaving. We had three weeks to make up our mind, but after a weekend of serious discussions, Joyce and I agreed it wasn't going to happen without someone taking care of her mom while we were away.

There was nothing more we could do but say no and it left us very disappointed! Don and his brother were understanding but the job was still open if I changed my mind.

Don resigned from the railroad after signing an 18-month contract to return to his old job in Lima. He and his family left Denver and returned to Silver City, New Mexico but his wife decided to stay behind. His two sons from his first marriage went with him to Silver City, and later, after his 18-month commitment ended, he and his wife divorced. He was a good railroad employee and friend but I lost contact with him and never saw him again.

A Change of Pace

I continued working for the Union Pacific till July of 1969, but lost my job when the Denver shops closed. We had a total of 400 jobs but only 55 men would survive; I was one of the unlucky. This put a sour taste in my mouth about the railroad that left me very upset. I had never been unemployed before, and here I was with a wife, three young daughters and one more due in just over a month.

After working more than 13 years for the railroad I thought it was time to find another job. Everyone who was laid off would now be offered a chance to exercise their rights and transfer to other location. The locations on offer were Los Angeles, Yermo, Las Vegas, Salt Lake City, Lincoln, and Omaha.

The only place I even considered was Lincoln, Nebraska, since my friend, Buddy Baker, was Superintendent in the recently built Bailey Train Yard. He had offered me a position as his assistant, which was a big temptation. I told him I would give it some thought and get back with him later.

This wasn't a decision I had to make right away, and I had also been offered a job at Coors Brewery in Golden, Colorado. My friend, Shorty Bernard, was the Superintendent of Construction and he offered me a construction job with better pay. It even sounded like something I might like. I gave it some thought, and because I was so upset about losing my railroad job, it didn't take long till I decided to take him up on his offer.

My connection with the Union Pacific would stay intact and I could take advantage of these other job locations for up to six months. My insurance would also stay active during this period and there would be plenty of time to make a decision. But if I didn't accept a job within six months, I would be paid a small severance package and be removed from the seniority roster without a chance of going back to the Union Pacific Railroad.

Joyce was due with our fourth daughter the last week of August and we couldn't afford to be without an income! My last day was Friday and I was able to start my new job the following Monday. I never lost any pay and still had one month's back pay coming.

Working for Coors paid $1.25 an hour more than the railroad but the benefits were fewer. I would be starting a new job and unfortunately, it would take two years before I would earn one week's vacation. I would now have to decide if I wanted to give up 13 years of railroading for a new trade that I had never worked in before.

My retirement was already vested after working 10 years with the railroad, and Coors didn't have a good retirement program like I already had. It was a big decision and I only had six months to make up my mind.

One thing that I found difficult to get accustomed to was that beer was available for all Coors constructions employees on their 9:00am break, during lunch and afternoon breaks, and all you could drink at the end of your shift. The free beer was only 3.2%, but it was enough to cloud your mind and create an unsafe work environment. I didn't drink alcohol myself, and on the railroad, I had served three one-year terms on the safety committee. On the railroad, any employee testing positive for alcohol or drugs would have been fired immediately.

For me, it was hard to accept this unsafe practice! Most of the men didn't go overboard, but there were some who would drink all they could on their morning break and do it all over again for lunch and their afternoon break. When their shift ended, many went to the cafeteria, drank all they wanted, and drove home drunk. One of the men I worked with was stopped by the Colorado State Highway Patrol; at the age of 64 and close to retirement, was arrested and taken to jail. His car was impounded, his license was taken away for one year, and he lost his job.

Another employee was killed two hours after his midnight shift ended. He was speeding on Coors property when he ran off the road, hit a tree, and died on the scene. This all happened before 9:00am. There ended up being a long court battle before Coors finally settled with the man's family for millions of dollars.

This was in 1969 and drinking often got out of hand. It really bothered me. The work was dangerous enough without being drunk so I gave much thought to whether I should leave or stay.

Shorty Bernard, the man who hired me, was a good friend and I felt bad about quitting, but I had been given an out if needed. He had told me if I ever decided to quit to give a written two-week notice, which I agreed to.

Being a railroader was an addiction in a way, but it was a job I always enjoyed even though I had worked at four locations and in three different states. A railroader traveling to different locations was called a *boomer*, and maybe at one time that fit me. But now, I was ready to get back and settle down.

I would carry out the wish of my friend and give two weeks' notice before resigning. In the last week of August, I wrote a letter of resignation to Coors Brewery and my last day was September 7th, 1969. I had already been offered a job with the Colorado and Southern Railroad and would begin on September 9th at the Colorado & Southern Rice Yard in Denver.

Before I left Coors, our fourth daughter, Kimberly Jo, was born on August 28th at Lutheran Hospital in Wheat Ridge. Joyce was given a special room for Coors employees and a beautiful bouquet of flowers was delivered to her room.

Coors was a great company in many ways that had close to 6,000 employees, but felt I was doing what was best for me and my family. I now had a strong urge to return to my old trade and make it a lifetime career.

Transferring to another location was still a temptation, but I decided to take my severance pay and give up my seniority and connection with the Union Pacific Railroad. For 13 years, it had been a great job and it taught me many lessons about what it took to be a good railroad employee.

My four-year apprenticeship program in Los Angeles had required eight hours of schooling each week and 32 hours of on-the-job training. I felt I had been taught a great trade and was thankful for an opportunity that provided an income and great benefits for me and my family.

I began my new job on the Colorado and Southern Railroad on September 9, 1969 and was thrilled to be back home. Being a railroader was the same on all lines no matter where you were. The men in my craft were called *cartoads* and we were a very special breed. It never took long for me to adjust to the job and the men.

In 1974, the Colorado and Southern Railroad merged with the Chicago, Burlington and Quincy, along with four other railroads and became the Burlington Northern. This gave me and many others better job protection, and after working 17 years on the afternoon and midnight shifts, I was able to work days, although I never got Saturdays and Sundays off until 1981.

During these mergers, many employees with the least amount of seniority were forced to other locations. Some chose to do what I did on the Union Pacific but were not as lucky as me and never made it back to Denver.

After 43 years, I had paid my dues and was now in the top

10 on the seniority roster. My job would be secure and protected for the next 19 years while I worked in Golden. I was a Burlington Northern, Santa Fe employee but worked on Coors property as an inspector and repair man. All cars used to transport beer from Golden across the U.S. would be inspected by me and my friend Ed Jacobs until I retired on May 1st, 2000. Ed was number one and I was number two on the roster and we had our pick of jobs in the Colorado seniority district, which included Denver and Golden, Colorado; Alliance, Nebraska; and Guernsey, Wyoming. After scrambling for job locations and getting the leftovers for 31 years, it was great being on top for a change.

Singing with The Gatlin Brothers

It was December 2002 and Larry Gatlin and the Gatlin Brothers Band would be performing a three-week Christmas special in Branson. Joyce and I were members of The Best Is Yet to Come choir and D.K. and Sherrie Brewster were asked to provide seven members from their choir to sing back-up. When Joyce and I were asked, we were not only thrilled but shocked and could hardly believe we would be a part of something so special. The Christmas show would be held at a local theater with two performances each day from December 1st till the 22nd. Other members in our choir who joined us were D.K. and Sherrie, along with their daughter, Jaimee, and Lois Baldsmeir.

The local Branson Baptist church would also provide seven members from their choir, but only eight at a time would perform on stage for each show. A list was made up in advance, so everyone knew what programs they would be performing in.

At first, most of us had stage fright, but not like it had been the year before for the three-day Dino, Spring, and Easter Spectacular. The entire 78-member, *The Best is Yet to Come* choir performed in all six shows and it got easier each time.

The theater held 750 and was always sold out. It was a big hit for everyone and a great thrill for the back-up singers every time we walked out on stage.

We wore bright-colored sweaters, scarfs and hats, and before each show, there was a half-hour practice session. No words or music were ever used since all the songs were old-time favorites.

We met Larry and his brothers, Steve and Rudy, along with the band, and refreshments were furnished for everyone after the last show. It was such a special event for everyone that Joyce and I never thought was possible and an experience we would never forget.

It was so much fun being a part of this special show and we had never thought there would be any pay for our services, but each performer was paid union scale. Everyone cashed their checks and framed the stubs for souvenirs.

After performing on stage for three weeks, we became much more relaxed, and our voices sounded better together. This experience allowed us to meet many new people and help us be confident singers for the audience.

Something did happen, however, that surprised us all and that was that the band members had instruments but went through the motions without ever making a sound. The soundtrack for the music was played and the only real performers were the Gatlin Brothers and the back-up singers.

Clem School Reunion

In September 2002, we attended my school reunion in Magee, Mississippi. It was our first to attend and we saw family friends I hadn't seen in 46 years. My four stepbrothers and two stepsisters also attended. It was great seeing them, but we had all changed.

Clem was a little country school that never had more than 200 kids attending each year throughout its history. The doors had closed in the spring of 1957 after the school year ended. It left an empty space in this little farm community and it was a sad day for all the kids and their families. This was not just a class reunion, but rather one for anyone who had ever attended our little school.

Joyce and I drove down from Branson the day before and rented a motel in Magee. Over the years, we had visited Mississippi many times but I hadn't been back to Magee since 1956.

From Branson, we drove south on Highway 65 across the

beautiful Ozarks down to Conway, Arkansas. We then took Interstate 40 to Little Rock and over to Memphis. From there, we headed south on Highway 61, better known as "The Blues Highway," down to Vicksburg. This was always home to me even though I was born in Meridian.

We made it to Magee in the late afternoon and took a drive through town before checking into our room. Nothing looked like I remembered it, but it was still a nice little country town.

The next day we arrived early for the reunion but so did all the others. The handshakes and hugs were many as Joyce and I made our way through strange faces, introducing ourselves. We were also strangers to them but Joyce had met my stepbrothers and stepsisters many years before, in the early years of our marriage.

Tables were assigned and soon everyone settled down and took their seats. The room became quiet and after a prayer was said, things got underway. One by one, each guest got up and introduced themselves and spoke a few words. After the introductions and speeches, a local band played while everyone went through the buffet line. We returned to our tables and enjoyed a great lunch while talking about old times.

Like us, some of my stepsiblings lived far away from the little farm community of Clem and didn't visit very often. Hiawatha lived in France, Ben was in south Texas, Marion lived in Houston, and Roosevelt, Margie, and Virgie still lived in the Clem community. At the time, my brother, Marshall, was in Utah and Alton Ray was in California. My only sister, Mae, and her husband, Gene, lived in northeast Texas. Not all the family made it to the reunion but those who did had a great time.

Over the years, I had lost my oldest brother, Kennie, along with three stepbrothers, M.L., Bilbo, and Johnnie Cecil Heggins. They were all young and left behind wives and many children. My mom and dad were also gone and so was my stepdad.

At 5:00pm, the reunion came to an end and everyone said goodbye. The parking lot was soon empty except for Joyce, Roosevelt, and me. For a while longer, we would swap a few more memories but then it was time to say goodbye. It had been a fun day but it was also sad as we drove away.

I would never see him or my other stepbrothers or sisters again. As I write this, all of them have passed away except Hiawatha, Marion, and Virgie. Like myself, they too are in their winter years. My three biological brothers are all gone. Mae and I are the only Stephenson kids left, but God has been good to us and we have much to be thankful for.

Attending the Clem School reunion holds many memories for me but someday we'll all be together again.

After filling up my car with gas and getting something to drink, we left Magee around 6:00pm and made it to Gulfport, Mississippi shortly after sundown. From there, we drove over to

Slidel, Louisiana, rented a motel, and later had dinner.

It was Labor Day weekend and we left for home early Monday morning. The weather was beautiful as we made our way north to Vicksburg and on to Memphis. From there, we followed the same route and it wasn't long till we could see our favorite Ozark mountains. We turned off on Highway 65 north at Conway, Arkansas and made it home before dark.

It had been a great trip and a fun time renewing old memories with family and friends! Joyce and I were happy to be home and we had missed our little Sycamore Log Church and friends in The Best Is Yet to Come ministry.

Changing Seasons

Summer was coming to an end and we were looking forward to cooler weather. Roark Ridge is one of the highest points in Missouri, and is beautiful in all seasons. It was impossible for me to keep the leaves raked, but at least mowing the lawn and raking leaves, along with all the other work, kept me from ever having to visit the gym. We continued our activities with The Best Is Yet to Come ministry, attended our little Sycamore Log Church each Sunday, and visited Silver Dollar City often! Fall in the Ozarks had been our favorite time since we had started visiting each October 20 years before.

The theme for Silver Dollar City was late 1800s and 1900s, with more tourists in the fall than any other time of the year. We bought season tickets our first year and attended 19 times but never got tired of going. It was the most peaceful, beautiful and interesting place we had ever lived in or visited, and folks were different from any place we had ever been. Yet though living in the Ozarks was our dream come true, it became a major health problem for Joyce after our first year.

She began having breathing problems and ultimately developed asthma. After many visits to her doctor, she was found to be highly allergic to most vegetation but the main cause was cedar trees. It was worse in the spring and fall, but the year-round high humidity compounded the problem. Even with all the prescribed medications, nothing seemed to work and she fought it every day.

She stayed inside most of the time. Before I would leave the house with Joyce, I would start the car and turn on the air a few minutes before she came out. This would help but it continued to be a problem for the rest of the time we lived there. We prayed she would get better but rarely was there a time when she felt good. Inside the house, we ran the air conditioning and dehumidifier most of the time and this helped keep the air dry. When we did venture out, she had to use an inhaler until we got to a place where there was air conditioning. Most of our activities were inside so I always dropped her off at the front door to escape the hot, humid air.

Spending two hours each Sunday morning at the Sycamore Log Church was also a problem. With no air conditioning and only two ceiling fans and four open windows, she always used an inhaler.

After more than three years of treatment by Dr. James Lukavsky, who was a friend but also a member of the Best is Yet to Come ministry, he suggested we move to a drier climate. If we didn't, Joyce would have to spend the rest of her life fighting a problem that would never go away.

This was a big disappointment for us and difficult to hear, but exhausted from the long battle, we began making plans to leave Missouri.

While living in Colorado, Joyce had had seasonal allergies but nothing like she had presently in Missouri. Our first thoughts were to move to Arizona or New Mexico, but we decided it would be best to go back to our old hometown of Arvada, where we had lived for 35 years. I called a realtor and together we decided on a listing price. Signs were posted on Highway 248 and in front of the house.

It was spring of 2004 and real estate prices were not at their best. After a workup on sales in the area, we listed it for $199,000.00. In Colorado, a home like ours was selling for a half million dollars on a small city lot; with 8.7 acres, the price would have been a million dollars. In addition to a large house, there was two acres of lawn with many huge shade trees and four fruit trees. It was in the country and 1000 feet off the highway, a perfect location where wildlife could be seen daily. There were turkeys, deer, coyotes, bears, possums, racoons, armadillos, along with many squirrels and rabbits. The birds were also plentiful, as were rattlesnakes and copperheads. The chiggers and ticks along with poison oak and ivy were everywhere but we learned to avoid them.

There was one extra thing the buyer was getting, and that was his own personal ghost. Bob had not quit strolling through the house and Joyce often saw him. I had never seen him but heard and felt his presence many times. We normally didn't experience destructive pranks from him, other than a sighting Joyce had a few weeks leading up to the move.

One night, she was having problems sleeping and went out to the guest bedroom and soon fell asleep. Later she woke up, turned over facing the window, and saw a figure lying on his side facing away from her. The room was brightly lit from the outside security light and she got a silhouette view of someone fully dressed, lying on the bed. She became terrified and ran into our bedroom, jumping in bed with me. She snuggled up close and woke me to tell me what she had seen. Now I was frightened so I got up and made another check of the house. Like always, nothing had been disturbed. Bob had simply showed his presence once again and disappeared. That was shortly after Christmas of 2004 and his presence was never seen or heard again. Our friendly ghost was known to most of our friends at church and the Best is Yet to Come ministry, including our neighbors, Tom and Jeannie. The previous owner, of course, also knew.

I think most everyone thought we made up the story but it

was true. Still, we thought it was best not to say anything to the new buyers. Even after moving back to Colorado, every time something strange happened in our house, Bob got the blame. We both had been skeptics but became believers after living on Roark Ridge for nearly five years.

A deal was made with the buyers to keep our dog, Rowdy. She lived out her life on the ridge and died at the age of 16! The family who bought our home still lives there but our neighbors, Tom and Jeannie, sold their place and moved away shortly after we left. If Bob still shows his presence, we haven't heard of it.

Before leaving Branson, our plan was to sell everything and buy new furnishings when we got to Colorado. All we planned on keeping was bedding, pictures, dishes and silverware, wall decorations, some decorative rugs and a few garden tools.

We didn't want to sell anything until we found someone interested in buying the house. Our life with The Best is Yet to Come ministry and the little Sycamore Log Church continued, but Joyce's health never got better. She was soon sleeping in a recliner or propped up in bed every night.

We continued to visit Colorado and each time the problem would go away until we got back to Missouri.

In the fall of 2004, a couple from New Hampshire was vacationing in Branson and the husband was close to retirement. He planned to retire in January of 2005 and Branson was a place of interest for them. He wanted to check out our house before leaving, so he got in touch with our realtor to set up an appointment for a showing.

It was a Saturday morning in August when they showed up with their daughter & son-in-law and two grandkids. We waited outside to answer their questions but they left after a two-hour tour. We thought they were just more lookers and pushed it out of our minds. Then a week went by and we got a call with an offer of full price, contingent upon the family selling their home first. We were hesitant about that arrangement and didn't want to take it off the market, but we decided after a week to accept. We wrote a contract but still worried something might cause the deal to fall through.

Everything was now for sale and we made plans to close before the end of the year. We began having garage sales on weekends and sold many items, holding back on the furniture and appliances. As the weeks and months passed, we decided to offer a special deal to the buyer and made out an itemized list of the furniture and appliances to give to our realtor. Shortly after Christmas of 2004, it was sent to the buyer and they agreed to take everything without questions. Over the phone a closing date was set and the sale was finalized.

On January 21st, we rented a small U-Haul truck and a car hauler for my pick-up and everything we planned on taking to Colorado was loaded. Joyce would drive her car. We were on our way back to Colorado before noon and arrived in Denver at 4:30

pm the following day, which was Joyce's 62nd birthday. We had reserved a storage shed in Wheat Ridge and with the help of my son-in-law, Loren, everything was unloaded and the truck and car hauler were returned before 7:00 that night.

For two months, we stayed with our daughter, Kim, and her husband, John, with plans of looking for a townhome. We began immediately and after a month, we found a beautiful three-story townhouse in Wheat Ridge. It was 1600 square feet and had a two-car garage, two bedrooms, two baths, a deck off each bedroom, plus a deck off the dining room and a front porch that faced the lake. It would be a step down from what we had in Missouri but we grew to love it! There was no furniture or appliances, so Joyce and I spent another month shopping for what we needed. It was fun for both of us.

On March 10th, 2005, we moved in and arrangements were made to have the furniture and appliances delivered. It was the easiest move we had ever made because we simply had everything brought from the storage shed and our home was complete.

After settling down in Colorado, we had to make another trip back to Branson and get our motor home. We took five days and visited our friends at the Sycamore Log Church and the Best is Yet to Come ministry before heading back. We had a good time but it was sad again when we left – perhaps not as sad as it was the first time.

Joyce drove her car and followed me in the motor home. We stopped often along the way for gas and food and spent the first night in a Walmart parking lot in Salina, Kansas. We left the next morning and arrived at an RV storage facility in Wheat Ridge late that evening.

Gas was nearly $4.00 a gallon so the motor home would stay in storage until it sold the following September. Large motor homes weren't very popular with gas prices out of sight and getting rid of a 38-foot motor home wasn't easy. On that trip back from Branson, we found it would be much cheaper to stay in the best hotels and motels than to pay such a high price for gas while getting only five to six miles per gallon. From Branson to Denver was 840 miles and that trip made us realize that a motorhome wasn't a cheap way to travel.

We settled down in our new home and right away, we began taking walks around Tomlinson Park. It was still under construction when we moved in but after a beautification project on the dam, which included building new walking paths and constructing several pieces of exercise equipment and a children's playground, it became very popular with local residents, including Joyce and me. Once around the lake is one-half mile and we walked at 7:00 every morning except Sunday, when we went to church. We started out with four laps but moved up to eight after a month. We met new friends and our group soon grew to seven. We started meeting for breakfast at Denny's every other Tuesday and still meet there from 8:30 till 11:00 am.

In October 2015, my granddaughter, Melanie Hafke, had plans to be married and her request for me was to perform her wedding. This took me by surprise, since I wasn't an ordained minister, but she wouldn't take no for an answer. After two months, with her help, I became an ordained Christian minster and performed the ceremony. It was a beautiful wedding and everything went like clockwork, completely legal and binding. There were many friends and family who attended and the reception was fun for everyone with great Mexican food and a beautiful cake. I have to say, I was very nervous but I pulled it off, and for an old grandpa, they say I did great.

These days, I get together once a month with my retired railroad friends for lunch at the Golden Corral. There are always 20 to 35 attending and we spend a few hours talking over old times. Our ages range from the 60s all the way to 90. Sharing memories with each other makes for a fun time for everyone, especially since some of us have known each other or worked together over 50 years. We've been together so long, it's more like a family reunion each month. The railroads we represent are the Burlington Northern/Santa Fe and the Colorado and Southern, including all crafts.

I'm still good friends with Ray Dizmang, who I met on Thanksgiving Day in 1965. He had a paint business and I was in need of a part-time job. I went to work for him in January of 1966 and the job lasted seven years. We have coffee at McDonald's together every Monday, Wednesday, and Friday. The two of us and our wives get together one each month for lunch at one of our favorite restaurants.

Joyce and I also have lunch together every Sunday and our favorite places are Red Lobster, Olive Garden, Red Robin, and Chili's. Sometimes we need a change and the Black-Eyed Pea will work, but then we go back to our favorites. Our fast food favorites are Taco Bell and McDonald's.

For a long time after moving back to Colorado in 2005, we attended Faith Bible Chapel, but later began to stay home and watch different preachers on TV. We started watching John Hagee on Sunday morning at 7:00 and that grew to become a habit that hasn't yet been broken. We also watch Hal Lindsey at 9:00 on Sunday night.

Our lifestyle has definitely changed with age, but both of us agree that makes it great. Old habits are hard to break and since we created them together over the last 58 years, we only occasionally have differences about where and what we will be doing each week.

Joyce loves to shop and I go with her sometimes, but she would prefer to go with our daughters or granddaughter, which is okay with me. But we always do grocery shopping together on the first day of the month. It takes all day since she goes to several stores for the bargains.

House cleaning is always on Friday and we both have a list of things to do. We try to finish up about 4:00 pm, and have dinner by 5:30. Joyce always makes her favorite hamburgers with lettuce, tomato, onion, and cheese and serves them with her favorite French fries along with chips and pickles. She's been doing this since I retired in May of 2000 and it's always a special night for us because her hamburgers are the very best!

As Joyce and I look back at our 58 years together and see where we came from, most of our memories make us happy. A few bring sadness to our hearts and tears in our eyes. Yet, if we had a chance to go back and do it over, there's very little we would change. From our four daughters, we were given 13 grandkids and 12 great-grandkids (though I'm sure that number will change) who we love very much. They are all good kids and we pray that they have a long, healthy, and prosperous life ahead of them. If there could only be one thing that I would like them to take away from this book, it is that although Joyce and I were young when we first met, we had enough love for each other to last forever, and that has made all the difference in the world.

PLAY THE SONGS

Chorus

Play the songs we always danced to,
Play the songs we used to sing,
Songs that always made us happy,
Songs that taught us many things!

Verse #1

Singers from the past have been our heroes,
Living out the songs they wrote and sang,
Teaching life before we ever lived it,
Helping us to understand most everything!

Verse #2

Hank Williams wrote about the many heartbreaks,
Teaching us about a cheating heart.
He made us think about what really happens,
When songs he sang were on the music chart.

Verse #3

409

The Grand Ole Opry entertained our family,
From Nashville, Tennessee on Saturday night,
We gathered round an ole-time Motorola
And listened to the stars by coal oil light!

Verse #4

From Minnie Pearl, a howdy always welcomed us,
Rod Brassfield, Grandpa Jones not far behind.
Lonzo & Oscar and many others,
Roy Acuff took us on the Wabash line.

Verse #5

The Possum taught us all about white lighting
And what it did when drinking way too much.
He's now a country music legend,
George Jones is known and loved by all of us.

Verse #6

Gone are many heroes and we miss them,
Left with memories never to forget.
Happy days of listening to their music
But never did they leave us with regrets!

ALL ABOARD

God's train is at the station,
It's ready for you to board.
Your ticket was paid at Calvary
And there's never an overload!
No waiting in line, just climb aboard
When it's time for you to leave.
Jesus is waiting there for you
But first you must believe.

Before your life is over
Accept Christ as your king,
He's ready to forgive you of your sins
And his heavenly choir will sing,
This train is run by angels
But God is in control,
He'll take you up to heaven
But first he must save your soul!

Just give your heart to Jesus
And say the sinner's prayer.

411

That's all it takes to make this trip
But faith will take you there.
Your sins will be forgiven
And never remembered again.
You'll meet your friends and loved ones
Over in glory land!

You're going home but it won't take long,
Just a twinkle of an eye.
This train is bound for glory land
And your mansion in the sky!
Your loved ones will be waiting there
When that glory train arrives.
You'll live with them forever
Where no one ever dies!

Face to face, you'll see Jesus
And walk those streets of gold.
There's no more pain or sorrow
Because God has saved your soul.
So climb aboard this heavenly train
And take that final ride!
You'll live in heaven forever
With Jesus by your side!

FRIENDS

You meet them on the Internet
And on your telephone.
You sometimes meet on Facebook
And never leave your home!

You meet them at a grocery store
Or in a shopping mall.
You meet them at your local church
Or when the pastor calls.

You sometimes meet in places
Where you never would expect,
Like at a local emission booth
While writing out a check!

They come in sizes big and small,
Red, yellow, black and white,
You meet because God loves us all
And making friends is right.

While at a weekend yard sale,

You see that special bike;
The owner is a friendly soul
And the asking price is right.

You pass the time with chit-chat,
But much more you will say.
He offers you a lower price
And it's your lucky day.

While at your local flower shop,
A question that you ask,
May lead to a special friendship
And one that just may last!

You spend time at a city park
Where strangers pass each day,
But if you stop and say hello,
Good friends are made this way.

So if you're not in a great hurry
And have some time to spare,
Stop and pass the time of day
And show someone you care.

Our Branson home

Our Branson house

First snow in Branson

Rowdy on Roark Ridge

Joyce and Rufus

Joyce and Rufus at Sycamore Log Church

Pastor Erma

Chloe

Pastor Erma and Hansel

Joyce in the Sycamore Log Church congregation

The Sunday morning congregation

Imogene, Cecil, and Joyce

Singing a goodbye to our friend, Willard Jones

Imogene and Cecil

Ann and Harold Tell

Rufus and Imogene

Our 45th wedding anniversary

Eating our anniversary cake

Joyce and Rufus in 2003

Rufus and George Bryant at the Ministry BBQ

George Jones and DK Brewster

Christmas Celebration at the rest home

Rufus, Joyce, and the rest home visitors

Flay and Ruby

Jaimee, Sherrie, DK, Rufus and Joyce

Cody Brewster, our sound man

Rufus the cameraman

Randy Plummer, DK, Sherrie, Rufus, and Joyce

Randy, Rufus, and Joyce

Rufus and Joyce with the choir

Sherrie, Bill, DK, and Gary Paxton

Rufus, Gary Paxton, and Joyce

Joyce and Santa

RUFUS AND THE

LADYBUGS

433

Written for my great-grandchildren and all the generations to come! I hope you find these stories amusing. Please pass it on to your kids and grandkids and let them know that Papa loves them.

Grandpa Rufus Franklin Stephenson

n a beautiful spring morning, Rufus was sent by his mother to gather vegetables for the evening meal. Everything in this special garden was organically grown and was healthy for his family.

He entered the garden through its big wooden gate. First on his list were tomatoes, which he could see brightly shining in the early morning sun. He picked four of the best and placed them in his basket. Next he needed lettuce, so he began picking the fresh, tender leaves. As he was finishing, strange sounds could be heard. He couldn't tell where they were coming from. After searching up and down the rows he finally discovered they were coming from beneath the lettuce. He began to separate the leaves and was shocked by what he found!

Sitting on a large rock was a bright, orange and black ladybug with wings drooping by its side. Rufus was surprised to see that this tiny creature had been crying. He noticed the dirt around the rock was wet and got up enough courage to speak. He was shocked again when he heard, "My name is Oscar. I'm lost and searching for a safe home for my family."

Finding it very difficult to communicate, Rufus told him to stay on the rock and wait till he returned. He lay the basket on the ground and went to his bedroom. There he found a large magnifying glass and hurried back with it to the garden.

Rufus was surprised once again to find the ladybug still waiting on the rock. With his powerful magnifying glass he could see and communicate much better. The dampness around the rock was much easier to see and Rufus could tell it was caused by Oscar's tears. Unable to fly with his wet wings, Rufus picked Oscar up and placed him in the basket.

Then he remembered a large tomato plant growing next to the old horse barn and hurried over to check it out. It would be a safe hiding place and Rufus told Oscar to stay there while he finished gathering vegetables for his mother. Oscar felt much safer knowing he had found a friend.

Rufus's mother soon called and he headed to the kitchen with his basket full of fresh vegetables. She met him at the door and asked him why it had taken so long. "Playing with ladybugs," he replied, and left the basket on the counter before asking permission to go outside again. His mothing told him it was okay, but to please not harm the ladybugs.

Back to the barn he was headed when he saw a bright, red breasted Robin sitting at the top of the tomato plant. Rufus was frightened, thinking his tiny friend had been eaten, and he began to search for Oscar. He was nowhere to be found!

Rufus sat on the ground and began to cry. But then, he heard a wee voice and was happy to see his tiny friend sitting on his shoulder. "Where have you been?" he asked. "I flew to a nearby fence, found a hiding place, and waited for you to return." Rufus's tiny friend was safe again and began to share more information about his search to find a new home for his family.

Just two days before, the ladybugs were happy and living in a large garden several miles to the north. In this garden, all the ladybugs except Oscar had become ill after eating vegetables contaminated with poison spray. It was an emergency situation but they were able to move to another location in the garden, not knowing how long they would be safe. Oscar was now in charge and he knew his family would surely die if the farmer sprayed again. He had to leave them behind for the time being but would return when a safe home was found for them!

The thoughts of leaving everyone behind made Oscar very sad but something had to be done before it was too late. His six sisters and one brother were named Lucy, Audrey, Cece, Madison, Bella, Riley and Max. He knew his parents would have a big responsibility taking care of them while he was away.

His father's name was Storm and Violet was his mother's name. His dad's name described him well. He was a rough, tough ladybug and was always able to take care of his family. He would continue to do his best. Oscar was heartbroken to leave, but had to try to help them.

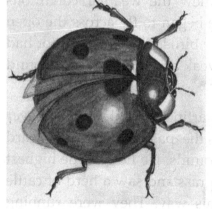

After saying goodbye, Oscar knew they were depending on him to return and take them away from what could surely be their fate. It was hard to keep from crying and he wanted to be brave, but he was also worried that the farmer would return with his poison spray before he found a new home.

Rufus tried to console Oscar and wanted to learn more about where his family was living.

Oscar thought long and hard, then spoke about everything he could remember, hoping something said would be useful.

His search had begun in the early morning hours when the weather was sunny and bright, but the skies became cloudy later in the afternoon and it began to rain. It had become nearly impossible for Oscar to fly, but he found a cornfield and stayed there the rest of the day and through the night. Heavy rain fell and the wind blew, making it hard for Oscar to hang on to the tall corn stalk. His time spent in the corn field was frightening and passed slowly. He also remembered being very cold and hungry.

Later that night the storm moved out and the skies became clear. He could hear the noisy animals and other creatures of the night, making it nearly impossible to fall asleep. His night didn't go very well but he woke up with bright sunlight shining in his eyes! He saw many birds and had to be careful as he flew south. In less than an hour, he was out of the cornfield. But what he was about to face made the cornfield seem like a much safer place.

In front of him was a large open pasture with many cows in it. The only protection was short grass and weeds. To the south, the air was calm and he knew the weather conditions would make flying much easier. He began to fly across the open pasture, keeping a sharp lookout for birds. Since he had not had much to drink or eat, he was very weak and tired but soon found a safe place to rest.

He was starting to think he may never get cross the pasture when he heard strange sounds. He flew to the highest blade of grass and saw a herd of cattle coming his way. They were running fast so he flew as high as he could and landed on the back of a big, red, Brahma Bull. Hiding in the bull's thick bushy hair gave Oscar a safe place to rest as well as a free ride across the empty field. The bull was fast and the distance he covered in a few minutes would have taken Oscar two hours or more. Then suddenly, the bull stopped and all the cattle gathered around bales of sweet smelling hay to eat.

There were swarms of flies everywhere and the cows kept swinging their tails back and forth, trying to keep them away. This was causing problems for Oscar but he kept watching for a chance to fly away without getting hit. When his break came, he began to fly from cow to cow, making a safe escape through all the swinging tails.

Oscar was at the edge of a cotton field when he saw a tractor with a huge white cloud behind it. This looked familiar to him and he knew it was poison spray being applied to the cotton plants. This brought back sad memories of why he had left his family behind. He knew he had to act fast before it was too late.

The tractor stopped at the end of the field and the driver got off. He walked over and got in a pickup truck. As he drove away, Oscar saw a chance for another ride and flew fast as he could, landing in the back. He hid under some loose hay.

After riding more than an hour the old farmer stopped for gas but Oscar stayed under the hay until the tank was filled. Once attendant was paid the truck entered a car wash! Slowly they moved through the big brushes and Oscar could hear the powerful sound of spraying water. He needed to find more protection, so he crawled under the spare tire just in time to be saved from the powerful spray. It seemed like forever before the washer finished, but then the farmer continued down the highway.

After driving a short distance, the truck turned off and the ride became very rough. Oscar knew he was on a gravel road. Soon they stopped again, the door opened and the farmer got out. Oscar wanted to check out the danger and flew to the top of a tall oak tree to get a better view.

It was getting late and the sun was going down. But it was still light enough to survey the farmer's yard. Oscar didn't like what he saw and kept flying south!

While riding in the truck, Oscar never knew how far west he had traveled but he continued south and was soon back on course. There was a little daylight left and he had to find a safe place to stay the night. A few yards away was a large rose bush growing on a wooden fence, which looked safe enough. There he found food to satisfy his hunger and droplets of fresh water to quench his thirst. He climbed down inside a rose and fell fast asleep.

As the evening passed, the sky got dark and the wind began to blow. Suddenly, Oscar woke up. The rose bush was being pulled from the ground! He was hanging on for his life when he heard a loud roaring sound coming from the north. This frightened him even more. He knew that a tornado must be pulling the rose bush out of the ground and blowing it high in the sky. It was spinning out of control but Oscar held on tightly with all his might.

He thought he would surely die as the storm moved south, yet in seconds everything began to calm down. He hung tightly to the rose and the soft breeze carried him to the ground. Where was he now? There had been no rain and it was very dark, so he crawled down under some vegetation and found a large rock where he stayed the night.

The bright sunlight woke him early the next morning. Oscar was still frightened and worried about his family. All he could do was cry. He was just about ready to give up when Rufus found him. Now at least he had some hope of finding a new home for his family!

Rufus explained that his parents owned a small vegetable farm where everything was grown organically. This meant there were no poison of any kind used. The water was pure there. Knowing this made Oscar very happy. It was time to go find his family.

After hearing Oscar's story, Rufus was sure he could find all the ladybugs but told Oscar to stay on the tomato vine until he could make arrangements for them to start searching.

To the house he ran. He told his mother he was going for a bike ride and that he would be home before dark. She said it was okay but to please not be late for supper.

With less than eight hours of daylight left, they would have to hurry and find Oscar's family before dark. The basket on the bike was filled with fresh grass and after Oscar was placed inside, they were on their way.

Rufus thought he knew where the family may be living

and began riding north fast as he could. He stopped often and took Oscar out of the basket to observe the area and Oscar began to recognize the landscape.

For two hours they rode. They stopped once so Rufus could eat the lunch his mother had prepared. Oscar was also taken out of the basket and placed in the tall, sweet clover where he found food and water. After they had finished eating, Oscar was more excited than ever and looking forward to seeing his family. He was anxious to leave so Rufus placed him in the basket and they continued their search.

Once while riding down the gravel road, Rufus looked down and to his surprise Oscar was on the handlebars surveying the farmland. Rufus often stopped and let Oscar look across the fields. Oscar was sure they were getting close.

Rufus reached down on the handlebars and Oscar crawled on the back of Rufus's hand, then Rufus placed him on his shoulder. He could hear much better that way as Oscar gave directions.

At a distance, Oscar recognized the farm, but there again was the farmer spraying more poison. He didn't think they would make it in time but Rufus pedaled as fast as he could in the hopes they would get to the ladybugs before the farmer and his tractor.

The garden was behind a big farmhouse so they rode very quietly, stopping by the garden gate. After leaning his bike against a fence post, Rufus removed the basket and placed it on the ground.

Oscar flew out and began flying from plant to plant! Rufus soon lost sight of him and lay down on the ground, hoping he wouldn't be seen. He knew there was nothing more he could do but wait.

Meanwhile, unknown to Rufus, Oscar had landed at the top of a tall beanpole. When he looked down he was surprised to see his family huddled together on the ground! He flew down and joined them. His dad was the first to see him soaring through the air and all the others saw him as he was landing.

Everyone was so happy he had returned that they gathered around and began to hug and kiss him. Oscar was happy too that his family had survived.

Soon the excitement was over and it was time to make their escape. The farmer was getting close with his poison spray. Oscar flew back and forth through the garden and soon found Rufus. Rufus took the basket, made his way to where everyone was hiding, and gently laid it on the ground while Oscar instructed his family to fly inside. One by one they made their way and were soon all safe.

Rufus picked up the basket and Oscar flew to his shoulder. They headed for the bike and reattached the basket. Oscar wanted to ride with his family and flew back into the basket.

Then a loud voice was heard coming from the big farmhouse. The farmer's wife had seen them! Rufus turned the bike around and as they rode away, she was screaming and waving her broom. But they escaped. When Rufus stopped to check on the ladybugs, he could hear them laughing and singing.

Oscar crawled from under the grass and flew back to Rufus's shoulder. He had one more request and that was to ride on the handlebars the rest of the way.

As they rode into Rufus's driveway, the sun was nearly down and Rufus's mother told him to get ready for supper. He asked if there was enough time to do one more chore before coming in and she said it was okay, but to please hurry and get washed up.

He continued to the garden, where Oscar flew to his shoulder again. Rufus opened the big gate and went to the place where he had first found Oscar and he flew back to the basket and joined his family. Rufus couldn't understand their chatter, but Oscar flew out with a message. They wanted to thank him for what he had done and the children all wanted to have a chance to sit on Rufus's shoulder before settling in to their new home.

One by one, they made the flight and when they were lined up, Violet and Storm joined the others and expressed their thanks as well.

Now it was time for Oscar to take them to their new home. He flew to the big rock where Rufus had found him and his family joined him there. Rufus took out his magnifying glass one more time and could see them sitting in a circle. They were now happy and began to dance and sing.

Soon, Rufus heard his mother's call and it was time for him to go. But before leaving, he made a promise to Oscar and his family that their new home would always be safe and that they would never have to live in fear again. He promised to visit them often!

Rufus stood with tears in his eyes. One fell on the rock below where he had found Oscar. As he left he made another promise to the ladybugs and to himself. There would never be any poison used in his family garden. He rode away with happiness in his heart.

Soon Rufus was washed up and sitting at the supper table. His father gave thanks for the food and Rufus said a special prayer for his ladybug friends, thanking God for what they do to help the farmers. When he began to eat his salad, a smile came across his face as he remembered the adventure he had that day. Again his mother asked what he had been doing, but he just smiled and said, "Playing with ladybugs". His father said that was okay, but to always remember to be gentle because ladybugs were great friends to the farmer.

As the days passed, Rufus was always looking for Oscar but he never saw him again. Every time he saw a ladybug, he called him Oscar, but he hoped he would someday see his friend again.

After Oscar and his family came to the garden, it became more beautiful and many ladybugs could be seen throughout. Rufus knew there were many Oscars there to take care of the family garden. He would always remember to take care of them too.

LEON THE HERO RABBIT

or weeks, Farmer Brown had been making plans to add an acre of land to his produce farm. Located just ten miles east of Vicksburg, Mississippi, this new addition would double the farm's size. His property was at the edge of Big Black Swamp. Many large trees and thick vegetation bordered his vegetable garden so all kinds of birds and animals of the forest made their home there.

Throughout their lives, these defenseless little critters depended on the forest for food and shelter. Some had built their homes in tall trees, some were deep underground or under rocks, and others lived in hollow logs. They didn't know of Farmer Brown's plan to extend his farm and were shocked to hear that everything above ground would soon be destroyed. Nothing could be done to stop it.

Early one spring morning, huge bulldozers and their operators arrived and within an hour, giant trees were being pushed to the ground and stacked in huge piles at the edge of the swamp. The animals and birds began to panic, flying and running to escape the danger. It was a nightmare for them. They barely escaped with their lives! Bit by bit, throughout the day, everything was destroyed, leaving no place for the animals to live. They were forced to retreat to an unexplored part of the forest.

At last, the long day came to an end and the sun disappeared behind the trees. The animals and birds were now alone in strange surroundings, just doing their best to survive. The small section of forest they once called home was gone and they would be spending the night among some of the most frightening and unfriendly critters in the swamp.

The large Alligator waited in the shadows to devour anything that moved, and the sounds of the swamp were unfamiliar. The big Bullfrog croaked and the wise old Owl sitting high in the tree made frightening sounds while the defenseless and homeless creatures sat silent in darkness, hoping to survive the night.

As evening passed, their fear become greater than ever. They began to gather away from the water where they thought they would be out of danger from the many unfriendly creatures.

One by one, the Rabbits hopped to safety under the guidance of Leon, who was the oldest and wisest member of his family. He had grown big and strong from eating the vegetables in Farmer Brown's garden and from being chased by his old hound dog, Luke.

Leon was brave and knew the best times to feast on Farmer Brown's garden. He also knew the best escape routes and could outsmart Ole Luke any day of the week. Other family members had also been taught these things and they too had become stronger and wiser in time.

As they gathered to make plans for their new homes, Brother Opossum and many of his family and friends were also ready to follow Leon, depending on him to be their leader. Raccoons and Squirrels showed up with their families as well but they would wait until daylight before venturing out and exploring on their own.

Throughout the evening, Skunks and Chipmunks arrived, along with many birds, and together they found safety away from the water. Leon spoke of his plans for the next day and much attention was given to what he had to say. With less than an hour of daylight left, he talked about the many dangers they faced and how they would be working together to build new homes. They now felt much safer knowing Leon would be in charge and they found special places to stay for the night.

Soon the animals were all sleeping despite the many strange and frightful sounds around them. After what seemed to be only minutes, the sun began to light the forest and the birds began to chirp and fly, while all the other animals and their families moved about on the ground and in the trees.

Leon soon called them together and had their attention. They were all anxiously waiting to hear his plan but their first question was, where would their new homes be built? He told them of a large pipe he once used while hiding from Ole Luke: It was twelve feet long and Farmer Brown had left it at the edge of the forest when making changes to his irrigation system. With their huge bulldozers, the operators had covered the pipe with tons of dirt and debris and if it was lying in the right direction, all their problems could be solved.

Earlier in the day, Leon had seen one end of the pipe sticking out on the north side and thought it was large enough for everyone to crawl through. If it went under the debris far enough, they might find a safe place for their new home at the other end. This needed to be investigated more and Leon was soon checking it out. They were all much more hopeful and exited now, anxiously waiting for him to make his final inspection.

As he hopped toward the clearing where Farmer Brown was planting his new vegetables, Leon heard Ole Luke barking. Ole Luke was smart, but Leon had outwitted him many times and knew he could do it again. Being very cautious, he continued out of the swamp watching out for Ole Luke, but also keeping an eye out for Brother Fox, the wise old Owl, the Hawk and the big Eagle.

He hopped a few yards then stopped. After looking in all directions, he continued and could see the big pipe sticking out from under the dirt and debris. It would be a fifty-yard run out in the open to get to the pipe, but there was no other way to carry out his plan.

Just as Leon was preparing for his fastest run ever, he heard Ole Luke barking off at a distance. He saw him digging in the fresh soil. Leon wanted to make his run while Farmer Brown was busy but he also had to keep his eyes on Ole Luke. Could he outrun him one more time?

Leon watched as Ole Luke would dig and nearly out of sight, back out for fresh air, then go back into his hole and continue to dig. Leon decided to wait for the moment after the dog caught his next breath to make his move.

At the speed of lighting, he ran toward the pipe. But just then, Farmer Brown called out for Ole Luke! Ole Luke stopped digging, backed out, and looked straight at Leon.

Ole Luke took off like a bullet and was gaining on Leon. Leon had to break his own record or become dog food. With only a few feet to go, it seemed as if he would surely fly. He won the race, making it to safety.

When he entered the pipe he was running so fast he couldn't stop, so he slid all the way through and landed on the ground inside a huge open room. To his surprise, bright sunlight was shining through a small opening at the top. This appeared to be a perfect place for Leon and his friends! It was sealed off on all four sides with the fallen trees from their old homes and the small opening at the top would keep out dangerous birds. His plan was coming together and he could hardly wait to tell everyone.

Ole Luke waited outside by the pipe for a few minutes but left when he realized it was no use. Farmer Brown called the dog away. Now that Leon's plan had worked, it was time to bring everyone to their new home. When Leon returned, they were all excited and thanked him for being their leader.

After things had calmed down, Leon told the animals about his narrow escape with Ole Luke and what he found at the end of the pipe. Everyone was happy to hear the good news.

Leon did have concerns about everyone fitting through the pipe, especially Mrs. Raccoon, who was too big because she was expecting babies. Mr. Raccoon was worried too.

After thinking it over, he decided to wait until the babies were born and big enough to join the others. In the safe area where everyone had been waiting, Brother Opossum, Brother Squirrel and their families got together and dug a large hole where Mrs. Raccoon could stay after everyone had left. None of the others would be taking any chances and would have to leave without them.

Leon's plan was to get everyone to safety as soon as possible. He thought it was best to take one animal from each family. There would be six animals on each trip: one each of rabbits, squirrels, opossums, raccoons, skunks and chipmunks. They all agreed and were very anxious to get started. Each trip would take less than five minutes, but first Leon needed time to rest. He found an old rotten log and crawled inside while the others waited. Soon he was ready and one member from each family got in line. Leon gave a signal to follow him.

The first trips went quickly with no problems and they continued until there were only six animals left. Leon had to rest before making the final trip. Again, he crawled inside the old rotten log and in thirty minutes he was ready to go.

Leon called the last six together and went to the edge of the forest, but high in the sky soared Brother Eagle, searching for his evening meal. Leon knew this would be the most dangerous trip of all and that any movement on the ground would get Brother Eagle's attention. Brother Fox would also be out and about looking for a meal!

It was time now to get the others to safety, but first Leon had to tempt Brother Eagle by running out in the clearing alone. If he flew after Leon, the other six animals would have a better chance of making it safely to the pipe. No one liked the idea, but Leon insisted and his plan was put into action. Leon quickly ran out in the clearing and as expected, Brother Eagle began diving to the ground. The others headed for the pipe, and one by one, made it without a problem.

Their leader wasn't as lucky. The giant Eagle swooped down and picked him up, but discovering that Leon was too heavy, he dropped him to the ground. The soft dirt cushioned Leon's fall but knocked the breath out of him. Within seconds, Leon was breathing again. To his surprise, he had landed a few feet from the big hole Ole Luke had dug earlier in the day. He quickly scrambled inside. When Brother Eagle realized he couldn't reach Leon, he soon gave up and flew away.

Leon discovered that he was bleeding where Brother Eagle's claws cut into his back, but the injury wasn't bad. With his heart pounding from fright, he lay inside the hole and rested. The bleeding soon stopped once fresh dirt got in his wound.

Leon was sad as he hopped across the open field, but he soon arrived at the pipe. He crawled inside. He found it much more slippery than before, since all the other animals had gone through before him. He began to slide, unable to stop himself, and shot out of the pipe where everyone was waiting. They were cheering and dancing and now that their hero had arrived safe and sound. Their only worry was for Mr. and Mrs. Raccoon. They all prayed their friends were safe and hoped they could join them soon.

Leon's wound was much better now but he was very tired and sore. It had been a long, busy day for everyone and it was now time to settle down for the night.

The danger of the outside world was locked away but the sadness of leaving their friends was heavy on their hearts. All the birds had flown to safety and were roosting in the upper chamber and the animals had found a new home. God had taken care of them.

Over the next few days, Farmer Brown planted his new garden and Ole Luke would bark at anything that moved. The animals were now safe inside their little hideaway but they anxiously waited for Farmer Brown's vegetable garden to produce so they could sample it from time to time.

Water was available when it rained but sometimes they had to go down to the edge of the swamp to drink. This was dangerous, but they had always lived with some danger, even in their old homes. The grass and other vegetation grew tall and gave more protection to them when they ventured outside their safety zone.

Late one evening, after all the animals had returned home, they were all settled in for the evening and the sun was still shining through the open roof. Then a noise was heard coming from the pipe. Everyone began to hide and climb high in the big room and all the birds became restless. They listened and watched. Suddenly, there was a big surprise when a tiny fur ball came sliding through the pipe!

One by one they came until three baby Raccoons were walking around inside. Before they knew what was happening, Mr. and Mrs. Raccoon came sliding through. The family was now reunited in the safety of their new home. Everyone joined in dancing and singing until late in the evening.

The days of summer slowly passed. One day, Leon and his family began to feast on the tender vegetables from Farmer Brown's garden. There was plenty for everyone, and since the garden was only twelve feet away, the danger of being caught was now very slim.

Ole Luke continued to chase the animals but his bark was always a warning to run and hide. Inside, their new home was safe and cozy and they all lived together in peace and harmony.

Leon had many kids and grandkids and saw Mr. and Mrs. Raccoon's babies grow into healthy adults. They too became grandparents many times.

Farmer Brown often complained about his vegetables being eaten and Ole Luke got older, dreaming often of chasing Leon and all the others.

All the animals and birds continued to enjoy the safety of the new homes that came about after their old homes had been destroyed.

Being kind to animals and birds was Farmer Brown's way of making up for destroying their old homes and food supply! The animals continued to be content and happy, and so was Farmer Brown. Ole Luke got fatter and slower every day but always enjoyed an early morning chase. The animals teased him often but this kept him active as he chased them around the garden.

Printed in the United States .
By Bookmasters